Taste of Home
Grandma's
FAVORITES

Over 350 Best-Loved Recipes Handed Down through the Generations, from Sunday Pot Roast to Oatmeal Cookies

The Reader's Digest Association, Inc.
Pleasantville, New York/Montreal

A READER'S DIGEST BOOK

Taste of Home Books
© 2006 Reiman Media Group, Inc.
5400 S. 60th Street, Greendale, WI 53129

Editor: Faithann Stoner
Art Director: Lori Arndt
Executive Editor, Books: Heidi Reuter Lloyd
Senior Editor, Books: Julie Schnittka
Associate Editors: Jean Steiner, Michelle Bretl
Proofreader: Julie Blume
Graphic Art Associates: Ellen Lloyd, Catherine Fletcher
Editorial Assistant: Barb Czysz

Food Editor: Janaan Cunningham
Associate Food Editors: Coleen Martin, Diane Werner
Assistant Food Editor: Karen Scales
Senior Recipe Editor: Sue A. Jurack
Recipe Editors: Janet Briggs, Mary King
Test Kitchen Director: Mark Morgan
Test Kitchen Home Economists: Peggy Fleming,
Nancy Fridirici, Tina Johnson, Ann Liebergen, Pat Schmeling,
Wendy Stenman, Amy Welk-Thieding
Test Kitchen Assistants: Suzanne Kern, Rita Krajcir,
Kris Lehman, Sue Megonigle, Megan Taylor

Food Photograpers: Rob Hagen, Dan Roberts, Jim Wieland
Set Stylists: Julie Ferron, Stephanie Marchese,
Sue Myers, Jennifer Bradley Vent
Food Stylists: Kristin Arnett, Sarah Thompson, Joylyn Trickel
Photographers Assistant: Lori Foy
Cover Designer: George McKeon

Senior Vice President, Editor in Chief: Catherine Cassidy
President: Barbara Newton
Chairman and Founder: Roy Reiman

International Standard Book Number: 0-89821-449-1
Library of Congress Control Number: 2005901781

For more Reader's Digest products and information, visit our
website at www.rd.com

Printed in China

3 5 7 9 10 8 6 4 2

Table of Contents

Pictured on the front cover: Herbed Beef Stew, p. 109; Angel Biscuits, p. 90; Emily's Spinach Salad, p. 52 and Carrot Cake, p. 172.

Pictured on the back cover: Savory Pot Roast, p. 103; Whole Wheat Refrigerator Rolls, p. 91; Molded Peach Gelatin, p. 53 and Citrus Cranberry Pie, p. 178.

Snacks & Beverages

At left: Homemade Orange Refresher (p. 14),
Mini Hamburgers (p. 9)
and Tater-Dipped Veggies (p. 15).

At right: Fresh Vegetable Dip (p. 13) and
Cheesy Sun Crisps (p. 7).

Tangy Meatballs

These hearty meatballs are a family favorite and a big hit wherever they go! In their delicious barbecue sauce, they're a perfect dish to pass and also work well as hors d'oeuvres.
—Jane Barta
St. Thomas, North Dakota

2 eggs, beaten
2 cups quick-cooking *or* old-fashioned oats
1 can (12 ounces) evaporated milk
1 cup chopped onion
2 teaspoons salt
1/2 teaspoon pepper
1/2 teaspoon garlic powder
3 pounds lean ground beef
SAUCE:
2 cups ketchup
1-1/2 cups packed brown sugar
1/2 cup chopped onion
1 to 2 teaspoons Liquid Smoke, optional
1/2 teaspoon garlic powder

In a large bowl, combine the first seven ingredients. Crumble beef over mixture and mix well. Shape into 1-1/2-in. balls. Place in two lightly greased 13-in. x 9-in. x 2-in. baking pans.

Bake, uncovered, at 375° for 30 minutes. Remove from the oven and drain. Place all of the meatballs in one of the pans.

In a saucepan, bring all sauce ingredients to a boil. Pour over meatballs. Return to the oven and bake, uncovered, for 20 minutes or until meatballs are no longer pink. **Yield:** 4 dozen.

During warm weather, Grandma would roll lemons back and forth between her hands. Then she'd cut those fragrant lemons in half and twist them on a glass juicer. I could hardly wait as she added sugar, water and ice and stirred up a big pitcher of lemonade!
—Shirley Mier-May, Olympia, Washington

Cinnamon-Raisin Granola

This granola recipe makes a great late-night or after-school snack. I like that it's nutritious, too.
—Tammy Neubauer, Ida Grove, Iowa

4 cups old-fashioned oats
1 cup flaked coconut
1/4 cup packed brown sugar
1/4 cup vegetable oil
1/4 cup honey
1 teaspoon ground cinnamon
1-1/2 teaspoons vanilla extract
1 cup raisins

In a large bowl, combine oats and coconut; set aside. In a saucepan, combine brown sugar, oil, honey and cinnamon; bring to a boil. Remove from the heat and stir in vanilla. Pour over oat mixture; stir to coat.

Spread in a large shallow baking pan. Bake at 350° for 15-20 minutes, stirring occasionally. Cool. Add raisins. Store in an airtight container. **Yield:** 6 cups.

Grandma's Favorites

Recipe for: *Cheesy Sun Crisps*

(Pictured on page 5)

These crackers have a great cheesy flavor and wholesome ingredients. They are perfect for snacking.

—Mary Detweiler, Farmington, Ohio

2 cups (8 ounces) shredded cheddar cheese
1/2 cup grated Parmesan cheese
1/2 cup butter, softened
3 tablespoons water
1 cup all-purpose flour
1/4 teaspoon salt
1 cup quick-cooking oats
2/3 cup roasted salted sunflower kernels

In a mixing bowl, combine cheddar and Parmesan cheeses, butter and water until well mixed. Combine flour and salt; add to cheese mixture. Stir in oats and sunflower kernels. Knead dough until it holds together. Shape into a 12-in. roll. Cover with plastic wrap; chill for 4 hours or overnight.

Allow to stand at room temperature for 10 minutes before cutting into 1/8-in. slices. Place on greased foil-lined baking sheets. Bake at 400° for 8-10 minutes or until edges are golden. Slide crackers and foil off baking sheets to wire racks to cool. **Yield:** 8 dozen.

Tomato Vegetable Juice

I've used this delicious recipe for many years, and it's always been a favorite. The tangy juice is refreshing on its own and also works great in any recipe calling for tomato juice. Because of all the vegetables, it's full of vitamins. —Sue Wille, Alexandria, Minnesota

10 pounds tomatoes, peeled and chopped (about 8 quarts)
3 garlic cloves, minced
2 large onions, chopped
2 carrots, cut into 1/2-inch slices
2 cups chopped celery
1/2 cup chopped green pepper
1/4 cup sugar
1 tablespoon salt
1 teaspoon Worcestershire sauce
1/2 teaspoon pepper
Lemon juice

Combine tomatoes, garlic, onions, carrots, celery and green pepper in a large Dutch oven or soup kettle. Bring to a boil; reduce heat and simmer for 20 minutes or until vegetables are soft. Cool.

Press mixture through a food mill or fine sieve. Return juice to the Dutch oven; add sugar, salt, Worcestershire sauce and pepper. Bring to a boil. Ladle hot juice into hot sterilized quart jars, leaving 1/4- in. headspace. Add 2 tablespoons lemon juice to each jar. Adjust caps. Process for 40 minutes in a boiling-water bath. **Yield:** 7-8 quarts.

Cozy Hot Chocolate

Steaming mugs of this smooth, chocolaty drink make a comforting treat anytime, especially during the colder months.
—Marie Hattrup
The Dalles, Oregon

    2 tablespoons baking cocoa
    2 tablespoons sugar
    1/4 cup water
    2 cups milk
    1/2 teaspoon vanilla extract
    Whipped cream
    Ground cinnamon, optional

In a saucepan, mix the cocoa and sugar; add water. Bring to a boil, stirring constantly; boil for 1 minute. Reduce heat; add milk and heat through.

Remove from the heat and stir in vanilla. Pour into two mugs; top with whipped cream and sprinkle with cinnamon if desired. **Yield:** 2 servings.

Banana Brunch Punch

A cold glass of refreshing punch really brightens a brunch or other gathering. It's nice to serve a crisp beverage like this that's more spectacular than plain juice. With bananas, orange juice and lemonade, it can add tropical flair to any day.
—Mary Anne McWhirter, Pearland, Texas

    6 medium ripe bananas
    1 can (12 ounces) frozen orange juice
        concentrate, thawed
    1 can (6 ounces) frozen lemonade
        concentrate, thawed
    3 cups warm water, *divided*
    2 cups sugar, *divided*
    1 can (46 ounces) pineapple juice
    3 bottles (2 liters *each*) lemon-lime soda
    Orange slices, optional

In a blender or food processor, blend bananas, and orange juice and lemonade concentrates until smooth. Remove half of the mixture and set aside. Add 1-1/2 cups of warm water and 1 cup sugar to mixture in blender; blend until smooth. Place in a large freezer container. Repeat with remaining banana mixture, water and sugar; add to container. Cover and freeze until solid.

One hour before serving, take punch base out of freezer. Just before serving, place in a large punch bowl. Add pineapple juice and soda; stir until well blended. Garnish with orange slices if desired. **Yield:** 60-70 servings (10 quarts).

Mini Hamburgers

(Also pictured on page 4)

I guarantee these delicious little burgers will be the first snack cleared from your table. —Judy Lewis
Sterling Heights, Michigan

1/2 cup chopped onion
1 tablespoon butter
1 egg, beaten
1/4 teaspoon seasoned salt
1/4 teaspoon rubbed sage
1/4 teaspoon salt
1/8 teaspoon pepper
1 pound lean ground beef
40 mini rolls, split
8 ounces process American cheese slices, cut into 1-1/2-inch squares, optional
40 dill pickle slices, optional

In a skillet, saute onion in butter. Transfer to a bowl; add egg and seasonings. Crumble beef over mixture and mix well. Spread over bottom halves of the rolls; replace tops. Place on baking sheets; cover with foil. Bake at 350° for 20 minutes or until meat is no longer pink.

If desired, place a cheese square and pickle on each hamburger; replace tops and foil and return to the oven for 5 minutes. **Yield:** 40 appetizers.

Recipe for: Spiced Pecans

These crunchy pecans are a family-favorite treat to munch on anytime and are very nice to serve when you have company. They also make a great gift. —Miriam Hershberger, Holmesville, Ohio

1 egg white
1 teaspoon cold water
1 pound (4 cups) pecan halves
1/2 cup sugar
1/4 teaspoon salt
1/2 teaspoon ground cinnamon

In a mixing bowl, lightly beat the egg white. Add water; beat until frothy but not stiff. Add pecans; stir until well coated. Combine sugar, salt and cinnamon. Sprinkle over pecans; toss to mix. Spread in a greased 15-in. x 10-in. x 1-in. baking pan. Bake at 250° for 1 hour, stirring occasionally. **Yield:** about 4 cups.

BLT Bites

These quick hors d'oeuvres may be mini, but their bacon and tomato flavor is full-size. I serve them at parties, brunches and picnics, and they're always a hit...even my kids love them.   —Kellie Remmen
Detroit Lakes, Minnesota

    16 to 20 cherry tomatoes
     1 pound bacon, cooked and crumbled
    1/2 cup mayonnaise
    1/3 cup chopped green onions
     3 tablespoons grated Parmesan cheese
     2 tablespoons snipped fresh parsley

Cut a thin slice off of each tomato top. Scoop out and discard pulp. Invert the tomatoes on a paper towel to drain.

   In a small bowl, combine all remaining ingredients; mix well. Spoon into tomatoes. Refrigerate for several hours. **Yield:** 16-20 appetizers.

Recipe for: # Sweet Minglers

This snack mix is perfect for a late-night treat or a pick-me-up any time of the day. I sometimes take a batch to work, and it's always eaten up quickly. It's a slightly different cereal snack because of the chocolate and peanut butter.   —Mary Obeilin, Selinsgrove, Pennsylvania

    1 cup (6 ounces) semisweet chocolate
      chips
    1/4 cup creamy peanut butter
     6 cups Corn *or* Rice Chex cereal
     1 cup confectioners' sugar

In a large microwave-safe bowl, melt chocolate chips on high for 1 minute. Stir; microwave 30 seconds longer or until the chips are melted. Stir in peanut butter. Gently stir in cereal until well coated; set aside.

   Place confectioners' sugar in a 2-gal. plastic storage bag. Add cereal mixture and shake until well coated. Store in an airtight container in the refrigerator. **Yield:** about 6 cups.

Buttermilk Shakes

These creamy, rich shakes taste just like liquid cheesecake! It's so easy to whip up a couple satisfying servings. —Gloria Jarrett, Loveland, Ohio

- 1 pint vanilla ice cream
- 1 cup buttermilk
- 1 teaspoon grated lemon peel
- 1/2 teaspoon vanilla extract
- 1 drop lemon extract

In a blender, blend all ingredients until smooth. Pour into glasses. Serve immediately. **Yield:** 2 servings.

How my grandma managed to turn out the good food she did on a wood stove is beyond me. I guess, like everything else, practice makes perfect. Most everything she cooked was what she raised on the farm. For a special treat, she parched corn. She placed ears of corn in the oven and left them until they became crispy and brown. That corn tasted wonderful. —Shelby Teaney, Rocky Mount, Missouri

Sweet Gingered Chicken Wings

I first tasted this delicious chicken dish many years ago when I attended a class on using honey in cooking. When I prepare this recipe for a party, it's one of the first dishes to disappear! —Debbie Dougal, Roseville, California

- 1 cup all-purpose flour
- 2 teaspoons salt
- 2 teaspoons paprika
- 1/4 teaspoon pepper
- 24 chicken wings

SAUCE:
- 1/4 cup honey
- 1/4 cup frozen orange juice concentrate, thawed
- 1/2 teaspoon ground ginger

Snipped fresh parsley, optional

In a bowl, combine flour, salt, paprika and pepper. Coat chicken wings in flour mixture; shake off excess. Place wings on a large greased baking sheet. Bake at 350° for 30 minutes. Remove from the oven and drain.

Combine honey, orange juice concentrate and ginger; brush generously over the chicken wings. Reduce heat to 325°. Bake for 30-40 minutes or until chicken is no longer pink, basting occasionally with more sauce. Sprinkle with parsley before serving if desired. **Yield:** 2 dozen.

Mini Apple Pizzas

My four children are now grown, but they still enjoy snacking on these sweet little pizzas...and so do my grandchildren. We use fresh apples from the small orchard on our dairy farm, and they're so easy to make. The warm cinnamon flavor and light crust make them delicious!
—Helen Lamb
Seymour, Missouri

> 1 tube (12 ounces) refrigerated buttermilk
>   biscuits, separated into 10 biscuits
> 1/2 cup packed brown sugar
>   2 tablespoons all-purpose flour
>   1 teaspoon ground cinnamon
>   2 tart apples, peeled, cored and shredded
>   1 cup (4 ounces) shredded cheddar
>   cheese, optional

Roll or pat biscuits into 3-1/2-in. circles; place on a lightly greased baking sheet. In a bowl, combine brown sugar, flour and cinnamon; mix well. Add apples and mix well; spoon rounded tablespoonfuls onto biscuits.

Bake at 350° for 15-20 minutes or until edges begin to brown. If desired, sprinkle each pizza with 1 tablespoon cheese. Serve warm. **Yield:** 10 servings.

I remember Grandma's moist spice cakes. She'd bake on Monday, and even several days later her cakes were still fresh. I think they stayed moist because she used real cream, butter and the juice of canned fruits.
—George Burke
Bonnerdale, Arkansas

Horseradish Cheese Spread

I got the recipe for this zippy, irresistible cheese spread from a friend. It makes a creamy, delicious evening snack. —Connie Simon, Reed City, Michigan

> 2 pounds process cheese (Velveeta),
>   cubed
> 1/2 cup prepared horseradish
> 1/3 cup mayonnaise
>   1 teaspoon hot pepper sauce

> 1/4 teaspoon garlic salt
> 1/4 teaspoon Worcestershire sauce
> Crackers *or* fresh vegetables

In the top of a double boiler over simmering water, melt cheese until smooth. Add the next five ingredients and stir until smooth. Spoon into containers; cover and refrigerate. Serve with crackers or fresh vegetables. **Yield:** 4 cups.

Grandma's Favorites

Recipe for: *Fresh Vegetable Dip*

(Pictured on page 5)

This cool and creamy dip is a real family favorite for snacking, especially when paired with fresh garden vegetables. It's also perfect for parties.
—Denise Goedeken, Platte Center, Nebraska

1-1/2 cups (12 ounces) sour cream
3/4 cup mayonnaise
1 tablespoon dried minced onion
1 teaspoon dill weed
1 teaspoon dried parsley flakes
1 teaspoon garlic salt
Dash Worcestershire sauce
Fresh vegetables

In a small bowl, combine sour cream, mayonnaise, onion, dill, parsley, garlic salt and Worcestershire sauce. Chill for at least 1 hour. Serve with fresh vegetables. **Yield:** 2 cups.

Aunt Frances' Lemonade

My sister and I spent a week each summer with Aunt Frances, who always had this thirst-quenching lemonade in a stoneware crock in the refrigerator. It tastes so much like fresh citrus and made a refreshing drink after a hot day on her farm.
—Debbie Blackburn, Camp Hill, Pennsylvania

5 lemons
5 limes
5 oranges
3 quarts water
1-1/2 to 2 cups sugar

Squeeze the juice from four of the lemons, limes and oranges; pour into a gallon container. Thinly slice the remaining fruit and set aside for garnish. Add water and sugar to juices; mix well. Store in the refrigerator. Serve on ice with fruit slices. **Yield:** 12-16 servings (about 1 gallon).

Homemade Orange Refresher

(Pictured on page 4)

Family and friends will thank you for serving this cool, tangy orange drink on warm evenings.
—Iola Egle, McCook, Nebraska

    1 can (6 ounces) frozen orange juice
      concentrate, thawed
  1/3 cup sugar
  1/3 cup nonfat dry milk powder
    2 teaspoons vanilla extract
  3/4 cup cold water
   10 to 12 ice cubes

Orange slices and mint, optional
Orange juice and sugar, optional

In a blender, combine the first five ingredients and process at high speed. Add ice cubes, a few at a time, blending until slushy. Garnish with orange slices and mint if desired. Serve immediately. **Yield:** 4 servings.

Editor's Note: For a fancy glass edge, invert glass and dip into orange juice and then sugar; let dry 1 hour before filling glass.

My grandma and grandpa lived on a farm in Arkansas. My cousins and I liked to visit them. We'd climb up into the loft of the barn where Grandpa stored his peanut crop. Then we'd sit in the middle of the peanut vines and eat raw peanuts until we were about to burst!
—Jean Haygood, Minden, Louisiana

Caramel Corn

For years I've taken this snack to our church retreat. I take it in two containers—one for each night—so it doesn't all disappear the first night. Other church members tell us that if we can't attend, we should just send the caramel corn.
—Nancy Breen
Canastota, New York

   12 quarts plain popped popcorn
    1 pound peanuts
    2 cups butter
    2 pounds packed brown sugar
  1/2 cup dark corn syrup
  1/2 cup molasses

Place popcorn in two large bowls. Mix 1/2 pound nuts into each bowl. In a 5-qt. saucepan, combine remaining ingredients. Bring to a boil over medium heat; boil and stir for 5 minutes. Pour half of syrup over each bowl of popcorn and stir to coat.

Turn coated popcorn into a large roasting pan. Bake at 250° for 1 hour. Remove from the oven and break apart while warm. Cool. Store in airtight containers. **Yield:** 12 quarts.

Puffed Wheat Balls

My Grandma Hunt is almost 90 years old. Whenever she comes over, she makes her famous Puffed Wheat Balls by the dozen. Her 82 grandchildren and 168 great-grandchildren all love them.
—Lucile Proctor, Panguitch, Utah

    12 cups puffed wheat cereal
     2 cups packed brown sugar
     1 cup corn syrup
     2 tablespoons butter
     1 cup evaporated milk
    1/3 cup sugar

Place cereal in a large bowl; set aside. In a heavy saucepan, bring brown sugar and corn syrup to a boil. Add butter. Combine evaporated milk and sugar; add to boiling mixture and continue cooking until a candy thermometer reads 240° (softball stage). Pour over cereal and stir to coat. Shape into 2-in. balls. **Yield:** 2-1/2 to 3 dozen.

Editor's Note: We recommend that you test your candy thermometer before each use by bringing water to a boil; the thermometer should read 212°. Adjust your recipe temperature up or down based on your test.

Recipe for: Tater-Dipped Veggies

(Pictured on page 4)

With this great recipe, you get the crispiness of deep-fried vegetables without the mess and fuss. Even picky eaters will dig into veggies prepared this way. —Earleen Lillegard, Prescott, Arizona

       1 cup mashed potato flakes
     1/3 cup grated Parmesan cheese
     1/2 teaspoon celery salt
     1/4 teaspoon garlic powder
     1/4 cup butter, melted and cooled
       2 eggs
       4 to 5 cups fresh bite-size vegetables
          (mushrooms, peppers, broccoli,
          cauliflower, zucchini *and/or*
          parboiled carrots)
    Prepared ranch salad dressing *or* dip,
       optional

In a small bowl, combine potato flakes, Parmesan cheese, celery salt, garlic powder and butter. In another bowl, beat eggs. Dip vegetables, one at a time, into egg, then into potato mixture; coat well.

Place on an ungreased baking sheet. Bake at 400° for 20-25 minutes. Serve with dressing or dip if desired. **Yield:** 6-8 servings.

Breakfast & Brunch

At left: Jellied Biscuits (p. 24), Hearty Egg Scramble (p. 20) and Ambrosia Fruit (p. 18).

At right: Feather-Light Muffins (p. 19).

Hash Brown Quiche

We love to have guests stay with us, and this is a great dish to serve for breakfast. To save time in the morning, I sometimes make the hash brown crust and chop the ham, cheese and peppers the night before. As a teacher and farm wife, I'm always looking for easy recipes like this one. —Jan Peters
Chandler, Minnesota

> 3 cups frozen shredded hash brown potatoes, thawed
> 1/3 cup butter, melted
> 1 cup diced fully cooked ham
> 1 cup (4 ounces) shredded cheddar cheese
> 1/4 cup diced green pepper
> 2 eggs
> 1/2 cup milk
> 1/2 teaspoon salt
> 1/4 teaspoon pepper

Press hash browns between paper towel to remove excess moisture. Press into the bottom and up the sides of an ungreased 9-in. pie plate. Drizzle with butter. Bake at 425° for 25 minutes.

Combine the ham, cheese and green pepper; spoon over crust. In a small bowl, beat eggs, milk, salt and pepper. Pour over all.

Reduce heat to 350°; bake for 25-30 minutes or until a knife inserted near the center comes out clean. Allow to stand for 10 minutes before cutting. **Yield:** 6 servings.

I loved spending the night at Grandmother's, as I knew her breakfast the next day was a special treat. Her cornmeal pancakes topped with homemade syrup were the best! —Rose Lee, Citra, Florida

Ambrosia Fruit

(Pictured on page 16)

For the wonderful taste of fresh fruit any time of year, give this simple yet special recipe a try. —Marsha Ransom, South Haven, Michigan

> 1 can (20 ounces) pineapple tidbits
> 1/4 cup packed brown sugar
> 1/2 teaspoon grated orange peel
> 2 medium navel oranges
> 2 medium apples, diced
> 1 tablespoon flaked coconut

Drain pineapple, reserving 1/4 cup juice; set pineapple aside. In a saucepan, mix brown sugar, orange peel and reserved juice; heat and stir until sugar dissolves.

Peel and section oranges into a large bowl. Add the apples and pineapple. Add pineapple juice mixture and stir gently. Chill. Just before serving, sprinkle with coconut. **Yield:** 6 servings.

Recipe for: *Feather-Light Muffins*

(Pictured on page 17)

Your family will likely gobble up these airy muffins, which won me a blue ribbon at our county fair! Pretty as well as tasty, their hint of spice will brighten breakfast, brunch or lunch for family or company.

—Sonja Blow, Groveland, California

1/3 cup shortening
1/2 cup sugar
1 egg
1-1/2 cups cake flour
1-1/2 teaspoons baking powder
1/2 teaspoon salt
1/4 teaspoon ground nutmeg
1/2 cup milk
TOPPING:
1/2 cup sugar
1 teaspoon ground cinnamon
1/2 cup butter, melted

In a mixing bowl, cream shortening, sugar and egg. Combine dry ingredients; add to creamed mixture alternately with milk. Fill greased muffin cups two-thirds full. Bake at 325° for 20-25 minutes or until golden. Let cool for 3-4 minutes.

Meanwhile, combine sugar and cinnamon in a small bowl. Roll warm muffins in melted butter, then in sugar mixture. Serve warm. **Yield:** 8-10 muffins.

Cinnamon Coffee Cake

I love the texture of this old-fashioned, streusel-topped coffee cake. Always a crowd pleaser, its sweet vanilla flavor enriched by sour cream may remind you of breakfast at Grandma's!

—Eleanor Harris, Cape Coral, Florida

1 cup butter, softened
2-3/4 cups sugar, *divided*
2 teaspoons vanilla extract
4 eggs
3 cups all-purpose flour
2 teaspoons baking powder
1 teaspoon baking soda
1 teaspoon salt
2 cups (16 ounces) sour cream
2 tablespoons ground cinnamon
1/2 cup chopped walnuts

In a large mixing bowl, cream the butter and 2 cups sugar until fluffy. Add the vanilla. Add the eggs, one at a time, beating well after each addition. Combine the flour, baking powder, baking soda and salt; add alternately with sour cream, beating just enough after each addition to keep batter smooth.

Spoon one-third of the batter into a greased 10-in. tube pan. Combine the cinnamon, nuts and remaining sugar; sprinkle one-third over batter in pan. Repeat layers two more times. Bake at 350° for 70 minutes or until a toothpick inserted near the center comes out clean. Cool for 10 minutes. Remove from pan to a wire rack to cool completely. **Yield:** 16-20 servings.

Hearty Egg Scramble

(Pictured on page 16)

This recipe makes a filling and flavorful egg dish. The ham and potatoes are comforting additions.
—Marsha Ransom, South Haven, Michigan

1/3 cup chopped onion
1/4 cup chopped green pepper
1/4 cup butter
  2 medium potatoes, peeled, cooked and cubed
1-1/2 cups julienned fully cooked ham

  6 eggs
  2 tablespoons water
Dash pepper

In a large skillet, cook onion and green pepper in butter until crisp-tender. Add potatoes and ham; cook and stir for 5 minutes.

In a bowl, beat eggs, water and pepper; pour over ham mixture. Cook over low heat, stirring occasionally, until eggs are set. **Yield:** 6 servings.

Overnight Apple French Toast

My in-laws own and operate an orchard, so we have an abundance of fruit fresh from the trees. This dish includes fresh apples, apple jelly and applesauce all in one recipe. It's a warm, hearty breakfast for busy days.
—Debra Blazer, Hegins, Pennsylvania

  1 cup packed brown sugar
1/2 cup butter
  2 tablespoons light corn syrup
  2 large tart apples, peeled and sliced 1/4 inch thick
  3 eggs
  1 cup milk
  1 teaspoon vanilla extract
  9 slices day-old French bread (3/4 inch thick)
SYRUP:
  1 cup applesauce
  1 jar (10 ounces) apple jelly
1/2 teaspoon ground cinnamon
1/8 teaspoon ground cloves

In a small saucepan, cook brown sugar, butter and syrup until thick, about 5-7 minutes. Pour into an ungreased 13-in. x 9-in. x 2-in. baking pan; arrange apples on top.

In a mixing bowl, beat eggs, milk and vanilla. Dip bread slices into the egg mixture for 1 minute; place over apples. Cover and refrigerate overnight.

Remove from the refrigerator 30 minutes before baking. Bake, uncovered, at 350° for 35-40 minutes. Combine syrup ingredients in a medium saucepan; cook and stir until hot. Serve syrup over French toast. **Yield:** 9 servings.

Sheepherder's Breakfast

My sister-in-law always made this delicious breakfast dish when we were camping. Served with toast, juice and milk or coffee, it's a sure hit with the breakfast crowd! One-dish casseroles like this were a big help while I was raising my nine children...now I've passed this recipe on to them. —Pauletta Bushnell
Albany, Oregon

   1 pound sliced bacon, diced
   1 medium onion, chopped
   2 packages (16 ounces *each*) frozen
     shredded hash brown potatoes, thawed
  10 eggs
Salt and pepper to taste
   2 cups (8 ounces) shredded cheddar
     cheese, optional
Chopped fresh parsley

In a large skillet, cook bacon and onion until bacon is crisp. Drain all but 1/2 cup of the drippings. Add hash browns to skillet; mix well. Cook over medium heat for 10 minutes, turning when browned. Make 10 "wells" evenly spaced in the hash browns. Place one egg in each well. Sprinkle with salt and pepper. Sprinkle with cheese if desired.

Cover and cook over low heat for about 10 minutes or until eggs are set. Garnish with parsley; serve immediately. **Yield:** 10 servings.

Recipe for: Crunchy Granola

This crisp, lightly sweet mixture is great as a breakfast cereal or an ice cream topping, or just eaten out of hand. Our children and grandchildren enjoy it. —Lorna Jacobsen, Arrowwood, Alberta

  2/3 cup honey
  1/2 cup vegetable oil
  1/3 cup packed brown sugar
    2 teaspoons vanilla extract
    4 cups old-fashioned oats
    1 cup sliced almonds
    1 cup flaked coconut
  1/2 cup sesame seeds
  1/2 cup salted sunflower kernels
    2 cups raisins

In a small saucepan, combine honey, oil and brown sugar; cook and stir over medium heat until the sugar dissolves. Remove from the heat; add vanilla. In a large bowl, combine the next five ingredients. Add honey mixture, stirring until evenly coated.

Spread onto two ungreased baking pans. Bake at 300° for 20 minutes, stirring frequently. Stir in raisins. Bake for 10 minutes. Cool, stirring occasionally. Store in an airtight container. **Yield:** 10 cups.

Sweet Broiled Grapefruit

I was never a fan of grapefruit until I had it broiled at a Florida restaurant—it was so tangy and delicious! I finally got the recipe and now make it often for husband Ron, myself and our children and grandchildren. —Terry Bray, Haines City, Florida

1 large grapefruit, sliced in half
2 tablespoons butter, softened
2 tablespoons sugar
1/2 teaspoon ground cinnamon
Maraschino cherry for garnish, optional

Cut membrane out of the center of each grapefruit half. Cut around each section so it will be easy to spoon out when eating.

Place 1 tablespoon butter in the center of each half. Combine sugar and cinnamon; sprinkle over each. Broil until butter is melted and sugar is bubbly. Garnish with a cherry if desired. Serve immediately. **Yield:** 2 servings.

Recipe for: Overnight Blueberry Coffee Cake

This cake, made with our own berries, stars at "welcome to Washington" breakfasts I serve out-of-town company. Since I prepare it the night before, there's no fuss the next morning. —Marion Platt
Sequim, Washington

1 egg
1/2 cup plus 2 tablespoons sugar, *divided*
1-1/4 cups all-purpose flour
2 teaspoons baking powder
3/4 teaspoon salt
1/3 cup milk
3 tablespoons butter, melted
1 cup fresh blueberries

In a mixing bowl, beat egg and 1/2 cup sugar. Combine flour, baking powder and salt; add alternately with milk to sugar mixture, beating well after each addition. Stir in butter. Fold in berries. Pour into a greased 8-in. square baking pan; sprinkle with the remaining sugar. Cover and chill overnight.

Remove from the refrigerator 30 minutes before baking. Bake at 350° for 30-35 minutes or until a toothpick inserted near the center comes out clean. **Yield:** 9 servings.

Sausage Gravy

This savory sausage gravy is a specialty among country folks in our area. It's best served over fresh, hot biscuits. It makes a real stick-to-the-ribs dish that we always enjoy and carries a traditional flavor that can showcase locally produced sausage.
> —Mrs. J. N. Stine, Roanoke, Virginia

 1 pound sage-flavored bulk pork sausage
 2 tablespoons finely chopped onion
 6 tablespoons all-purpose flour
 1 cup milk
1/2 teaspoon poultry seasoning
1/2 teaspoon ground nutmeg
1/4 teaspoon salt
Dash Worcestershire sauce
Dash hot pepper sauce
 12 biscuits

Crumble the sausage into a large saucepan; cook over medium-low heat. Add the onion; cook and stir until transparent.

Drain, discarding all but 2 tablespoons of drippings. Stir in the flour; cook over medium-low heat about 6 minutes or until mixture bubbles and turns golden. Stir in the milk. Add the seasonings; cook, stirring, until thickened.

To serve, slice biscuits and spoon gravy over halves. **Yield:** 4-6 servings.

Stuffed Apricot French Toast

In our family, this special recipe is often served for our Christmas Day brunch. I was always looking for something unique to serve, and this rich, colorful dish certainly fills the bill. It tastes so good!
> —Deb Leland, Three Rivers, Michigan

 1 package (8 ounces) cream cheese,
  softened
1-1/2 teaspoons vanilla extract, *divided*
 1/2 cup finely chopped walnuts
 1 loaf (1-1/2 pounds) French bread
 4 eggs
 1 cup heavy whipping cream
 1/2 teaspoon ground nutmeg
 1 jar (12 ounces) apricot preserves
1/2 cup orange juice

In a mixing bowl, beat cream cheese and 1 teaspoon vanilla until fluffy. Stir in nuts; set aside. Cut bread into 1-1/2-in. slices; cut a pocket in the top of each slice. Fill each pocket with about 2 tablespoons of cream cheese mixture.

In another bowl, beat eggs, cream, nutmeg and remaining vanilla. Dip both sides of bread into egg mixture, being careful not to squeeze out the filling. Cook on a lightly greased griddle until golden brown on both sides. Place on an ungreased baking sheet; bake at 300° for 20 minutes.

Meanwhile, combine preserves and orange juice in a small saucepan; heat through. Drizzle over hot French toast. **Yield:** about 8 servings.

Jellied Biscuits

(Pictured on page 16)

These biscuits taste special and look lovely.
—Marsha Ransom, South Haven, Michigan

2 cups all-purpose flour
4 teaspoons baking powder
2 teaspoons sugar
1/2 teaspoon salt
1/2 teaspoon cream of tartar
1/2 cup shortening
3/4 cup milk
1/3 cup jelly

In a bowl, combine flour, baking powder, sugar, salt and cream of tartar. Cut in shortening until the mixture resembles coarse crumbs. Add milk; stir quickly with a fork just until mixed.

Drop by rounded tablespoonfuls onto a greased baking sheet. Make a deep thumbprint in tops; fill each with 1 teaspoon of jelly. Bake at 450° for 10-12 minutes or until biscuits are browned. **Yield:** about 1 dozen.

Cream Cheese Coffee Cake

These impressive loaves really sparkle on the buffet.
—Mary Anne McWhirter, Pearland, Texas

1 cup (8 ounces) sour cream
1/2 cup sugar
1/2 cup butter
1 teaspoon salt
2 packages (1/4 ounce *each*) active dry yeast
1/2 cup warm water (110° to 115°)
2 eggs, beaten
4 cups all-purpose flour

FILLING:
2 packages (8 ounces *each*) cream cheese, softened
3/4 cup sugar
1 egg, beaten
2 teaspoons vanilla extract
1/8 teaspoon salt
GLAZE:
2-1/2 cups confectioners' sugar
1/4 cup milk
1 teaspoon vanilla extract
Toasted sliced almonds, optional

In a saucepan, combine sour cream, sugar, butter and salt. Cook over medium-low heat, stirring constantly, for 5-10 minutes or until well blended. Cool to room temperature.

In a mixing bowl, dissolve yeast in water. Add sour cream mixture and eggs; mix well. Gradually stir in flour. (Dough will be very soft.) Cover and refrigerate overnight.

The next day, combine filling ingredients in a mixing bowl until well blended. Turn dough onto a floured surface; knead 5-6 times. Divide into four equal portions. Roll each portion into a 12-in. x 8-in. rectangle. Spread 1/4 of the filling on each to within 1 in. of edges.

Roll up jelly-roll style from long side; pinch seams and ends to seal. Place seam side down on greased baking sheet. Cut six X's on top of loaves. Cover and let rise until nearly doubled, about 1 hour. Bake at 375° for 20-25 minutes or until golden brown. Cool on wire racks.

Combine the first three glaze ingredients; drizzle over loaves. Sprinkle with almonds if desired. Store in the refrigerator. **Yield:** 20-24 servings.

Oatmeal Waffles

This recipe can be used to make pancakes as well as waffles. Both are delicious because of their hearty, whole-grain flavor. For a special treat, serve them topped with fruit or a flavored syrup.
—Mrs. Francis Stoops, Stoneboro, Pennsylvania

2 eggs, beaten
2 cups buttermilk
1 cup quick-cooking oats
1 tablespoon molasses
1 tablespoon vegetable oil
1 cup whole wheat flour
1/2 teaspoon salt
1 teaspoon baking soda
1 teaspoon baking powder
Milk, optional

In a large bowl, mix eggs and buttermilk. Add oats and mix well. Stir in molasses and oil. Combine flour, salt, baking soda and baking powder; stir into the egg mixture. If batter becomes too thick, thin with a little milk. Pour about 3/4 cup batter onto a greased preheated waffle maker. Bake according to manufacturer's directions.

To make pancakes: Drop batter by 1/4 cupfuls onto a hot greased griddle. Turn when bubbles begin to form on top of pancake. **Yield:** 5 waffles (7 inches) or about 15 standard-size pancakes.

Recipe for: Grandma's Cinnamon Rolls

The secret to these rolls is the brown sugar sauce they're baked in. I serve them as dinner rolls as well as for a special breakfast treat.
—Della Talbert, Howard, Colorado

DOUGH:
  1 package (1/4 ounce) active dry yeast
1/4 cup sugar, *divided*
  1 cup warm water (110° to 115°), *divided*
  2 tablespoons butter, softened
  1 egg
  1 teaspoon salt
3-1/4 to 3-3/4 cups all-purpose flour
TOPPING:
  1 cup heavy whipping cream
  1 cup packed brown sugar
FILLING:
  1/2 cup sugar
  2 teaspoons ground cinnamon
  1/2 cup butter, softened

In a large bowl, dissolve yeast and 1/2 teaspoon sugar in 1/4 cup warm water. Add the remaining sugar and water, butter, egg, salt and 1-1/2 cups of flour; beat until smooth. Stir in enough remaining flour to form a soft dough. Turn onto a lightly floured surface; knead until smooth and elastic, about 6-8 minutes. Place in a greased bowl, turning once to grease top. Cover and let rise in a warm place until doubled, about 1 hour.

Meanwhile, combine topping ingredients; pour into a greased 13-in. x 9-in. x 2-in. baking pan; set aside. Combine filling ingredients; set aside. Punch dough down and turn onto a lightly floured surface. Roll into a 15-in. x 8-in. rectangle; spread filling over dough.

Roll up from the long side. Seal seam. Slice into 15 rolls; place with cut side down over topping. Cover and let rise until nearly doubled, about 30-45 minutes. Bake at 375° for 25 minutes or until golden brown. Cool 3 minutes; invert pan onto a serving plate. **Yield:** 15 rolls.

Apple-Topped Oatcakes

During the week we have quick breakfasts...but on Saturday I like to make something special. This is one of our favorite recipes because the oatcakes and apple topping are a tasty, wholesome combination. They also can be made ahead so a hungry family doesn't have to wait long. —Lois Hofmeyer
Aurora, Illinois

1-1/2 cups hot milk
  3/4 cup old-fashioned oats
    1 egg, beaten
    2 tablespoons vegetable oil
    2 tablespoons molasses

      1 cup all-purpose flour
1-1/2 teaspoons baking powder
  3/4 teaspoon ground cinnamon
  1/4 teaspoon ground ginger
  1/4 teaspoon baking soda
  1/4 teaspoon salt
    3 egg whites
LEMON APPLES:
    2 tablespoons butter
    5 medium tart apples, peeled and sliced
    1 tablespoon lemon juice
    1 teaspoon grated lemon peel
  1/2 cup sugar
    1 tablespoon cornstarch
  1/8 teaspoon ground nutmeg

In a large bowl, combine milk and oats; let stand for 5 minutes. Stir in egg, oil and molasses. Combine dry ingredients; stir into oat mixture just until moistened. Beat egg whites until soft peaks form; fold gently into batter. Set aside.

Heat butter in a skillet until foamy. Add apples, lemon juice and peel; cook, uncovered, for 8-10 minutes, stirring occasionally.

Meanwhile, cook oatcakes: Pour batter by 1/4 cupfuls onto a hot greased griddle. Cook until bubbles form; turn and cook until browned on other side.

For apple topping, combine sugar, cornstarch and nutmeg; add to apple mixture and cook 2 minutes longer or until tender. Serve warm over oatcakes. **Yield:** 6-8 servings.

Pork Patties

These delightful patties provide a taste-bud wake-up call with a variety of herbs and spices. Plus, they're quick to put together. —Lois Fetting
Nelson, Wisconsin

1-1/2 teaspoons salt
  1/2 teaspoon rubbed sage
  1/4 teaspoon pepper
  1/4 teaspoon ground nutmeg

  1/4 teaspoon dried thyme
Pinch ground ginger
    2 tablespoons water
    1 pound ground pork

In a bowl, combine first seven ingredients; crumble pork over mixture and mix well. Shape into six patties. In a skillet, cook patties over medium heat until no longer pink. **Yield:** 6 servings.

Breakfast Bread Pudding

Recipe for:

I assemble this dish the day before our grandchildren visit, giving me more time for fun with them! They look forward to it every visit.
—Alma Andrews, Live Oak, Florida

12 slices white bread, crusts removed
1 package (8 ounces) cream cheese, cubed
12 eggs
2 cups milk
1/3 cup maple syrup
1/4 teaspoon salt

Cut bread into cubes. In a bowl, toss bread lightly with cream cheese cubes; place in a greased 13-in. x 9-in. x 2-in. baking pan. In a large mixing bowl, beat eggs. Add milk, syrup and salt; mix well. Pour over bread mixture. Cover and refrigerate 8 hours or overnight.

Remove from refrigerator 30 minutes before baking. Bake, uncovered, at 375° for 40-45 minutes or until a knife inserted near the center comes out clean. Let stand 5 minutes before cutting. **Yield:** 6-8 servings.

Asparagus Cheese Strata

We visited old friends who served this egg dish for Sunday breakfast before church. I thought it was wonderful. Besides, it's easy to make ahead.
—Betty Jacques, Hemet, California

1-1/2 pounds fresh asparagus, cut into 2-inch pieces
3 tablespoons butter, melted
1 loaf (1 pound) sliced bread, crusts removed
3/4 cup shredded cheddar cheese, *divided*
2 cups cubed fully cooked ham
6 eggs
3 cups milk
2 teaspoons dried minced onion
1/2 teaspoon salt
1/4 teaspoon ground mustard

In a saucepan, cover asparagus with water; cover and cook until just tender but still firm. Drain and set aside. Lightly brush butter over one side of bread slices. Place half of the bread, buttered side up, in a greased 13-in. x 9-in. x 2-in. baking dish. Sprinkle with 1/2 cup cheese. Layer with asparagus and ham. Cover with remaining bread, buttered side up. In a bowl, lightly beat eggs; add milk, onion, salt and mustard; pour over bread. Cover and refrigerate overnight.

Bake, uncovered, at 325° for 50 minutes. Sprinkle with remaining cheese. Return to oven for 10 minutes or until cheese is melted and a knife inserted near the center comes out clean. Let stand 5 minutes before cutting. **Yield:** 10-12 servings.

Elephant Ears

Reaction from those who eat these makes them worth the effort!　—*Suzanne McKinley, Lyons, Georgia*

>   1 package (1/4 ounce) active dry yeast
>   1 cup warm water (110° to 115°)
>   1 cup warm milk (110° to 115°)
>   3 tablespoons sugar
>   1 tablespoon salt
>   3 tablespoons shortening
> 4 to 4-1/2 cups all-purpose flour
> Oil for deep-fat frying
> TOPPING:
>   1 cup sugar
>   1 teaspoon ground cinnamon

Dissolve yeast in water. Add milk, sugar, salt, shortening and 2 cups flour; beat until smooth. Stir in enough remaining flour to form a soft dough. On a floured surface, knead until smooth and elastic, about 6-8 minutes. Place in a greased bowl; turn once to grease top. Cover and let rise in a warm place until doubled, about 1 hour.

Punch down and shape into 15 ovals, 5-1/2 in. round by 1/8 in. thick. Heat 3-4 in. of oil to 375° in deep-fat fryer. Fry ovals, one at a time, 3 minutes per side or until golden brown. Drain. Mix sugar and cinnamon; sprinkle over warm pastries. **Yield:** 15 servings.

Scrambled Egg Casserole

There's nothing nicer than a delicious egg dish you can prepare the night before so you're not "scrambling" when guests arrive. With satisfying ingredients like ham and a creamy cheese sauce, this dish is really special.
　—*Mary Anne McWhirter*
Pearland, Texas

>   1/2 cup butter, *divided*
>   2 tablespoons all-purpose flour
>   1/2 teaspoon salt

>   1/8 teaspoon pepper
>   2 cups milk
>   1 cup (4 ounces) shredded process
>   cheese (Velveeta)
>   1 cup cubed fully cooked ham
> 1/4 cup sliced green onions
>   12 eggs, beaten
>   1 can (4 ounces) sliced mushrooms,
>   drained
> 1-1/2 cups soft bread crumbs
> Additional sliced green onions, optional

In a medium saucepan, melt 2 tablespoons butter. Add flour, salt and pepper; cook and stir until mixture begins to bubble. Gradually stir in milk; cook until thickened and bubbly, stirring constantly. Remove from the heat. Add cheese; mix well and set aside.

In a large skillet, saute ham and onions in 3 tablespoons butter until onions are tender. Add eggs; cook and stir until they begin to set. Add the mushrooms and cheese sauce; mix well. Pour into a greased 11-in. x 7-in. x 2-in. baking dish. Melt remaining butter; toss with bread crumbs. Sprinkle over top of casserole. Cover and refrigerate for 2-3 hours or overnight.

Bake, uncovered, at 350° for 25-30 minutes or until top is golden brown. Sprinkle with onions if desired. **Yield:** 6-8 servings.

Delicious Potato Doughnuts

I first tried these tasty treats at my sister's house and thought they were the best I'd ever had. They're easy to make, and the fudge frosting tops them off well. When I make them for friends, the recipe is always requested. —Pat Davis, Beulah, Michigan

2 cups hot mashed potatoes (mashed with milk and butter)
2-1/2 cups sugar
2 cups buttermilk
2 eggs, lightly beaten
2 tablespoons butter, melted
2 teaspoons baking soda
2 teaspoons baking powder
1 teaspoon ground nutmeg
1/2 teaspoon salt
6-1/2 to 7 cups all-purpose flour
Oil for frying
FAST FUDGE FROSTING:
    4 cups (1 pound) confectioners' sugar
    1/2 cup baking cocoa
    1/4 teaspoon salt
    1/3 cup boiling water
    1/3 cup butter, melted
    1 teaspoon vanilla extract

In a large bowl, combine potatoes, sugar, buttermilk and eggs. Stir in butter, baking soda, baking powder, nutmeg, salt and enough of the flour to form a soft dough. Turn onto a lightly floured surface; pat out to 3/4-in. thickness. Cut with a 2-1/2-in. floured doughnut cutter.

In an electric skillet, heat 1 in. of oil to 375°. Fry the doughnuts, a few at a time for 2 minutes per side or until browned. Place on paper towels. For frosting, sift sugar, cocoa and salt into a large bowl. Stir in water, butter and vanilla. Dip tops of warm doughnuts in frosting. **Yield:** 4 dozen.

Recipe for: Spinach Bacon Quiche

This versatile dish fits nicely into a menu for brunch or supper. The colorful pie slices easily.
—Lois Sundheim, Fairview, Montana

4 eggs
2 cups milk
1-1/4 cups (5 ounces) shredded cheddar cheese, *divided*
1/4 cup finely chopped onion
4 bacon strips, cooked and crumbled
1/2 teaspoon salt
1/2 teaspoon ground mustard
1/4 teaspoon paprika
1 package (10 ounces) frozen chopped spinach, cooked and drained
1 unbaked pastry shell (9 inches)

In a large bowl, beat eggs; whisk in milk, 1 cup cheese, onion, bacon, salt, mustard and paprika. Add spinach. Pour into pie shell. Sprinkle with the remaining cheese.

Bake at 400° for 40 minutes or until a knife inserted near the center comes out clean. Allow to stand for 10 minutes before cutting. **Yield:** 6 servings.

Quiche Lorraine

Ideal for a brunch or luncheon, this classic recipe highlights a delicious meal. Try serving a wedge with fresh fruit of the season and homemade muffins for a plate that will look as good as the food tastes!
—Marcy Cella, L'Anse, Michigan

CRUST:
    2 cups all-purpose flour
    1/2 teaspoon salt
    3/4 cup butter-flavored shortening
    3 to 4 tablespoons cold water
FILLING:
    12 bacon strips, cooked and crumbled
    4 eggs
    2 cups half-and-half cream
    1/4 teaspoon salt
    1/8 teaspoon ground nutmeg
    1-1/4 cups (5 ounces) shredded Swiss cheese

In a mixing bowl, combine flour and salt. Cut in shortening until mixture is crumbly. Gradually add water, tossing with a fork until dough forms a ball. Divide in half.

On a lightly floured surface, roll half of dough to fit a 9-in. pie plate; transfer to pie plate. Trim and flute edges. Chill. Wrap remaining dough; chill or freeze for another use.

For filling, sprinkle crumbled bacon in the chilled pie crust. In a bowl, beat eggs, cream, salt and nutmeg. Stir in cheese. Pour into crust. Bake at 425° for 15 minutes.

Reduce temperature to 325°; continue to bake for 30-40 minutes or until a knife inserted near the center comes out clean. Let stand 10 minutes before cutting. **Yield:** 6 servings.

Zucchini Scramble

This dish has a garden-fresh taste that's sure to please. I like this recipe because I can change it as other fresh vegetables become available. It also makes a tasty light lunch or dinner.
—Betty Claycomb, Alverton, Pennsylvania

    2 to 3 small zucchini (about 1 pound), sliced
    1 medium onion, chopped
    2 tablespoons butter
Salt and pepper to taste

    6 to 8 eggs, beaten
    1/2 cup shredded cheddar cheese
Tomato wedges, optional

In a skillet, saute zucchini and onion in butter until tender. Season with salt and pepper. Add the eggs; cook and stir until set. Sprinkle with cheese. Remove from the heat; cover until cheese melts. Serve with tomato wedges if desired. **Yield:** 4-6 servings.

Recipe for: Ham 'n' Cheese Pie

There's no need to make a crust for this eye-opening quiche. My family and friends love it for brunch or anytime.

—*Iris Posey, Albany, Georgia*

1 cup diced fully cooked ham
3/4 cup shredded Swiss cheese
5 bacon strips, cooked and crumbled
3/4 cup shredded sharp cheddar cheese
3 tablespoons chopped onion
3 tablespoons chopped green pepper
1 cup milk
1/4 cup biscuit/baking mix
2 eggs
1/4 teaspoon salt
1/8 teaspoon pepper

In a greased 10-in. quiche dish or pie plate, layer ham, Swiss cheese, bacon, cheddar cheese, onion and green pepper. Place the remaining ingredients in a blender in the order given; blend for 30-40 seconds. Pour over meat, cheese and vegetables; do not stir.

Bake, uncovered, at 350° for 30-35 minutes or until lightly browned and a knife inserted near the center comes out clean. Let stand 5 minutes before cutting. **Yield:** 6-8 servings.

Buttermilk Pecan Waffles

I like cooking with buttermilk. These nutty, golden waffles are my husband's favorite breakfast, so we enjoy them often. They're as easy to prepare as regular waffles, but their unique taste makes them exceptional. —*Edna Hoffman, Hebron, Indiana*

2 cups all-purpose flour
1 tablespoon baking powder
1 teaspoon baking soda
1/2 teaspoon salt
4 eggs
2 cups buttermilk
1/2 cup butter, melted
3 tablespoons chopped pecans

Combine flour, baking powder, baking soda and salt; set aside. In a mixing bowl, beat eggs until light. Add buttermilk; mix well. Add dry ingredients and beat until batter is smooth. Stir in butter.

Pour about 3/4 cup batter onto a lightly greased preheated waffle iron. Sprinkle with a few pecans. Bake according to manufacturer's directions until golden brown. Repeat until batter and pecans are gone. **Yield:** 7 waffles (about 8 inches each).

Breakfast & Brunch

Soups

At left: Hearty Minestrone (p. 36).

At right: Creamy Vegetable Soup (p. 34).

Cheesy Chicken Chowder

I like to serve this hearty chowder with garlic bread and a salad. It's a wonderful dish to prepare when company drops in. The rich, mild flavor and tender chicken and vegetables appeal even to children and picky eaters. —*Hazel Fritchie, Palestine, Illinois*

  3 cups chicken broth
  2 cups diced peeled potatoes
  1 cup diced carrots
  1 cup diced celery
  1/2 cup diced onion
1-1/2 teaspoons salt
  1/4 teaspoon pepper
  1/4 cup butter
  1/3 cup all-purpose flour
  2 cups milk
  2 cups (8 ounces) shredded cheddar
    cheese
  2 cups diced cooked chicken

In a 4-qt. saucepan, bring chicken broth to a boil. Reduce heat; add potatoes, carrots, celery, onion, salt and pepper. Cover and simmer for 15 minutes or until vegetables are tender.

Meanwhile, melt the butter in a medium saucepan; add flour and mix well. Gradually stir in milk; cook over low heat until slightly thickened. Stir in cheese and cook until melted; add to broth along with chicken. Cook and stir over low heat until heated through. **Yield:** 6-8 servings.

Creamy Vegetable Soup

(Pictured on page 33)

When I couldn't get a written recipe for this delicious soup, I began to experiment on my own. Finally, I came up with this blend, which is very close to the one I remember. The secret ingredient, I think, is sweet potatoes!
—*Audrey Nemeth*
Mount Vernon, Maine

  1 large onion, chopped
1/4 cup butter
  3 medium sweet potatoes, peeled and
    chopped
  3 medium zucchini, chopped
  1 bunch broccoli, chopped
  2 quarts chicken broth
  2 medium potatoes, peeled and shredded
  1 teaspoon celery seed
  1 to 2 teaspoons ground cumin
  2 teaspoons salt
  1 teaspoon pepper
  2 cups half-and-half cream

In a large soup kettle or Dutch oven, saute onion in butter until transparent but not browned. Add the sweet potatoes, zucchini and broccoli; saute lightly for 5 minutes or until crisp-tender.

Stir in broth; simmer for a few minutes. Add potatoes and seasonings; cook another 10 minutes or until vegetables are tender. Stir in cream and heat through but do not boil. **Yield:** 12-16 servings (4 quarts).

Recipe for: Chicken Soup with Spaetzle

This flavorful, hearty chicken soup with its tender spaetzle has old-world goodness that's hard to beat.

—Elaine Lange, Grand Rapids, Michigan

1 broiler-fryer chicken (2 to 3 pounds), cut into pieces
2 tablespoons vegetable oil
2 quarts chicken broth
2 bay leaves
1/2 teaspoon dried thyme
1/4 teaspoon pepper
1 cup *each* sliced carrots and celery
3/4 cup chopped onion
1 garlic clove, minced
1/3 cup medium pearl barley
2 cups sliced fresh mushrooms
SPAETZLE:
1-1/4 cups all-purpose flour
1/8 teaspoon baking powder
1/8 teaspoon salt
1 egg, lightly beaten
1/4 cup water
1/4 cup milk

In a large kettle or Dutch oven, brown chicken pieces in oil. Add the broth, bay leaves, thyme and pepper. Simmer until chicken is tender. Cool broth and skim off fat.

Skin and bone chicken and cut into bite-size pieces; return to broth along with carrots, celery, onion, garlic and barley. Bring to a boil. Reduce heat; cover and simmer for 35 minutes. Add mushrooms and simmer 8-10 minutes longer. Remove bay leaves.

In a small bowl, combine first three spaetzle ingredients. Stir in egg, water and milk; blend well. Drop batter by 1/2 teaspoonfuls into simmering soup. Cook for 10 minutes. **Yield:** 8-10 servings (2-1/2 quarts).

French Onion Soup

I adapted a basic recipe to copy an onion soup I had tried and enjoyed. Now I can make it whenever I like. It's a meal in itself or an impressive beginning to a full-course meal.
—Barbara Brunner
Steelton, Pennsylvania

2 medium onions, chopped
1 teaspoon sugar
6 tablespoons butter, *divided*
1 tablespoon all-purpose flour
1/8 teaspoon pepper
Dash ground nutmeg
2-1/2 cups beef broth
2 tablespoons grated Parmesan cheese
2 slices French bread (1 inch thick)
4 slices provolone cheese

In a saucepan, saute onions and sugar in 3 tablespoons of butter until golden brown. Stir in the flour, pepper and nutmeg until blended. Gradually stir in broth. Bring to a boil; cook and stir for 2 minutes. Reduce heat; cover and simmer for 30 minutes. Stir in the Parmesan cheese.

Meanwhile, in a skillet, melt remaining butter; add bread. Cook until golden brown on both sides. Ladle soup into two ovenproof bowls. Place a slice of cheese in each bowl; top with bread and remaining cheese. Bake at 375° for 10 minutes or until the cheese is bubbly. **Yield:** 2 servings.

Hearty Minestrone

(Pictured on page 32)

This soup is a fresh-tasting main dish that gets its zesty flavor from Italian sausage. When you want to use up your garden bounty of zucchini, try this soup. —Donna Smith, Victor, New York

1 pound bulk Italian sausage
2 cups sliced celery
1 cup chopped onion
6 cups chopped zucchini
1 can (28 ounces) whole tomatoes,
**   undrained, cut up**
1-1/2 cups chopped green pepper
1-1/2 teaspoons Italian seasoning

1-1/2 teaspoons salt
** 1 teaspoon dried oregano**
** 1 teaspoon sugar**
1/2 teaspoon dried basil
1/4 teaspoon garlic powder

In a large saucepan, brown the sausage. Remove with a slotted spoon to paper towel to drain, reserving 1 tablespoon of drippings. Saute celery and onion in the drippings for 5 minutes.

    Add sausage and remaining ingredients; bring to a boil. Reduce heat; cover and simmer for 20-30 minutes or until the vegetables are tender. **Yield:** 9 servings.

Five-Bean Soup

Prepare a big batch of the beans, then just add a few ingredients each time you want a pot of soup. Sometimes we like to grate mozzarella cheese over the individual bowls just before serving. —Lynne Dodd Mentor, Ohio

5 packages (16 ounces *each*) dry lima
**   beans, great northern beans, kidney**
**   beans, pinto beans and split peas**
**   (enough for four batches of soup)**
ADDITIONAL INGREDIENTS:
** 3 tablespoons dried chives**
** 1 teaspoon dried savory**
** 1 teaspoon salt, optional**
1/2 teaspoon ground cumin
1/2 teaspoon pepper
** 1 bay leaf**
** 3 beef bouillon cubes**
2-1/2 quarts water
** 1 can (14-1/2 ounces) stewed tomatoes**

Combine beans and peas. Store in an airtight container in a cool dry place for up to 1 year. **Yield:** 4 batches (15 cups total).

    To prepare soup: Wash 3-3/4 cups of beans and peas. Place in a large kettle; add enough water to cover. Bring to a boil; cook for 3-4 minutes. Remove from heat; cover and let stand 1 hour.

    Tie spices in a cheesecloth bag. Drain and rinse beans and peas. Return to kettle; add bouillon, spices and water. Bring to boil. Reduce heat; cover and simmer 1-1/2 hours or until beans and peas are tender, stirring occasionally. Remove spices. Add tomatoes and heat through. **Yield:** 14 servings (3-1/2 quarts) per batch.

Creamy Carrot Soup

When I serve this creamy soup, people are amazed by the bright carrot color and are hooked by the deliciously different flavor. A hint of rosemary adds spark to a slightly sweet soup. —Grace Yaskovic
Branchville, New Jersey

   1 cup chopped onion
 1/4 cup butter
4-1/2 cups sliced carrots (1/4 inch thick)
   1 large potato, peeled and cubed
   2 cans (14-1/2 ounces *each*) chicken
     broth
   1 teaspoon ground ginger
   2 cups heavy whipping cream
   1 teaspoon dried rosemary, crushed
 1/2 teaspoon salt
 1/8 teaspoon pepper

In a 5-qt. Dutch oven, saute the onion in butter until tender. Add the carrots, potato, broth and ginger. Cover and cook over medium heat for 30 minutes or until the vegetables are tender. Cool 15 minutes.

Puree in small batches in a blender or food processor until smooth. Return all to the saucepan; add cream, rosemary, salt and pepper. Cook over low heat until heated through but do not boil. **Yield:** 6-8 servings (2-1/2 quarts).

Recipe for: Mushroom and Potato Chowder

My daughter shared this delightful recipe with me. Its rich broth, big mushroom taste and medley of vegetables make this chowder a little different from ordinary mushroom soup. —Romaine Wetzel
Lancaster, Pennsylvania

 1/2 cup chopped onion
 1/4 cup butter
   2 tablespoons all-purpose flour
   1 teaspoon salt
 1/2 teaspoon pepper
   3 cups water
   1 pound fresh mushrooms, sliced
   1 cup chopped celery
   1 cup diced peeled potatoes
 1/2 cup chopped carrots
   1 cup half-and-half cream
 1/4 cup grated Parmesan cheese

In a large kettle, saute onion in butter until tender. Add flour, salt and pepper; stir to make a smooth paste. Gradually add water, stirring constantly. Bring to a boil; cook and stir for 1 minute.

Add the mushrooms, celery, potatoes and carrots. Reduce heat; cover and simmer for 30 minutes or until vegetables are tender. Add the cream and Parmesan cheese; heat through but do not boil. **Yield:** 4-6 servings.

Potato Cheese Soup

My father was Swiss, so cheese has been a basic food in our family as long as I can remember. With its big cheese taste, you'll want to prepare this soup often. A steaming bowl plus a salad and slice of bread makes a wonderful light meal. —Carol Smith
New Berlin, Wisconsin

3 medium potatoes (about 1 pound),
  peeled and quartered
1 small onion, finely chopped
1 cup water
1 teaspoon salt
3 cups milk
3 tablespoons butter, melted
2 tablespoons all-purpose flour
2 tablespoons minced fresh parsley
1/8 teaspoon white pepper
1 cup (4 ounces) shredded Swiss cheese

In a large saucepan, bring potatoes, onion, water and salt to a boil. Reduce heat; cover and simmer until potatoes are tender. Do not drain; mash slightly. Stir in milk.

In a small bowl, blend butter, flour, parsley and pepper; stir into the potato mixture. Cook and stir over medium heat until thickened and bubbly. Remove from the heat; add cheese and stir until almost melted. **Yield:** 6 servings (1-1/2 quarts).

Recipe for: Old-World Tomato Soup

This hearty soup has been in our family for four generations, and I've never seen another recipe like it. Each spoonful brings back memories. —Linda Pandolfo, East Haddam, Connecticut

3 quarts water
4 beef short ribs (about 2 pounds)
2 to 3 meaty soup bones (about 2
  pounds)
1 can (28 ounces) whole tomatoes,
  undrained
3 celery ribs, halved
1 large onion, quartered
1/2 cup chopped fresh parsley, *divided*
1 tablespoon salt
1-1/2 teaspoons pepper
4 carrots, cut into 1-inch pieces
2 parsnips, peeled and quartered
2 cups (16 ounces) sour cream
1/2 cup all-purpose flour
1/2 teaspoon ground nutmeg, optional
1 package (8 ounces) egg noodles,
  cooked and drained

In a large kettle, combine water, ribs, soup bones, tomatoes, celery, onion, 1/4 cup parsley, salt and pepper. Cover and simmer for 2 hours. Add carrots and parsnips; cover and simmer for 1 hour or until meat and vegetables are tender.

With a slotted spoon, remove meat, bones and vegetables. Strain broth and skim off fat; return all but 1 cup broth to kettle. Set reserved broth aside. Remove meat from the bones; dice and return to kettle. Discard celery and onion. Cut parsnips, carrots and tomatoes into 1/2-in. pieces and return to kettle. Add remaining parsley.

In a bowl, combine sour cream, flour, nutmeg if desired and reserved broth; stir into soup. Add noodles. Cook and stir until thickened and heated through (do not boil). **Yield:** 16-20 servings.

Sausage Lentil Soup

This savory soup gets wonderful flavor from sausage and vegetables. Lentils make it satisfying.
—Kathy Anderson, Casper, Wyoming

    1/2 pound bulk Italian sausage
      1 large onion, chopped
      1 medium green pepper, chopped
      1 large carrot, chopped
      2 cans (10-1/2 ounces *each*) chicken broth
      1 can (14-1/2 ounces) diced tomatoes,
        undrained
      1 cup water
      1 garlic clove, minced
      1 teaspoon salt
    1/2 teaspoon pepper
    3/4 cup dry lentils, rinsed

In a Dutch oven or soup kettle, brown and crumble sausage; drain. Add next nine ingredients; bring to a boil. Add lentils. Reduce heat; cover and simmer for 60-70 minutes or until the lentils are tender. **Yield:** 6-8 servings (2 quarts).

Grandma most always had a pot of soup simmering on the wood stove. When my brother and I came in from sledding, we'd get a bowl, and sometimes Grandma would ask all the neighbor kids in for soup. Hoboes would stop by for a bowl, too. Grandma fed her soup to anyone who was hungry, any time day or night.
—Joe Snyder
Bellevue, Washington

Vegetable Beef Soup

When we come in from playing in the snow, I serve this classic comforting soup. *—Nancy Soderstrom*
Roseville, Minnesota

      1 beef chuck roast (2-1/2 to 3 pounds)
      4 quarts water
      1 cup medium pearl barley
    1-1/2 cups chopped onion
    1-1/2 cups chopped celery
      1 tablespoon salt
      1 teaspoon pepper
      1 can (28 ounces) diced tomatoes,
        undrained
    1-1/2 cups chopped carrots
      1 package (16 ounces) frozen mixed
        vegetables
    1/4 cup minced fresh parsley
    1/2 teaspoon dried basil
    1/4 teaspoon dried thyme
    1/4 teaspoon garlic salt

In a large Dutch oven or soup kettle, place roast, water, barley, onion, celery, salt and pepper; bring to a boil. Reduce heat; cover and simmer for 1 hour and 15 minutes or until meat is tender. Remove meat; cool. Cut meat into bite-size pieces. Skim fat from broth. Add beef and remaining ingredients; bring to a boil. Reduce heat; cover and simmer for 45 minutes or until vegetables are tender. **Yield:** 15-20 servings (6 quarts).

Broccoli Soup

This thick creamy soup has wonderful fresh broccoli flavor with just a hint of nutmeg. —Marion Tipton
Phoenix, Arizona

4 cups chicken broth
2 to 2-1/2 pounds broccoli, cut into
   florets
1/2 cup chopped green onions
1 tablespoon olive oil
1/4 cup all-purpose flour
1 teaspoon salt
1/4 teaspoon ground nutmeg
1/8 teaspoon pepper
1 cup half-and-half cream

In a large saucepan, bring the broth to a boil; add broccoli. Reduce heat; cover and simmer until tender, about 10 minutes.

Meanwhile, in a small skillet, saute onions in oil until tender; stir into broth. Remove from the heat; cool 10-15 minutes. Puree in small batches in a blender or food processor until smooth. Return all to the saucepan; set aside.

In a bowl, combine flour, salt, nutmeg and pepper. Slowly add cream, stirring constantly. Gradually stir into broccoli mixture. Return to the heat; cook over medium until heated through, stirring occasionally. **Yield:** 4 servings.

Creamy Corn Chowder

Corn really stars in this delectable recipe. It hits the spot whenever you crave a rich, hearty soup.
—Carol Sundquist, Rochester, New York

2 chicken bouillon cubes
1 cup hot water
5 bacon strips
1 cup chopped green pepper
1/2 cup chopped onion
1/4 cup all-purpose flour
3 cups milk
1-1/2 cups fresh *or* frozen whole kernel corn
1 can (14-3/4 ounces) cream-style corn
1-1/2 teaspoons seasoned salt
1/4 teaspoon salt
1/8 teaspoon white pepper
1/8 teaspoon dried basil

Dissolve bouillon in water; set aside. In a 5-qt. Dutch oven, cook bacon until crisp. Remove bacon; crumble and set aside.

In the drippings, saute green pepper and onion until tender. Add flour; cook and stir until bubbly. Cook 1 minute longer. Gradually stir in milk and dissolved bouillon; bring to a boil. Reduce heat; cook and stir until thickened.

Add corn and seasonings. Cook for 10 minutes or until heated through. Sprinkle with bacon. **Yield:** 6-8 servings (2 quarts).

Tomato Dill Bisque

My family really enjoys this soup when we make it from our garden tomatoes. When those tomatoes are plentiful, I make a big batch (without mayonnaise) and freeze it. Then we can enjoy it even after the garden is gone for the season. —Susan Breckbill
Lincoln Univ., Pennsylvania

2 medium onions, chopped
1 garlic clove, minced
2 tablespoons butter
2 pounds tomatoes, peeled and chopped
1/2 cup water
1 chicken bouillon cube
1 teaspoon sugar
1 teaspoon dill weed
1/2 teaspoon salt
1/4 teaspoon pepper
1/2 cup mayonnaise, optional

In a large saucepan, saute onions and garlic in butter until tender. Add tomatoes, water, bouillon, sugar and seasonings. Cover and simmer 10 minutes or until tomatoes are tender. Remove from heat; cool.

Puree in a blender or food processor. Return to saucepan. If a creamy soup is desired, stir in mayonnaise. Cook and stir over low heat until heated through. Serve warm. **Yield:** 5 servings (5 cups).

Recipe for: Savory Cheese Soup

This delicious soup recipe was shared by a friend and instantly became a hit with my husband. Its big cheese flavor blends wonderfully with the flavor of the vegetables. I first served this creamy soup as part of a holiday meal, but now we enjoy it throughout the year. —Dee Falk, Stromsburg, Nebraska

1/4 cup chopped onion
3 tablespoons butter
1/4 cup all-purpose flour
1/4 teaspoon salt
1/8 teaspoon pepper
1/8 teaspoon garlic powder
2 cups milk
1 can (14-1/2 ounces) chicken broth
1/2 cup shredded carrots
1/2 cup finely chopped celery
1-1/2 cups (6 ounces) shredded cheddar cheese
3/4 cup shredded mozzarella cheese
Fresh *or* dried chives, optional

In a large saucepan, saute onion in butter until tender. Add flour, salt, pepper and garlic powder; stir until smooth. Gradually add milk; cook and stir over medium heat until thickened and bubbly.

Meanwhile, bring chicken broth to a boil in a small saucepan. Add carrots and celery; simmer for 5 minutes or until vegetables are tender. Add to milk mixture and stir until blended. Add cheeses. Cook and stir until melted (do not boil). Garnish with chives if desired. **Yield:** about 4 servings.

Scotch Broth

Early in winter, I make up big pots of this hearty soup to freeze in plastic containers. Then I can bring out one or two containers at a time. I heat the frozen soup in a saucepan on low all morning. By lunchtime, it's hot and ready to serve my hungry family!
—Ann Main, Moorefield, Ontario

2 pounds meaty beef soup bones
2 quarts water
6 whole peppercorns
1-1/2 teaspoons salt
1 cup chopped carrots
1 cup chopped turnips
1 cup chopped celery
1/2 cup chopped onion
1/4 cup medium pearl barley

In a large soup kettle or Dutch oven, combine soup bones, water, peppercorns and salt. Cover and simmer for 2-1/2 hours or until the meat comes easily off the bones.

Remove bones. Strain broth; cool and chill. Skim off fat. Remove meat from bones; dice and return to broth along with remaining ingredients. Bring to a boil. Reduce heat; cover and simmer about 1 hour or until vegetables and barley are tender. **Yield:** 6-8 servings (2 quarts).

Recipe for: Creamy Squash Soup

I simmer this smooth full-flavored soup featuring whatever winter squash is available. Serve with rolls, fruit and cheese.
—Gayle Lewis, Yucaipa, California

3 bacon strips
1 cup finely chopped onion
2 garlic cloves, minced
2 cups mashed cooked winter squash
2 tablespoons all-purpose flour
1 can (12 ounces) evaporated milk,
    divided
3 cups chicken broth
1/2 teaspoon curry powder
1/2 teaspoon salt
1/4 teaspoon pepper
1/8 teaspoon ground nutmeg
Sour cream, optional

In a saucepan or Dutch oven, cook bacon until crisp; crumble and set aside. Drain all but 1 tablespoon drippings; saute onion and garlic in drippings until tender.

In a blender or food processor, puree squash, flour, 1/3 cup milk and onion mixture; add to pan. Add broth, curry powder, salt, pepper, nutmeg and remaining milk; bring to a boil over medium heat. Boil for 2 minutes. Top servings with a dollop of sour cream if desired. Sprinkle with bacon. **Yield:** 6-8 servings.

Spinach Garlic Soup

During the years I owned and operated a deli, this was one of the most popular soups I served.
—*Marilyn Paradis, Woodburn, Oregon*

    1 package (10 ounces) fresh spinach,
       trimmed and coarsely chopped
    4 cups chicken broth
  1/2 cup shredded carrots
  1/2 cup chopped onion
    8 garlic cloves, minced
  1/3 cup butter
  1/4 cup all-purpose flour
  3/4 cup heavy whipping cream
  1/4 cup milk
  1/2 teaspoon pepper
  1/8 teaspoon ground nutmeg

In a 5-qt. Dutch oven, bring spinach, broth and carrots to a boil. Reduce heat; simmer 5 minutes, stirring occasionally. Remove from the heat; cool to lukewarm.

Meanwhile, in a skillet, saute onion and garlic in butter until onion is soft, about 5-10 minutes. Add flour; cook and stir over low heat for 3-5 minutes. Add to spinach mixture.

Puree in small batches in a blender or food processor until finely chopped. Place in a large saucepan. Add cream, milk, pepper and nutmeg; heat through but do not boil. **Yield:** 4-6 servings.

Basic Turkey Soup

I simmer a rich broth using the turkey carcass, then add favorite vegetables and sometimes noodles.
—*Katie Koziolek, Hartland, Minnesota*

TURKEY BROTH:
    1 leftover turkey carcass
    2 quarts water
    1 chicken bouillon cube
    1 celery rib with leaves
    1 small onion, halved
    1 carrot
    3 whole peppercorns
    1 garlic clove
    1 teaspoon seasoned salt
  1/4 teaspoon dried thyme
TURKEY VEGETABLE SOUP:
    8 cups turkey broth
    2 chicken bouillon cubes
  1/2 to 3/4 teaspoon pepper
    4 cups sliced carrots, celery *and/or* other
       vegetables
  3/4 cup chopped onion
    4 cups diced cooked turkey

In a large soup kettle, place all broth ingredients; cover and bring to a boil. Reduce heat; simmer for 25 minutes. Strain broth; discard bones and vegetables. Cool; skim fat. Use immediately for turkey vegetable soup or refrigerate and use within 24 hours.

For soup, combine broth, bouillon, pepper, vegetables and onion in a large soup kettle. Cover and simmer for 15-20 minutes or until the vegetables are tender. Add turkey and heat through. **Yield:** 8-10 servings.

Beef Noodle Soup

This recipe takes just minutes to prepare but tastes like it simmered all day. —Margery Bryan
Royal City, Washington

1 pound ground beef
1/2 cup chopped onion
2 cans (14-1/2 ounces *each*) Italian stewed tomatoes
2 cans (10-1/2 ounces *each*) beef broth
1 can (15 ounces) mixed vegetables, drained
1 teaspoon dried oregano
1/2 teaspoon salt
1/4 teaspoon pepper
1 cup uncooked egg noodles

In a Dutch oven or soup kettle, cook beef and onion over medium heat until meat is no longer pink; drain. Add tomatoes, broth, vegetables and seasonings. Bring to a boil; add noodles.

Reduce heat to medium-low; cover and cook for 10-15 minutes or until the noodles are tender. **Yield:** 6-8 servings (2 quarts).

The scent of dill takes me back to Grandma's kitchen. She always spent much time tending the coal cookstove and the pot of dill-flavored chicken soup, which seemed to be constantly simmering on the back burner.
—Helen Catherine Smith, Tampa, Florida

Hearty Potato Soup

Having grown up on a dairy farm in Holland, I love our country life here in Idaho's "potato country."

This potato soup originally called for whipping cream and bacon fat, but I've trimmed down the recipe.
—Gladys DeBoer, Castleford, Idaho

6 medium potatoes, peeled and sliced
2 medium carrots, diced
6 celery ribs, diced
2 quarts water
1 medium onion, chopped
6 tablespoons butter
6 tablespoons all-purpose flour
1 teaspoon salt
1/2 teaspoon pepper
1-1/2 cups milk

In a large soup kettle or Dutch oven, cook potatoes, carrots and celery in water until tender, about 20 minutes. Drain, reserving liquid and setting vegetables aside.

In the same kettle, saute onion in butter until tender. Stir in flour, salt and pepper; gradually add milk, stirring constantly until thickened. Gently stir in cooked vegetables. Add 1 cup or more of reserved cooking liquid until soup is desired consistency. **Yield:** 8-10 servings (about 2-1/2 quarts).

Stuffed Roast Pepper Soup

After sampling a similar soup at a summer resort, my daughter and I invented this version. Using a colorful variety of peppers makes it especially appealing.
—Betty Vig, Viroqua, Wisconsin

2 pounds ground beef
1/2 medium onion, chopped
6 cups water
8 beef bouillon cubes
2 cans (28 ounces *each*) diced tomatoes, undrained
2 cups cooked rice
2 teaspoons salt
1/2 teaspoon pepper
1/2 teaspoon paprika
3 green, yellow *or* sweet red peppers, seeded and chopped

In a large Dutch oven or soup kettle, cook ground beef and onion over medium heat until the meat is no longer pink and the onion is tender; drain.

Add water, bouillon cubes, tomatoes, rice and seasonings. Bring to a boil; reduce heat and simmer, covered, for 1 hour. Add chopped peppers; cook, uncovered, for 10-15 minutes or until peppers are tender. **Yield:** 14-16 servings (4 quarts).

Recipe for: U.S. Senate Bean Soup

Chock-full of ham, beans and celery, this hearty soup makes a wonderful meal at any time of year. Freeze the bone from a holiday ham until you're ready to make soup. Plus, once prepared, this soup freezes well for a great make-ahead supper!
—Rosemarie Forcum, White Stone, Virginia

1 pound dried great northern beans
1 meaty ham bone *or* 2 smoked ham hocks
3 medium onions, chopped
3 garlic cloves, minced
3 celery ribs, chopped
1/4 cup chopped fresh parsley
1 cup mashed potatoes *or* 1/3 cup mashed potato flakes
Salt and pepper to taste
Parsley *or* chives for garnish

In a saucepan, place beans and enough water to cover; bring to a boil and boil for 2 minutes. Remove from the heat and soak for 1 hour.

Drain and rinse beans. In a large kettle, place beans, ham bone and 3 qts. water. Bring to boil. Reduce heat; cover and simmer for 2 hours. Skim fat if necessary. Add onions, garlic, celery, parsley, potatoes, salt and pepper; simmer 1 hour longer.

Remove meat and bones from the soup. Remove meat from the bones; dice and return to kettle. Heat through. Garnish with parsley or chives. **Yield:** 8-10 servings (2-1/2 quarts).

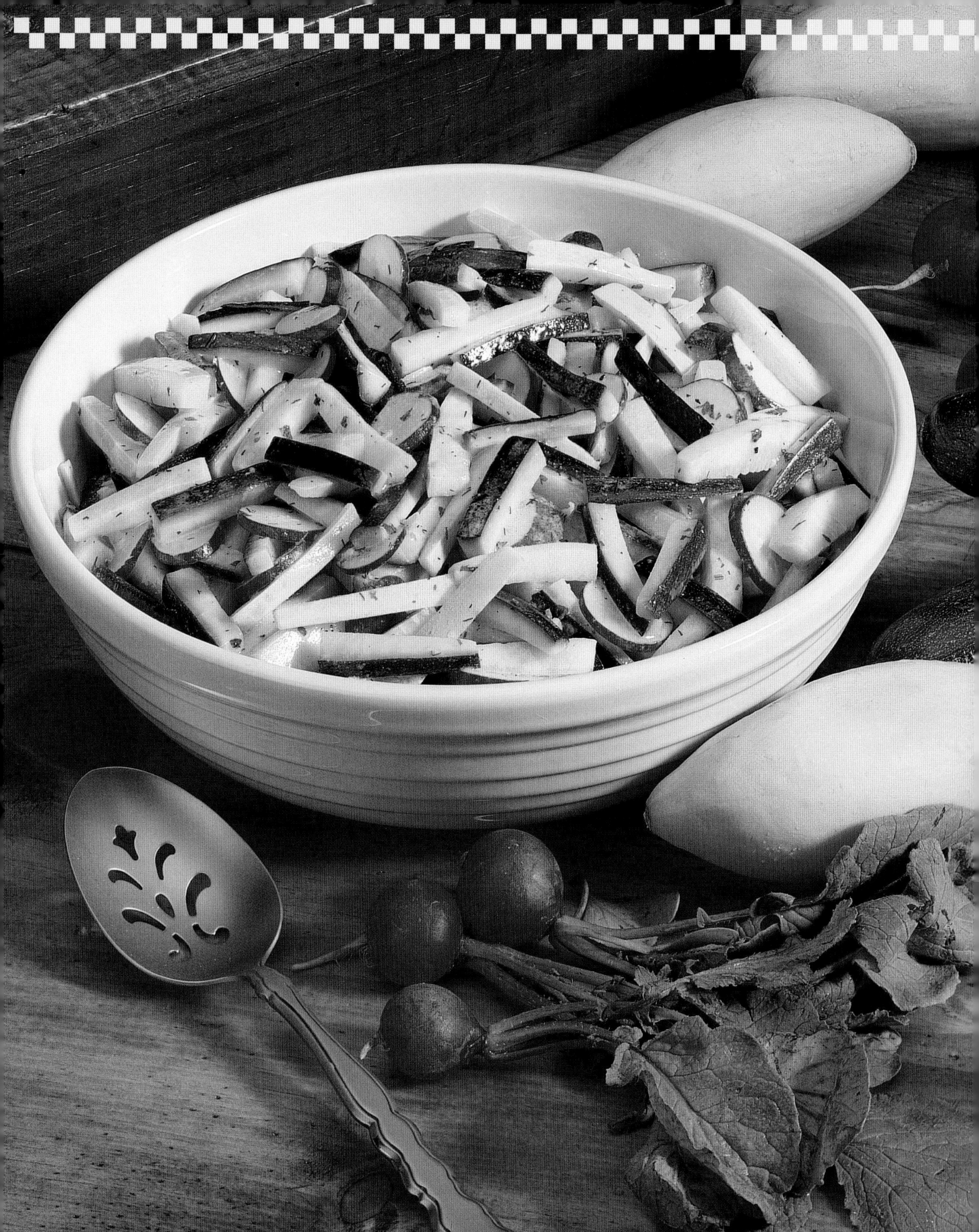

Salads

At left: Summer Squash Salad (p. 48).

At right: Lime Gelatin Salad (p. 51).

Gazpacho Salad

Here's a beautiful and tasty way to use garden vegetables. This fresh, colorful salad is great to make ahead and take to a potluck later, after the flavors have had a chance to blend. It's sure to be a success! —Florence Jacoby, Granite Falls, Minnesota

4 tomatoes, seeded and diced
2 cucumbers, peeled and diced
2 green peppers, seeded and diced
1 medium onion, diced
1 can (2-1/4 ounces) sliced ripe olives, drained
1 teaspoon salt
1/2 teaspoon pepper
DRESSING:
1/2 cup olive oil
1/4 cup cider vinegar
Juice of 1 lemon (about 1/4 cup)
1 tablespoon chopped fresh parsley
2 garlic cloves, minced
2 teaspoons chopped green onions
1/2 teaspoon salt
1/4 teaspoon ground cumin

In a 1-1/2-qt. glass jar or bowl, layer one-third to one-half of the tomatoes, cucumbers, green peppers, onion, olives, salt and pepper. Repeat layers two or three more times.

In a small bowl, combine all dressing ingredients. Pour over vegetables. Cover and chill several hours or overnight. **Yield:** 10-12 servings.

Summer Squash Salad

(Pictured on page 46)

This is a colorful and tasty alternative to coleslaw. Like most gardeners, we usually have an abundance of squash and zucchini in summer, so this dish is inexpensive to prepare and a great way to put this fresh produce to use. —Diane Hixon, Niceville, Florida

4 cups julienned zucchini
4 cups julienned yellow squash
2 cups sliced radishes
1 cup vegetable oil
1/3 cup cider vinegar
2 tablespoons Dijon mustard
2 tablespoons snipped fresh parsley
1-1/2 teaspoons salt
1 teaspoon dill weed
1/2 teaspoon pepper

In a bowl, toss the zucchini, squash and radishes. In a small bowl or jar with tight-fitting lid, combine all remaining ingredients; shake or mix well. Pour over vegetables. Cover and refrigerate for at least 2 hours. **Yield:** 12-16 servings.

Recipe for: Pineapple Gelatin Salad

My family enjoys this lovely layered salad in the summer with grilled hamburgers. It's always a favorite. A good friend shared it with me, and every time I make it, I think of her. —Susan Kirby, Tipton, Indiana

1 can (20 ounces) crushed pineapple
1 package (6 ounces) lemon gelatin
3 cups boiling water
1 package (8 ounces) cream cheese, softened
1 carton (16 ounces) frozen whipped topping, thawed
3/4 cup sugar
3 tablespoons lemon juice
3 tablespoons water
2 tablespoons all-purpose flour
2 egg yolks, lightly beaten

Drain pineapple, reserving juice. Dissolve gelatin in water; add pineapple. Pour into a 13-in. x 9-in. x 2-in. dish; chill until almost set, about 45 minutes.

In a mixing bowl, beat cream cheese and whipped topping until smooth. Carefully spread over gelatin; chill for 30 minutes.

Meanwhile, in a saucepan over medium heat, combine sugar, lemon juice, water, flour, egg yolks and reserved pineapple juice; bring to a boil, stirring constantly. Cook 1 minute or until thickened. Cool. Carefully spread over cream cheese layer. Chill for at least 1 hour. **Yield:** 12-16 servings.

Garden Bean Salad

My mother gave me this crunchy bean salad recipe many years ago, and I often take it to covered-dish dinners. It looks especially attractive served in a glass bowl to show off the colorful vegetables.
—Bernice McFadden, Dayton, Ohio

2 cans (17 ounces *each*) lima beans
1 can (16 ounces) cut green beans
1 can (16 ounces) kidney beans
1 can (16 ounces) wax beans
1 can (15 ounces) garbanzo beans
1 large green pepper, chopped
3 celery ribs, chopped
1 jar (2 ounces) sliced pimientos, drained
1 bunch green onions, sliced
2 cups vinegar
2 cups sugar
1/2 cup water
1 teaspoon salt

Drain all six cans of beans; place in a large bowl. Add green pepper, celery, pimientos and green onions; set aside. In a heavy saucepan, bring the remaining ingredients to a boil. Boil for 5 minutes. Remove from the heat and immediately pour over the vegetables. Refrigerate several hours or overnight. **Yield:** 12-16 servings.

Tomato Basil Salad

Tomatoes team up with red onion and fresh basil in this pleasant salad. —*Joyce Brown, Genesee, Idaho*

6 tomato slices (1/4 inch thick)
6 red onion slices
2 tablespoons olive oil
4 teaspoons red wine vinegar
2 tablespoons chopped fresh basil
1 teaspoon sugar

Place tomatoes in a shallow dish; top each slice with an onion. In a small jar with tight-fitting lid, combine remaining ingredients; shake well. Pour over tomatoes and onions. Cover and refrigerate for at least 1 hour. **Yield: 2 servings.**

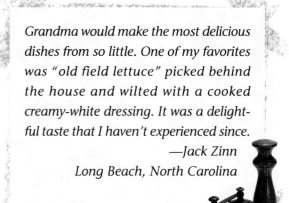

Grandma would make the most delicious dishes from so little. One of my favorites was "old field lettuce" picked behind the house and wilted with a cooked creamy-white dressing. It was a delightful taste that I haven't experienced since.
—*Jack Zinn*
Long Beach, North Carolina

Overnight Coleslaw

This has been a favorite salad from my recipe box for a long, long time. Before I retired, when my office had a get-together, I was always asked to bring my tangy coleslaw. My family loves it, too.
—*Fern Hammock, Garland, Texas*

12 cups shredded cabbage (1 medium head)
1 medium green pepper, chopped
1 medium red onion, chopped
2 medium carrots, shredded
1 cup sugar
DRESSING:
2 teaspoons sugar
1 teaspoon ground mustard
1 teaspoon celery seed
1 teaspoon salt
1 cup cider vinegar
3/4 cup vegetable oil

In a large bowl, combine the first four ingredients. Sprinkle with sugar; set aside.

In a saucepan, combine dressing ingredients; bring to a boil. Remove from heat; pour over vegetables, stirring to cover evenly. Cover and refrigerate overnight. Stir well before serving. **Yield: 12-16 servings.**

Favorite Broccoli Salad

"Fresh tasting...so colorful...delicious dressing" are some of the compliments I get whenever I serve this broccoli salad with a meal or take it to a church dinner. Although I have many other good salad recipes, I'm especially fond of this one.
—Esther Shank, Harrisonburg, Virginia

1 bunch broccoli, separated into florets
1 head cauliflower, separated into florets
8 bacon strips, cooked and crumbled
1/3 cup chopped onion
1 cup chopped seeded tomatoes
2 hard-cooked eggs, sliced
1 cup mayonnaise
1/3 cup sugar
2 tablespoons cider vinegar

In a large salad bowl, combine broccoli, cauliflower, bacon, onion, tomatoes and eggs; set aside. In another bowl, combine mayonnaise, sugar and vinegar; mix until smooth. Just before serving, pour dressing over salad and toss. **Yield:** 6-8 servings.

Recipe for: # Lime Gelatin Salad

(Pictured on page 47)

I've made this refreshing recipe more than 100 times over the past 15 years! It can be a salad or dessert. When I take it to a potluck, it's always one of the first things to disappear. —Louise Harding
Newburgh, New York

1 package (6 ounces) lime gelatin
1 cup boiling water
1 package (8 ounces) cream cheese, softened
1/2 teaspoon vanilla extract
1 can (15 ounces) mandarin oranges, drained
1 can (8 ounces) crushed pineapple, drained
1 cup lemon-lime soda
1/2 cup chopped pecans
1 carton (8 ounces) frozen whipped topping, thawed, *divided*

Dissolve gelatin in water. In a mixing bowl, beat cream cheese until fluffy. Stir in gelatin mixture and beat until smooth. Stir in vanilla, oranges, pineapple, soda and pecans. Chill until mixture mounds slightly when dropped from a spoon.

Fold in three-fourths of the whipped topping. Pour into a 13-in. x 9-in. x 2-in. dish. Refrigerate for 3-4 hours or until firm.

Cut into squares; garnish with the remaining whipped topping. **Yield:** 16-20 servings.

Emily's Spinach Salad

(Also pictured on front cover)

I made up this recipe to enter in a spinach cooking contest. I was delighted when my colorful, tangy salad took the grand prize! —Emily Fields
Santa Ana, California

2/3 cup vegetable oil
1/4 cup red wine vinegar
2 teaspoons lemon juice
2 teaspoons soy sauce
1 teaspoon sugar
1 teaspoon ground mustard
1/2 teaspoon curry powder
1/2 teaspoon salt
1/2 teaspoon seasoned pepper
1/4 teaspoon garlic powder
1 package (10 ounces) fresh spinach, torn
5 bacon strips, cooked and crumbled
2 hard-cooked eggs, sliced

In a jar with a tight-fitting lid, combine the first 10 ingredients; mix well. Set aside. Place the spinach in a large salad bowl.

Just before serving, pour the dressing over the spinach and toss gently. Garnish with the crumbled bacon and egg slices. **Yield:** 6-8 servings.

Recipe for: Special Potato Salad

Vinegar and yogurt give this salad a refreshing tang that's unlike typical potato salads with heavy creamy dressings. My family loves the crispness of the onion and celery and the heartiness that comes from the eggs and crumbled bacon. —Page Alexander, Baldwin City, Kansas

2-1/2 pounds red potatoes
2 tablespoons red wine vinegar
1 tablespoon olive oil
1 tablespoon Dijon mustard
1/2 teaspoon dried basil
1/2 teaspoon pepper
1/4 teaspoon salt
1/2 cup plain yogurt
1/4 cup sour cream
1 teaspoon garlic salt
3/4 cup chopped red onion
1/2 cup diced celery
4 bacon strips, cooked and crumbled
2 hard-cooked eggs, chopped

In a saucepan, cook potatoes in boiling salted water until tender. Meanwhile, in a large bowl, combine vinegar, oil, mustard, basil, pepper and salt; mix well. Drain the potatoes; cut into 1-in. chunks and add to the vinegar and oil mixture while still warm. Toss to coat; cool completely.

In another bowl, combine yogurt, sour cream and garlic salt. Add onion, celery, bacon and eggs; mix well. Add to potato mixture; toss gently. Cover and chill for several hours. **Yield:** 6-8 servings.

Summer Apple Salad

This crunchy salad goes great alongside sandwiches and is especially nice in summer and fall.
—Kim Stoller, Smithville, Ohio

        3 medium tart red apples, cored and
          diced
        1 can (8 ounces) pineapple tidbits,
          drained
  1-1/2 cups sliced celery
        1 cup grape halves
        1 carrot, shredded
      1/2 cup coarsely chopped almonds
      3/4 cup sour cream
        1 tablespoon sugar
      1/2 teaspoon lemon juice

In a large salad bowl, combine apples, pineapple, celery, grapes, carrot and almonds. In a small bowl, combine sour cream, sugar and lemon juice; mix well. Add to apple mixture and toss to coat. Chill. **Yield:** 12 servings.

After he finished lunch, Grandpa would say to Grandma, "That was the best meal I ever ate!" Then, turning to me he'd say, "Your grandmother has cooked me 16,425 meals so far and every one of them has been delicious!"   —Suzanne Beard
Kings Mountain, North Carolina

Molded Peach Gelatin

This is an eye-catching, refreshing salad that's perfect with any dinner. It's a convenient do-ahead dish when preparing for a busy day.—Betty Howard
Wheeler, Texas

        1 can (15-1/4 ounces) sliced peaches
      1/2 cup sugar
      1/4 to 1/2 teaspoon ground nutmeg
        1 package (3 ounces) peach gelatin

Drain peaches, reserving the juice; add enough water to juice to measure 1 cup. Place peaches in a blender. Cover and process until smooth; set aside.

In a saucepan, combine the sugar, nutmeg and reserved juice mixture. Bring to a boil over medium heat; cook and stir for 1 minute or until sugar is dissolved. Remove from the heat; stir in gelatin until dissolved. Stir in the peach puree.

Pour into a 3-cup mold coated with nonstick cooking spray. Refrigerate until set. Just before serving, unmold onto a serving plate. **Yield:** 4-6 servings.

Caesar Salad

This crunchy, refreshing salad has a zesty dressing that provides a burst of flavor with each bite. It's a great salad to perk up any meal.
—Schelby Thompson, Winter Haven, Florida

    1 large bunch Romaine lettuce, torn
3/4 cup olive oil
    3 tablespoons red wine vinegar
    1 teaspoon Worcestershire sauce
1/2 teaspoon salt
1/4 teaspoon ground mustard
    1 large garlic clove, minced

    1/2 lemon
Dash pepper
    1/4 to 1/2 cup shredded Parmesan cheese
Caesar-flavored *or* garlic croutons

Place lettuce in a large salad bowl. Combine the next six ingredients in a blender; process until smooth. Pour over lettuce and toss. Squeeze lemon juice over lettuce. Sprinkle with pepper, Parmesan cheese and croutons. Serve immediately. **Yield:** 6-8 servings.

Vegetable Pasta Salad

This light, multicolored salad is an original. When I serve it at potlucks, I'm always asked for the recipe. It's also a standby for the "snowbirds" who gather with us in Arizona each winter.   *—Kathy Crow Cordova, Alaska*

1-1/2 cups thinly sliced carrots
   12 ounces rotini pasta, cooked and drained

    6 green onions, thinly sliced
    1 to 2 small zucchini, thinly sliced
    2 cups frozen broccoli and cauliflower, thawed and drained
    1 cup thinly sliced celery
1/2 cup frozen peas, thawed
    1 can (2-1/4 ounces) sliced ripe olives, drained
    1 jar (6 ounces) marinated artichoke hearts, drained and quartered
DRESSING:
  1/2 cup mayonnaise
  1/2 cup Italian salad dressing
  1/2 cup sour cream
    1 tablespoon prepared mustard
  1/2 teaspoon dried Italian seasoning

In a small saucepan, bring 1 inch of water to a boil. Add carrots; cover and simmer for 2 minutes or until crisp/tender. Drain and immediately place carrots in ice water. Drain and pat dry. In a large bowl, combine carrots, pasta, onions, zucchini, broccoli and cauliflower, celery, peas, olives and artichoke hearts.

   In a small bowl, combine dressing ingredients; mix well. Pour over pasta and vegetables and toss. Cover and refrigerate for at least 1 hour. **Yield:** 16-18 servings.

Layered Fruit Salad

This colorful salad is a real eye-catcher, and it tastes as good as it looks. Fresh fruit is always a welcome side dish with a summer meal. The addition of oranges and grapefruit gives this salad a different twist. —*Page Alexander, Baldwin City, Kansas*

1/2 cup orange juice
1/4 cup lemon juice
1/4 cup packed brown sugar
1/2 teaspoon grated orange peel
1/2 teaspoon grated lemon peel
1 cinnamon stick
2 cups fresh *or* drained canned pineapple chunks
1 cup seedless red grapes
2 medium bananas, sliced
2 medium oranges, sectioned
1 medium grapefruit, sectioned
1 pint strawberries, sliced
2 kiwifruit, peeled and sliced

In a medium saucepan, combine the first six ingredients; bring to a boil. Reduce heat; simmer, uncovered, for 5 minutes. Remove from the heat; cool completely.

Meanwhile, layer fruit in a glass serving bowl. Remove cinnamon stick from the sauce; pour sauce over fruit. Cover and chill for several hours. **Yield:** 6-8 servings.

Recipe for: Pat's Potato Salad

I came up with this recipe when we wanted a salad that would complement a barbecue sandwich and to use up day-old baked potatoes. It keeps well and seems to taste even better after being refrigerated.
—*Patricia Maul, Bartlesville, Oklahoma*

12 medium red potatoes, boiled, peeled and cubed
1 medium red onion, chopped
1 cup chopped fresh parsley
1-1/2 cups mayonnaise
1 cup (8 ounces) sour cream
1/4 cup sugar
1/4 cup cider vinegar
4 teaspoons ground mustard
1 teaspoon salt

In a large bowl, combine potatoes, onion and parsley. In a small bowl, combine remaining ingredients. Pour over potatoes and mix well. Refrigerate at least 1 hour before serving. **Yield:** 12-16 servings.

1 medium fresh pineapple
3 medium apples (1 red, 1 yellow and 1
   green), cubed
1 small cantaloupe, cubed
1 large firm banana, sliced
1 pint strawberries, halved
1 pint blueberries
4 cups seedless red and green grapes
3 kiwifruit, peeled and sliced
DRESSING:
1 package (3 ounces) cream cheese,
   softened
1/2 cup confectioners' sugar
2 teaspoons lemon juice
1 carton (8 ounces) frozen whipped
   topping, thawed
Additional berries for garnish, optional

Festive Fruit Salad

This refreshing, beautiful salad has become a favorite of everyone who's tried it. My bowl always comes home empty when I take this salad to a party or cookout. This recipe is a great way to take advantage of fresh fruit at its best. —Gail Sellers
Savannah, Georgia

Peel and core pineapple; cut into cubes. Place in a 3- or 4-qt. glass serving bowl. Add remaining fruit and stir to mix.

In a mixing bowl, beat the cream cheese until smooth. Gradually add sugar and lemon juice; mix well. Fold in whipped topping. Spread over fruit. Garnish with additional berries if desired. Store leftovers in the refrigerator. **Yield:** 16-20 servings.

Tomato Spinach Salad

When I serve this fresh spinach salad tossed with a creamy dill dressing, I receive plenty of compliments. The recipe is a longtime favorite.
—Ruth Seitz, Columbus Junction, Iowa

1/2 cup mayonnaise
1/2 cup grated Parmesan cheese
1/4 cup milk
1-1/2 teaspoons dill weed
1-1/2 teaspoons dried minced onion
1-1/2 teaspoons lemon-pepper seasoning

1 package (10 ounces) fresh spinach, torn
2 cups cherry tomatoes

In a small bowl or a jar with tight-fitting lid, combine first six ingredients; mix or shake well. Chill for at least 1 hour. Just before serving, combine spinach and tomatoes in a large salad bowl. Whisk or shake dressing; pour over salad and toss. **Yield:** 6-8 servings.

Editor's Note: If dressing thickens, thin with additional milk if desired.

Recipe for: *German Potato Salad*

I'd always loved my German grandmother's potato salad. So when I married a potato farmer—and had spuds in abundance—I played with several recipes that were similar and came up with this salad, which reminds me of hers.
—Sue Hartman, Parma, Idaho

5 bacon strips
3/4 cup chopped onion
2 tablespoons all-purpose flour
1 teaspoon salt
1/8 teaspoon pepper
2/3 cup cider vinegar
1-1/3 cups water
1/4 cup sugar
6 cups sliced cooked peeled potatoes

In a large skillet, fry bacon until crisp; remove and set aside. Drain all but 2-3 tablespoons of drippings; cook onion in drippings until tender. Stir in flour; blend well. Add vinegar and water; cook and stir until bubbly and slightly thick.

Add sugar and stir until it dissolves. Crumble bacon; gently stir in bacon and potatoes. Heat through, stirring lightly to coat potato slices. Serve warm. **Yield:** 6-8 servings.

Ruby Red Raspberry Salad

A refreshing and attractive side dish, this salad adds a festive touch to a special dinner.
—Marge Clark, West Lebanon, Indiana

1 package (3 ounces) raspberry gelatin
2 cups boiling water, *divided*
1 package (10 ounces) frozen raspberries in syrup
1-1/2 cups sour cream
1 package (3 ounces) cherry gelatin
1 can (20 ounces) crushed pineapple, drained
1 can (16 ounces) whole-berry cranberry sauce
Lettuce leaves
Mayonnaise, optional
Mint leaves, optional

Dissolve raspberry gelatin in 1 cup boiling water. Add raspberries and stir until berries are thawed and separated. Pour into a 13-in. x 9-in. x 2-in. pan; chill until set. Carefully spread with sour cream; chill.

Dissolve cherry gelatin in remaining boiling water. Add pineapple and cranberry sauce; mix well. Allow to thicken slightly. Carefully spoon over sour cream mixture; chill. Cut into squares and serve on lettuce leaves.

If desired, top each with a dollop of mayonnaise and garnish with a mint leaf. **Yield:** 12-16 servings.

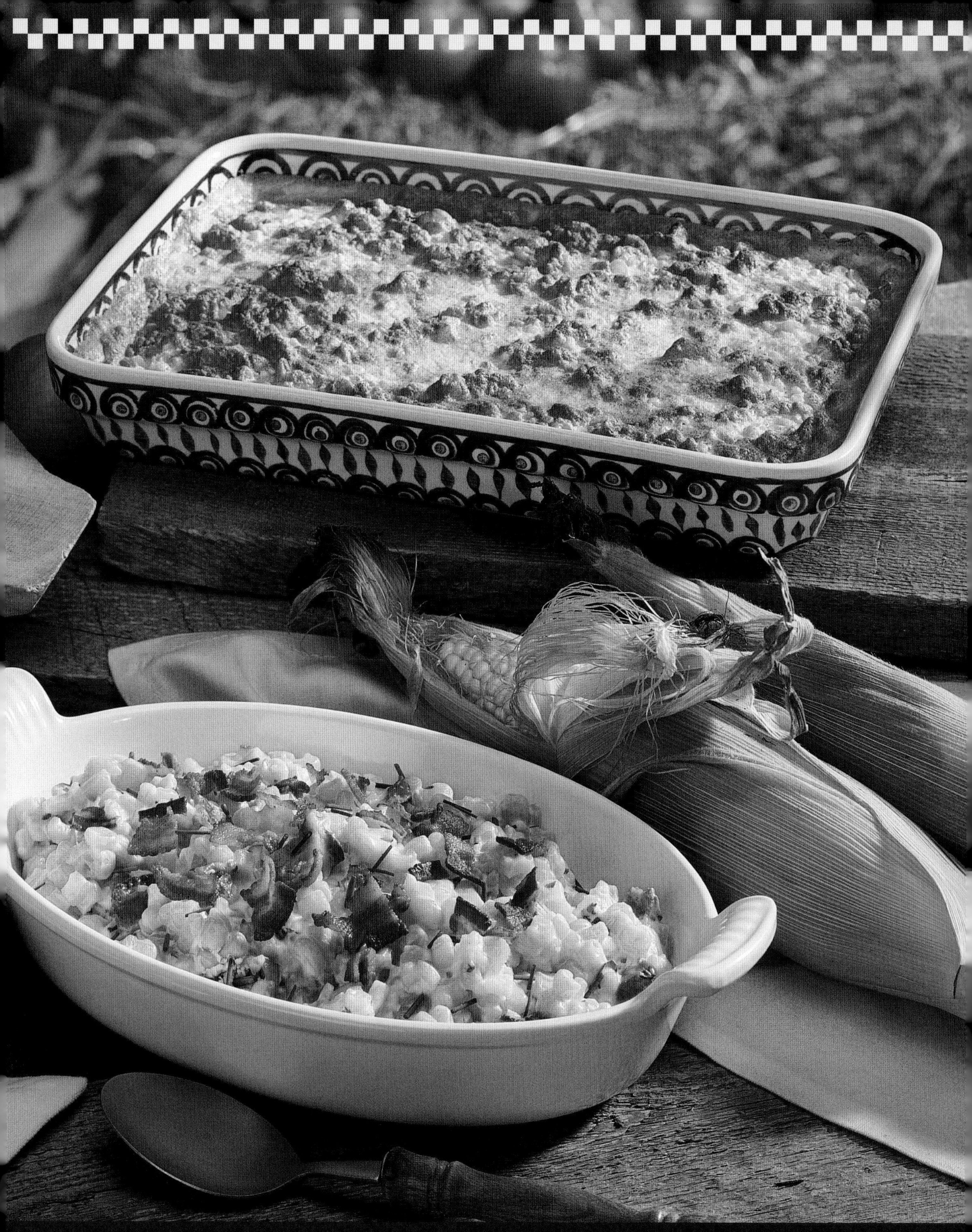

Side Dishes

At left: Delicious Corn Pudding (p. 65) and Corn and Bacon Casserole (p. 63).

At right: Tomato Dumplings (p. 61).

Onion Potato Pancakes

When Grandma prepared potato pancakes, she used an old-fashioned grater, great for potatoes but not for knuckles! With homemade applesauce, this side dish complements a meal so well. I made these pancakes for my own family and often served them as a main dish for light suppers.
—*Joan Hutter*
Warnick, Rhode Island

    2 eggs
    1 medium onion, quartered
    2 tablespoons all-purpose flour
  3/4 teaspoon salt
  1/4 teaspoon pepper
  1/4 teaspoon baking powder
    4 medium potatoes, peeled and cubed
      (about 1-1/2 pounds)
    2 tablespoons chopped fresh parsley
    3 to 4 tablespoons vegetable oil

In a blender or food processor, place the eggs, onion, flour, salt, pepper, baking powder and 1/2 cup of potatoes. Cover and process on high until smooth. Add parsley and remaining potatoes; cover and pulse 2-4 times until potatoes are chopped.

Pour 1 to 2 tablespoons oil onto a hot griddle or skillet. Pour batter by 1/3 cupfuls onto griddle; flatten slightly to a 4-in. to 5-in. diameter. Cook over medium heat until golden on both sides. Add oil as needed until all pancakes are cooked. **Yield:** 6-8 servings (12 pancakes).

Sage Dressing for Chicken

This classic dressing is a satisfying side dish that makes a chicken dinner extra special.
—*Bobbie Talbott, Veneta, Oregon*

    2 cups unseasoned dry bread cubes
  1/2 cup chopped onion
  1/4 cup chopped fresh parsley
    3 tablespoons chopped fresh sage *or* 1
      tablespoon rubbed sage
  1/4 cup egg substitute
  1/2 to 3/4 cup chicken broth
    1 roasting chicken (3 to 4 pounds)
Melted butter, optional

In a large bowl, combine bread cubes, onion, parsley, sage and the egg substitute. Add enough broth until stuffing is moistened and holds together. Stuff loosely into chicken. Fasten with skewers to close.

Place with breast side up on a shallow rack in roasting pan. Brush with butter if desired. Bake, uncovered, at 375° for 1-3/4 to 2-1/4 hours or until a meat thermometer reads 180° for chicken and 165° for dressing. Baste several times with pan juices or butter. Prepare gravy if desired. **Yield:** 6 servings.

Recipe for: Tomato Dumplings

(Pictured on page 59)

The wonderful fresh tomato taste of the sauce complements these light savory dumplings. They make a perfect side dish for a meal with beef. My family enjoys them very much. —Lucille Tucker, Clinton, Illinois

1/2 cup finely chopped onion
1/4 cup finely chopped green pepper
1/4 cup finely chopped celery
1/4 cup butter
1 bay leaf
1 can (28 ounces) diced tomatoes, undrained
1 tablespoon brown sugar
1/2 teaspoon dried basil
1/2 teaspoon salt
1/4 teaspoon pepper
DUMPLINGS:
1 cup all-purpose flour
1-1/2 teaspoons baking powder
1/2 teaspoon salt
1 tablespoon cold butter

1 tablespoon snipped fresh parsley
2/3 cup milk

In a medium skillet, saute onion, green pepper and celery in butter until tender. Add bay leaf, tomatoes, brown sugar, basil, salt and pepper; cover and simmer for 5-10 minutes.

Meanwhile, for dumplings, combine flour, baking powder and salt in a bowl. Cut in butter. Add parsley and milk; stir just until mixed.

Drop by tablespoonfuls into six mounds onto bubbling tomato mixture; cover tightly and simmer for 12-15 minutes or until a toothpick inserted into dumpling comes out clean. Remove and discard the bay leaf. Serve immediately. **Yield:** 6 servings.

Broccoli Bake

This tasty side dish is always a big hit when my son, daughter-in-law and granddaughter come for dinner or when I'm hosting a shower or party. At Easter, it's a great way to use up hard-cooked eggs!
—Carolyn Griffin, Macon, Georgia

2 packages (10 ounces *each*) frozen cut broccoli
1/2 cup chopped onion
1 tablespoon butter
1 can (10-3/4 ounces) condensed cream of mushroom soup, undiluted
1/2 teaspoon ground mustard
1/2 teaspoon salt
4 hard-cooked eggs, chopped
1-1/2 cups (6 ounces) shredded cheddar cheese
1 can (2.8 ounces) french-fried onions

Cook broccoli according to package directions; drain and set aside. In a skillet or saucepan, saute onion in butter until tender. Stir in soup, mustard and salt; heat until bubbly.

In a 1-1/2-qt. casserole, arrange half of broccoli; top with half of the eggs, half of the cheese and half of the mushroom sauce. Repeat layers. Bake at 350° for 20 minutes. Sprinkle onions on top and bake 5 minutes more. **Yield:** 6 servings.

Paprika Potatoes

These tasty potatoes are golden and crusty on the outside and tender on the inside. I've served them with many kinds of meat. When a meal needs a comforting, homey touch, I whip up a batch.
—Ruth Andrewson, Leavenworth, Washington

4 large potatoes, peeled, cooked and quartered
3 tablespoons butter
1/2 teaspoon paprika

In a large skillet, slowly saute potatoes in butter until golden brown, about 10-15 minutes. Sprinkle with paprika. **Yield:** 4-6 servings.

As a young girl, I felt privileged when my grandmother asked me to shop for her. I walked to the creamery for some butter and then stopped by the meat market for 25 cents worth of German bologna. I'd proudly carry them back to Grandma in a little basket.
—Helen Dillson
Hixson, Tennessee

Cheese Potato Puff

I enjoy entertaining and always look for recipes that can be made ahead of time. I got this comforting potato recipe from my mother-in-law. It contains basic ingredients that everyone loves like milk and cheddar cheese. —Beverly Templeton, Garner, Iowa

12 medium potatoes, peeled (about 5 pounds)
1 teaspoon salt, *divided*
3/4 cup butter
2 cups (8 ounces) shredded cheddar cheese
1 cup milk
2 eggs, beaten
Fresh *or* dried chives, optional

In a large kettle, cover potatoes with water. Add 1/2 teaspoon salt; cook until tender. Drain; mash potatoes until smooth. In a saucepan, cook and stir butter, cheese, milk and remaining salt until smooth. Stir into potatoes; fold in eggs.

Pour into a greased 3-qt. baking dish. Bake, uncovered, at 350° for 40 minutes or until puffy and golden brown. Sprinkle with chives if desired. **Yield:** 8-10 servings.

Butternut Squash Bake

If I ask our two girls what to fix for a special meal, this dish is always requested. I discovered this slightly sweet and crunchy-topped casserole at a church dinner about 10 years ago, and now I take it to potluck dinners and come home with an empty dish! —Julie Jahn, Decatur, Indiana

1/3 cup butter, softened
3/4 cup sugar
2 eggs
1 can (5 ounces) evaporated milk
1 teaspoon vanilla extract
2 cups mashed cooked butternut squash

TOPPING:
1/2 cup crisp rice cereal
1/4 cup packed brown sugar
1/4 cup chopped pecans
2 tablespoons butter, melted

In a mixing bowl, cream butter and sugar. Beat in eggs, milk and vanilla. Stir in squash (mixture

will be thin). Pour into a greased 11-in. x 7-in. x 2-in. baking pan.

Bake, uncovered, at 350° for 45 minutes or until almost set. Combine topping ingredients; sprinkle over casserole. Return to the oven for 5-10 minutes or until bubbly. **Yield:** 6-8 servings.

Recipe for: Corn and Bacon Casserole

(Pictured on page 58)

Corn is my three boys' favorite vegetable, so we eat a lot of it. This recipe is a family favorite. My husband, Bob, and the boys really enjoy it. —Marcia Hostetter, Canton, New York

6 bacon strips
1/2 cup chopped onion
2 tablespoons all-purpose flour
2 garlic cloves, minced
1/2 teaspoon salt
1/2 teaspoon pepper
1 cup (8 ounces) sour cream
3-1/2 cups fresh *or* frozen whole
kernel corn
1 tablespoon chopped fresh parsley
1 tablespoon chopped fresh chives

In a large skillet, cook bacon until crisp. Drain, reserving 2 tablespoons of drippings. Crumble bacon; set aside. Saute onion in drippings until

tender. Add flour, garlic, salt and pepper. Cook and stir until bubbly; cook and stir 1 minute more. Remove from the heat and stir in sour cream until smooth. Add corn, parsley and half of the bacon; mix well.

Pour into a 1-qt. baking dish. Sprinkle with remaining bacon. Bake, uncovered, at 350° for 20-25 minutes or until heated through. Sprinkle with chives. **Yield:** 6-8 servings.

Creamed Peas

I can still taste these wonderful peas in Mama's delicious white sauce. Our food was pretty plain during the week, so I thought this white sauce made the peas "extra fancy" and fitting for a Sunday meal.
—Imogene Hutton, Norton, Texas

   1 tablespoon butter
   1 tablespoon all-purpose flour
1/4 teaspoon salt
1/8 teaspoon pepper
1/2 cup milk
   1 teaspoon sugar
   1 package (10 ounces) frozen peas

In a medium saucepan, melt the butter. Add flour, salt and pepper; cook over low heat until bubbly. Gradually add milk and sugar; cook and stir until thickened. Cook peas according to package directions; drain. Stir into the sauce and heat through. **Yield:** 3-4 servings.

Recipe for: Caraway Sauerkraut

This simple side dish has wonderful old-world flavor that's perfect with a pork roast or chops.
—Trudy Johnson, Hixson, Tennessee

6 bacon strips, chopped
1 medium onion, chopped
2 bags *or* jars (32 ounces *each*)
   sauerkraut, rinsed and drained
1 tablespoon caraway seed
2 cups water
1 large potato, peeled and shredded

In a 5-qt. Dutch oven, cook bacon and onion until onion is golden brown, about 8-10 minutes. Add sauerkraut and caraway; mix well. Add water; bring to a boil. Reduce heat; cover and simmer for 1-1/2 hours, stirring occasionally. Add potato. Cook for 20 minutes or until potato is tender. **Yield:** 18-20 servings.

Delicious Corn Pudding

(Pictured on page 58)

Nothing beats Grandma's corn pudding! This comforting recipe has been in my family for years and is shared at many gatherings. —Paula Marchesi
Rocky Point, New York

>   4 eggs, *separated*
>   2 tablespoons butter, melted and cooled
>   1 tablespoon sugar
>   1 tablespoon brown sugar
>   1 teaspoon salt
> 1/2 teaspoon vanilla extract
> Pinch *each* ground cinnamon and nutmeg
>   2 cups fresh whole kernel corn (4 medium ears)

1 cup half-and-half cream
1 cup milk

In a mixing bowl, beat egg yolks until thick and lemon-colored, 5-8 minutes. Add butter, sugars, salt, vanilla, cinnamon and nutmeg; mix well. Add corn. Stir in cream and milk. Beat egg whites until stiff; fold into yolk mixture. Pour into a greased 1-1/2-qt. baking dish.

Bake, uncovered, at 350° for 35 minutes or until a knife inserted near the center comes out clean. Cover loosely during last 10 minutes of baking if necessary to prevent overbrowning. **Yield:** 8 servings.

Norwegian Parsley Potatoes

I love to use parsley in many dishes, and it suits the fresh taste of small red potatoes well. Even though they're easy to prepare, they look fancy and go great with baked ham. —Eunice Stoen
Decorah, Iowa

>   2 pounds small red new potatoes
> 1/2 cup butter
> 1/4 cup chopped fresh parsley
> 1/4 teaspoon dried marjoram

Cook potatoes in boiling salted water for 15 minutes or until tender. Cool slightly. With a sharp knife, remove one narrow strip of skin around the middle of each potato.

In a large skillet, melt butter; add parsley and marjoram. Add the potatoes and stir gently until coated and heated through. **Yield:** 6-8 servings.

Mashed Potatoes with Horseradish

These creamy zippy potatoes are a bit unexpected and a delicious addition to any meal.
—Cynthia Gobeli, Norton, Ohio

6 medium potatoes, peeled and cubed
1/4 cup butter, melted
3/4 teaspoon salt
1/8 teaspoon pepper

1/2 cup sour cream
2 tablespoons prepared horseradish

Cook the potatoes in boiling salted water until tender, about 8-10 minutes; drain. Add butter, salt and pepper. Whip with an electric mixer on low speed or mash with a potato masher. Add sour cream and horseradish; mix well. Serve immediately. **Yield:** 6-8 servings.

When Mom fried potatoes, she would moisten bread under the faucet, squeeze out the water, then break the bread into the potatoes. It would fry up brown and crunchy. When I got married, I made potatoes the same way. When my daughter got married, so did she.

Not long ago, Mom came for a visit. She decided to fry potatoes. I was stunned when she did not add the bread to the pan. When

I asked where the bread was, she said she didn't know what I was talking about. So I explained that when I was a child in the early 1940s, she always fried potatoes that way. She started to laugh. She told me the only reason she did that was because we didn't have enough potatoes!
—Judie DuMont
Walton, Indiana

German-Style Spinach

Grandma's spinach dish is flavored with her Austrian heritage. It's tasty and always looks so pretty on the plate. We children never had to be told to eat our spinach at Grandma's house! —Joan Hutter
Warnick, Rhode Island

2 packages (10 ounces *each*) frozen
 chopped spinach
1 large onion, chopped
2 garlic cloves, minced
2 tablespoons butter
6 bacon strips, cooked and crumbled
1/2 teaspoon ground nutmeg
1/2 teaspoon salt
Pepper to taste

Cook spinach according to package directions. Drain well and set aside. In a large skillet, saute onion and garlic in butter until tender. Stir in the spinach, bacon, nutmeg, salt and pepper; heat through. **Yield:** 6-8 servings.

Asparagus with Sesame Butter

The first fresh asparagus is a delightful springtime treat. This light butter sauce lets the asparagus flavor come through, and the sprinkling of sesame seeds adds a delicate crunch. This is an easy yet delicious dish. —Eunice Stoen, Decorah, Iowa

    2 pounds fresh asparagus
    1 cup boiling water
1/2 teaspoon salt
    1 tablespoon cornstarch
1/4 cup cold water
1/4 cup butter
    3 tablespoons sesame seeds, toasted

In a large skillet, place asparagus spears, boiling water and salt. Cook for 5-7 minutes or until tender. Remove asparagus and keep warm.

Drain cooking liquid, reserving 1/2 cup in a small saucepan. Combine cornstarch and cold water; stir into liquid. Cook and stir over medium heat until thickened and bubbly; cook and stir 1 minute more. Stir in butter until melted. Spoon over asparagus; sprinkle with sesame seeds and serve immediately. **Yield:** 6-8 servings.

Recipe for: **Herbed Rice Pilaf**

This savory side dish has been a family favorite for years. We sure enjoy this simple tasty rice dish in the summer alongside a grilled entree. —Jeri Dobrowski, Beach, North Dakota

    1 cup uncooked long grain rice
    1 cup chopped celery
3/4 cup chopped onion
1/4 cup butter
2-1/2 cups water
    1 package (2 to 2-1/2 ounces) dry
      chicken noodle soup mix
    2 tablespoons minced fresh parsley
1/2 teaspoon dried thyme
1/4 teaspoon rubbed sage
1/4 teaspoon pepper
    1 tablespoon chopped pimientos,
      optional

In a large skillet, cook the rice, celery and onion in butter, stirring constantly, until rice is browned. Stir in the next six ingredients; bring to a boil.

Reduce heat; cover and simmer for 15 minutes. Stir in the pimientos if desired. Remove from the heat and let stand, covered, for 10 minutes. **Yield:** 6 servings.

Hungarian Noodle Side Dish

I first served this creamy, rich casserole at our ladies meeting at church. Everyone liked it and many of the ladies wanted the recipe. The original recipe was from a friend, but I changed it a bit to suit our tastes.
—Betty Sugg, Akron, New York

3 chicken bouillon cubes
1/4 cup boiling water
1 can (10-3/4 ounces) condensed cream
  of mushroom soup, undiluted
1/2 cup chopped onion
2 tablespoons Worcestershire sauce
2 tablespoons poppy seeds
1/8 to 1/4 teaspoon garlic powder
1/8 to 1/4 teaspoon hot pepper sauce
2 cups (16 ounces) cottage cheese
2 cups (16 ounces) sour cream
1 package (16 ounces) medium egg
  noodles, cooked and drained
1/4 cup shredded Parmesan cheese
Paprika

In a large bowl, dissolve bouillon in water. Add the next six ingredients; mix well. Stir in cottage cheese, sour cream and noodles and mix well.

Pour into a greased 2-1/2-qt. baking dish. Sprinkle with the Parmesan cheese and paprika. Cover and bake at 350° for 45 minutes or until heated through. **Yield:** 8-10 servings.

Harvard Beets

This is a pretty and flavorful side dish that's also quick to prepare. —Jean Ann Perkins
Newburyport, Massachusetts

1 can (16 ounces) sliced beets
1/4 cup sugar
1-1/2 teaspoons cornstarch
2 tablespoons white vinegar
2 tablespoons orange juice
1 tablespoon grated orange peel

Drain beets, reserving 2 tablespoons juice; set beets and juice aside. In a saucepan, combine sugar and cornstarch. Add vinegar, orange juice and beet juice; bring to a boil.

Reduce heat and simmer for 3-4 minutes or until thickened. Add beets and orange peel; heat through. **Yield:** 4-6 servings.

Recipe for: Party Potatoes

These creamy, tasty potatoes can be made the day before and stored in the refrigerator until you're ready to pop them in the oven. The garlic powder and chives add zip, and the shredded cheese adds color.

—Sharon Mensing, Greenfield, Iowa

4 cups mashed potatoes (about 8 to 10 large) *or* 4 cups prepared mashed potato flakes
1 cup (8 ounces) sour cream
1 package (8 ounces) cream cheese, softened
1 teaspoon dried chives *or* 1 tablespoon snipped fresh chives
1/4 teaspoon garlic powder
1/4 cup dry bread crumbs
1 tablespoon butter, melted
1/2 cup shredded cheddar cheese

In a large bowl, combine potatoes, sour cream, cream cheese, chives and garlic powder. Turn into a greased 2-qt. casserole. Combine bread crumbs and butter; sprinkle over potatoes.

Bake at 350° for 50-60 minutes. Top with cheese and serve immediately. **Yield:** 10-12 servings.

Continental Zucchini

Zucchini are big and plentiful here, and people often joke about using them up before they multiply! Sharing zucchini—and zucchini recipes—is a good-neighbor policy. This colorful and easy recipe wins raves at church and school gatherings.

—Martha Fehl, Brookville, Indiana

1 pound zucchini (about 3 small), cubed
1 to 2 garlic cloves, minced
1 tablespoon vegetable oil
1 jar (2 ounces) chopped pimiento, drained
1 can (15-1/2 ounces) whole kernel corn, drained
1 teaspoon salt, optional
1/4 teaspoon lemon-pepper seasoning
1/2 cup shredded mozzarella cheese

In a large skillet, saute zucchini and garlic in oil for 3-4 minutes. Add pimiento, corn, salt if desired and lemon-pepper; cook and stir for 2-3 minutes or until zucchini is tender. Sprinkle with cheese and heat until cheese melts. **Yield:** 6 servings.

Scalloped Pineapple Casserole

This is a sweet, satisfying side dish that's very good with ham or chicken. —*Judy Howle*
Columbus, Mississippi

3/4 cup butter
1-1/4 cups sugar
3 eggs
1 can (20 ounces) crushed pineapple, well-drained
1-1/2 teaspoons lemon juice
4 cups firmly packed cubed white bread (crusts removed)

In a mixing bowl, cream butter and sugar. Add eggs, one at a time, beating well after each addition. Stir in the pineapple and lemon juice. Gently fold in bread cubes.

Spoon into a greased 2-qt. baking dish. Bake, uncovered, at 350° for 40-45 minutes or until top is lightly golden. Serve warm. **Yield:** 6 servings.

Stuffed Baked Potatoes

These special potatoes are a hit with my whole family, from the smallest grandchild on up. I prepare them up to a week in advance, wrap them well and freeze. Their flavorful filling goes so nicely with juicy ham slices. —*Marge Clark, West Lebanon, Indiana*

3 large baking potatoes (1 pound *each*)
1-1/2 teaspoons vegetable oil, optional
1/2 cup sliced green onions
1/2 cup butter, *divided*
1/2 cup half-and-half cream
1/2 cup sour cream
1 teaspoon salt
1/2 teaspoon white pepper
1 cup (4 ounces) shredded cheddar cheese
Paprika

Rub potatoes with oil if desired; pierce with a fork. Bake at 400° for 1 hour and 20 minutes or until tender. Allow potatoes to cool to the touch.

Cut potatoes in half lengthwise; carefully scoop out pulp, leaving a thin shell. Place pulp in a large bowl. Saute onions in 1/4 cup butter until tender. Add to potato pulp along with half-and-half cream, sour cream, salt and pepper. Beat until smooth. Fold in cheese.

Stuff potato shells and place in a 13-in. x 9-in. x 2-in. baking pan. Melt remaining butter; drizzle over the potatoes. Sprinkle with paprika. Bake at 350° for 20-30 minutes or until heated through. **Yield:** 6 servings.

Zesty Carrot Bake

For a fun vegetable dish, try these tender carrots in a sauce that gets its zip from horseradish. With a crunchy crumb topping and comforting sauce, it will tempt even those who usually don't care for cooked carrots.
—Grace Yaskovic
Branchville, New Jersey

    1 pound carrots, cut into 1/2-inch slices
    2 tablespoons minced onion
3/4 cup mayonnaise
1/3 cup water
    1 tablespoon prepared horseradish
1/4 teaspoon pepper
1/2 cup dry bread crumbs
    2 tablespoons butter, melted
1/2 cup shredded sharp cheddar cheese

On stovetop or in a microwave oven, cook carrots until tender. Place in a 1-qt. baking dish; set aside. In a small bowl, combine the next five ingredients; mix well. Pour over carrots. Combine bread crumbs and butter; sprinkle on top. Bake, uncovered, at 350° for 25-30 minutes. Sprinkle with cheese. Return to the oven for 2-3 minutes or until the cheese melts. **Yield:** 6 servings.

Recipe for: Western Beans

I've made these beans many times for picnics and potlucks—they're hearty and zesty with chili peppers and the extra flavor of lentils in the bean mix. The recipe can be made ahead and heated before serving.
—Arthur Morris, Washington, Pennsylvania

    4 bacon strips, diced
    1 large onion, chopped
1/3 cup dry lentils
1-1/3 cups water
    2 tablespoons ketchup
    1 teaspoon garlic powder
3/4 teaspoon chili powder
1/2 teaspoon ground cumin
1/4 teaspoon crushed red pepper flakes
    1 bay leaf
    1 can (16 ounces) diced tomatoes, undrained
    1 can (16 ounces) kidney beans, rinsed and drained
    1 can (15 ounces) pinto beans, rinsed and drained

Lightly fry bacon in a heavy 3-qt. saucepan. Add onion; cook until transparent. Stir in remaining ingredients. Cook over medium heat for 45 minutes or until lentils are tender, stirring twice. Remove bay leaf before serving. **Yield:** 8-10 servings.

Peas with Mushrooms

This is a savory side dish with a fresh taste, even though it calls for convenient frozen peas.
—*Mary Dennis, Bryan, Ohio*

1/2 pound fresh mushrooms, sliced
2 tablespoons sliced green onions
1 tablespoon butter
1/4 teaspoon dried marjoram
1/4 teaspoon salt, optional
1/8 teaspoon pepper
Dash ground nutmeg
1 package (10 ounces) frozen peas, cooked

In a skillet over medium heat, saute the mushrooms and onions in butter for 3-5 minutes. Add marjoram, salt if desired, pepper and nutmeg; mix well. Add peas and heat through. **Yield:** 4 servings.

Recipe for: Creamy Sweet Potatoes

I took my mother's delicious sweet potato casserole recipe and gave it a new twist by adding the tempting taste of orange—a fruit very abundant in our state. The flavors are wonderful together and make this dish a favorite of my children and grandchildren.
—*Norma Poole, Auburndale, Florida*

5 pounds sweet potatoes, peeled and cooked
4 eggs, lightly beaten
1/2 cup orange juice
1/2 cup butter, softened
1/2 cup sugar
1 teaspoon vanilla extract
1/2 teaspoon ground nutmeg
Dash salt
Large marshmallows

In a large bowl, mash sweet potatoes. Add eggs, orange juice, butter, sugar, vanilla, nutmeg and salt; mix well. Transfer to a greased 3-qt. baking dish. Bake at 350° for 35-40 minutes or until set.

Top with marshmallows; return to oven until they just begin to puff and melt, about 5-10 minutes. **Yield:** 10-12 servings.

Broccoli-Pasta Side Dish

With broccoli, garlic and cheese, this is a popular side dish with an Italian twist. I come from a line of great Italian cooks. —Judi Lacourse, Mesa, Arizona

2-1/2 pounds fresh broccoli
  2 garlic cloves, minced
  1/3 cup olive oil
    1 tablespoon butter
    1 teaspoon salt
  1/4 teaspoon pepper
Pinch cayenne pepper

8 ounces linguine *or* thin spaghetti, cooked and drained
Grated Romano *or* Parmesan cheese

Cut florets and tender parts of broccoli stems into bite-size pieces. In a large skillet, saute broccoli with garlic, oil, butter, salt, pepper and cayenne over medium heat for about 10 minutes or until just tender, stirring frequently.

Place hot pasta in a serving dish; top with the broccoli mixture. Sprinkle with cheese. **Yield:** 4-6 servings.

Garden Casserole

This delicious cheesy casserole is made with the bounty from my garden. The dish includes a sunny medley of summer vegetables like eggplant, zucchini and tomatoes. It's so nice to cook with those abundant crops. —Phyllis Hickey, Bedford, New Hampshire

  2 pounds eggplant, peeled
  5 teaspoons salt, *divided*
1/4 cup olive oil
  2 medium onions, finely chopped
  2 garlic cloves, minced
  2 medium zucchini, sliced 1/2 inch thick
  5 medium tomatoes, peeled and chopped
  2 celery ribs, sliced
1/4 cup minced fresh parsley
1/4 cup minced fresh basil *or* 1 tablespoon dried basil
1/2 teaspoon pepper
1/2 cup grated Romano cheese
  1 cup dry Italian bread crumbs
  2 tablespoons butter, melted
  1 cup (4 ounces) shredded mozzarella cheese

Cut eggplant into 1/2-in.-thick slices; sprinkle both sides with 3 teaspoons salt. Place in a deep dish; cover and let stand for 30 minutes. Rinse with cold water; drain and dry on paper towels. Cut into 1/2-in. cubes and saute in oil until lightly browned, about 5 minutes. Add onions, garlic and zucchini; cook 3 minutes. Add tomatoes, celery, parsley, basil, pepper and remaining salt; bring to a boil. Reduce heat; cover and simmer for 10 minutes.

Remove from heat; stir in Romano cheese. Pour into a greased 13-in. x 9-in. x 2-in. baking dish. Combine crumbs and butter; sprinkle on top. Bake, uncovered, at 375° for 15 minutes. Sprinkle with mozzarella cheese. Return to the oven for 5 minutes or until cheese is melted. **Yield:** 12 servings.

Breads

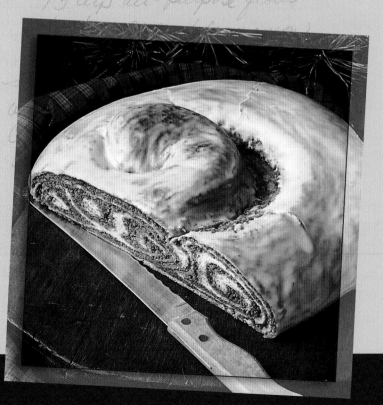

At left: Dutch Apple Bread (p. 78), Cheddar-Dill Bread (p. 81) and Lemon Blueberry Bread (p. 77).

At right: Poteca Nut Roll (p. 82).

Pop-Up Rolls

For lightly sweet, biscuit-like rolls that aren't dry, you can't beat Pop-Up Rolls. They're so easy to make.
—Judi Brinegar, Liberty, North Carolina

1-1/2 cups self-rising flour
3/4 cup milk
3 tablespoons sugar
1-1/2 tablespoons mayonnaise

In a bowl, stir together all ingredients until thoroughly combined. Fill greased muffin cups half full. Bake at 375° for 18-20 minutes or until lightly browned. **Yield:** 9 rolls.

 Editor's Note: As a substitute for self-rising flour, place 2-1/4 teaspoons baking powder and 3/4 teaspoon salt in a measuring cup. Add enough all-purpose flour to equal 1-1/2 cups.

My grandmother made a doughnut-shaped bread, which she called "pretzel buck." She would deep-fry it like doughnuts and sprinkle cinnamon and sugar on it. You can't buy bread that tastes as good as that old pretzel buck.
—David Kidd
Waterford, Michigan

Apricot Walnut Bread

Orange juice and oat bran add flavor and texture to this recipe. —Diane Hixon, Niceville, Florida

4 egg whites
2/3 cup water
1/2 cup orange juice
1/4 cup vegetable oil
1 teaspoon vanilla extract
3/4 cup uncooked oat bran hot cereal
1/2 cup chopped dried apricots
1-1/4 cups all-purpose flour
1/2 cup packed brown sugar

1 teaspoon baking powder
1/2 teaspoon baking soda
1/4 cup chopped walnuts

In a bowl, combine the first five ingredients. Stir in oat bran and apricots. Combine flour, brown sugar, baking powder and soda; stir into apricot mixture just until moistened. Fold in nuts.

 Pour into a greased 8-in. x 4-in. x 2-in. loaf pan. Bake at 350° for 50-55 minutes or until a toothpick comes out clean. Cool in pan 10 minutes; remove to wire rack. **Yield:** 1 loaf (16 slices).

Recipe for: Lemon Blueberry Bread

(Pictured on page 74)

Of all the quick breads we had growing up, this beautifully glazed, berry-studded loaf is the best!
—Julianne Johnson, Grove City, Minnesota

1/3 cup butter, melted
1 cup sugar
3 tablespoons lemon juice
2 eggs
1-1/2 cups all-purpose flour
1 teaspoon baking powder
1/2 teaspoon salt
1/2 cup milk
2 tablespoons grated lemon peel
1/2 cup chopped nuts
1 cup fresh *or* frozen blueberries
GLAZE:
2 tablespoons lemon juice
1/4 cup sugar

In a mixing bowl, beat butter, sugar, juice and eggs. Combine flour, baking powder and salt; stir into egg mixture alternately with milk. Fold in peel, nuts and blueberries.

Pour into a greased 8-in. x 4-in. x 2-in. loaf pan. Bake at 350° for 60-70 minutes or until a toothpick comes out clean. Cool in pan for 10 minutes.

Meanwhile, combine glaze ingredients. Remove bread from pan and drizzle with glaze. Cool on a wire rack. **Yield:** 1 loaf.

Irish Soda Bread

An Irish meal wouldn't be complete without a lovely loaf of Irish Soda Bread. This recipe makes a beautiful high loaf of bread dotted with sweet raisins. It doesn't last long at our house on St. Patrick's Day.
—Gloria Warczak, Cedarburg, Wisconsin

2 cups all-purpose flour
2 tablespoons brown sugar
1 teaspoon baking powder
1/2 teaspoon baking soda
1/4 teaspoon salt
3 tablespoons butter
2 eggs
3/4 cup buttermilk
1/3 cup raisins

In a bowl, combine flour, brown sugar, baking powder, baking soda and salt. Cut in butter until crumbly. Combine 1 egg and buttermilk; stir into flour mixture just until moistened. Fold in raisins. Knead on a floured surface for 1 minute.

Shape into a round loaf; place on a greased baking sheet. Cut a 1/4-in.-deep cross in top of loaf. Beat remaining egg; brush over loaf. Bake at 375° for 30-35 minutes or until golden brown. **Yield:** 6-8 servings.

Dutch Apple Bread

(Pictured on page 74)

This fruity streusel-topped bread is delightful for brunch. It's a great make-ahead treat that freezes well, too. —June Formanek, Belle Plaine, Iowa

  1/2 cup butter, softened
    1 cup sugar
    2 eggs
    1 teaspoon vanilla extract
    2 cups all-purpose flour
    1 teaspoon baking soda
  1/2 teaspoon salt
  1/3 cup buttermilk
    1 cup chopped peeled apple
  1/3 cup chopped walnuts
TOPPING:
  1/3 cup all-purpose flour
    2 tablespoons sugar
    2 tablespoons brown sugar
  1/2 teaspoon ground cinnamon
    3 tablespoons butter

In a mixing bowl, cream butter and sugar. Beat in eggs and vanilla. Combine flour, baking soda and salt; stir into the creamed mixture alternately with buttermilk. Fold in apple and nuts.

Pour into a greased 9-in. x 5-in. x 3-in. loaf pan. For topping, combine the first four ingredients; cut in butter until crumbly. Sprinkle over batter. Bake at 350° for 55-60 minutes or until a toothpick comes out clean. Cool in pan 10 minutes before removing to a wire rack. **Yield:** 1 loaf.

Blueberry Streusel Muffins

What a joy to set out a basket of these moist blueberry muffins topped with streusel on the brunch buffet. People rave when they taste them for the first time. —Mary Anne McWhirter, Pearland, Texas

  1/4 cup butter, softened
  1/3 cup sugar
    1 egg, beaten
2-1/3 cups all-purpose flour
    4 teaspoons baking powder
  1/2 teaspoon salt
    1 cup milk
    1 teaspoon vanilla extract
1-1/2 cups fresh *or* frozen blueberries
STREUSEL:
  1/2 cup sugar
  1/3 cup all-purpose flour
  1/2 teaspoon ground cinnamon
  1/4 cup butter

In a mixing bowl, cream butter and sugar. Add egg; mix well. Combine flour, baking powder and salt; add to the creamed mixture alternately with milk. Stir in vanilla. Fold in blueberries.

Fill 12 greased or paper-lined muffin cups two-thirds full. In a small bowl, combine sugar, flour and cinnamon; cut in butter until crumbly. Sprinkle over muffins. Bake at 375° for 25-30 minutes or until browned and a toothpick comes out clean. Cool for 5 minutes before removing from pan to a wire rack. **Yield:** 1 dozen.

Poppy Seed Bread

This moist, rich bread is so delicious. It gets golden brown and looks great sliced for a buffet. I also like to make miniature loaves to give as gifts.
—*Faye Hintz, Springfield, Missouri*

   3 cups all-purpose flour
2-1/4 cups sugar
1-1/2 tablespoons poppy seeds
1-1/2 teaspoons baking powder
1-1/2 teaspoons salt
   3 eggs, lightly beaten
1-1/2 cups milk
   1 cup vegetable oil
1-1/2 teaspoons vanilla extract
1-1/2 teaspoons almond extract
1-1/2 teaspoons butter flavoring
GLAZE:
   3/4 cup sugar
   1/4 cup orange juice
   1/2 teaspoon vanilla extract
   1/2 teaspoon almond extract
   1/2 teaspoon butter flavoring

In a large bowl, combine first five ingredients. In another bowl, beat eggs, milk, oil, extracts and butter flavoring. Stir into dry ingredients just until moistened. Pour into two greased 8-1/2-in. x 4-1/2-in. x 2-1/2-in. loaf pans. Bake at 350° for 60-65 minutes or until a toothpick comes out clean. Cool completely in pans.

In a saucepan, bring all glaze ingredients to a boil. Pour over bread in pans. Cool for 5 minutes before removing from pans to wire racks to cool completely. **Yield:** 2 loaves.

Recipe for: Pumpkin Bread

This is a deliciously spicy pumpkin-rich quick bread. I keep my freezer stocked with home-baked goodies like this winner for our harvest crew.
—*Joyce Jackson, Bridgetown, Nova Scotia*

1-1/2 cups sugar
   1 cup canned pumpkin
   1/2 cup vegetable oil
   1/2 cup water
   2 eggs
1-2/3 cups all-purpose flour
   1 teaspoon baking soda
   1 teaspoon ground cinnamon
   3/4 teaspoon salt
   1/2 teaspoon baking powder
   1/2 teaspoon ground nutmeg
   1/4 teaspoon ground cloves
   1/2 cup chopped walnuts
   1/2 cup raisins, optional

In a mixing bowl, combine sugar, pumpkin, oil, water and eggs; beat well. Combine dry ingredients; gradually add to pumpkin mixture and mix well. Stir in nuts and raisins if desired.

Pour into a greased 9-in. x 5-in. x 3-in. loaf pan. Bake at 350° for 65-70 minutes or until a toothpick comes out clean. Cool 10 minutes in pan before removing to a wire rack. **Yield:** 1 loaf.

Raspberry Lemon Muffins

These are my all-time favorite muffins, and I have a hard time eating just one. With their pretty color and tangy flavor, they're delectable. Serve them with brunch or as a tasty snack. —*Sharon Shine Bradford, Pennsylvania*

2 cups all-purpose flour
1 cup sugar
1 tablespoon baking powder
1/2 teaspoon salt
2 eggs, lightly beaten
1 cup half-and-half cream
1/2 cup vegetable oil
1 teaspoon lemon extract
1-1/2 cups fresh *or* frozen raspberries

In a large bowl, combine flour, sugar, baking powder and salt. Combine the eggs, cream, oil and lemon extract; stir into dry ingredients just until moistened. Fold in raspberries.

Spoon into 18 greased or paper-lined muffin cups. Bake at 400° for 18-20 minutes or until a toothpick comes out clean. Cool for 5 minutes before removing from pan to wire racks. **Yield:** 1-1/2 dozen.

Recipe for: Glazed Cinnamon Biscuits

I often make this easy, delicious variation of glazed cinnamon rolls for our family as a breakfast treat on weekends. —*Sue Gronholz, Columbus, Wisconsin*

2 cups all-purpose flour
4 teaspoons baking powder
1/2 teaspoon salt
6 tablespoons butter, *divided*
3/4 cup milk
1/4 cup sugar
1 teaspoon ground cinnamon
GLAZE:
1 cup confectioners' sugar
1 tablespoon butter, melted
5 to 6 teaspoons milk
1/8 teaspoon vanilla extract

In a large bowl, combine dry ingredients. Cut in 4 tablespoons of the butter until mixture resembles coarse crumbs. Stir in milk just until moistened. Turn onto a lightly floured surface; knead gently 8-10 times.

Roll into an 11-in. x 8-in. rectangle about 1/2 in. thick. Melt remaining butter; brush 1 tablespoon over dough.

Combine sugar and cinnamon; sprinkle over butter. Roll up jelly-roll style, starting with long edge. Cut into 12 equal slices. Place with cut side down in a greased 8-in. square baking pan. Brush with remaining butter.

Bake at 450° for 18-20 minutes or until golden brown. Cool for 5 minutes. Combine glaze ingredients; spread over warm biscuits. Serve immediately. **Yield:** 1 dozen.

Cheddar-Dill Bread

(Pictured on page 74)

With soup and salad, this savory cheese bread sparked with dill makes a terrific meal.
—*Karen Gardiner, Eutaw, Alabama*

>   2 cups self-rising flour
>   1 tablespoon sugar
>   1/4 cup butter
>   1 cup (4 ounces) shredded sharp cheddar
>   cheese
>   2 teaspoons dill weed
>   1 egg
>   3/4 cup milk

In a large bowl, combine flour and sugar. Cut in butter until crumbly; stir in the cheese and dill. In a small bowl, beat egg and milk; pour into dry ingredients and stir just until moistened. (Batter will be very thick.)

Pour into a greased 8-in. x 4-in. x 2-in. loaf pan. Bake at 350° for 35-40 minutes or until a toothpick comes out clean. Cool in pan 10 minutes before removing to a wire rack. **Yield:** 1 loaf.

Editor's Note: As a substitute for self-rising flour, place 1 tablespoon baking powder and 1 teaspoon salt in a measuring cup. Add enough all-purpose flour to equal 2 cups.

Chocolate Mini Loaves

The moist texture of these mini loaves resembles a pound cake. Each bite is rich and succulent, making this perfect for dessert as well as snacking.
—*Elizabeth Downey, Evart, Michigan*

>   1/2 cup butter, softened
>   2/3 cup packed brown sugar
>   1 cup (6 ounces) semisweet chocolate
>   chips, melted
>   2 eggs
>   2 teaspoons vanilla extract
>   2-1/2 cups all-purpose flour
>   1 teaspoon baking powder
>   1 teaspoon baking soda
>   1-1/2 cups applesauce
>   1/2 cup miniature semisweet chocolate
>   chips
> GLAZE:
>   1/2 cup semisweet chocolate chips
>   1 tablespoon butter
>   5 teaspoons water
>   1/2 cup confectioners' sugar
>   1/4 teaspoon vanilla extract
> Dash salt

In a mixing bowl, cream butter and brown sugar. Add melted chocolate chips, eggs and vanilla; mix well. Combine the flour, baking powder and baking soda; add to creamed mixture alternately with applesauce. Fold in miniature chocolate chips.

Divide batter among five greased 5-3/4-in. x 3-in. x 2-in. loaf pans, about 1 cup in each. Bake at 350° for 30-40 minutes or until a toothpick comes out clean. Cool for 10 minutes before removing from pans to wire racks.

For glaze, combine chocolate chips, butter and water in a saucepan; cook and stir over low heat until chocolate is melted. Remove from the heat; stir in confectioners' sugar, vanilla and salt. Drizzle over cooled loaves. **Yield:** 5 mini loaves.

Editor's Note: Two 8-in. x 4-in. x 2-in. loaf pans may be used; bake for 50-55 minutes.

Poteca Nut Roll

(Pictured on page 75)

My mother-in-law brought this recipe from Yu-goslavia in the early 1900s. It was a tradition in her family to serve it for holidays and special occasions. Now it's my tradition. Family members often help roll out the dough and add the filling.
—Mrs. Anthony Setta, Saegertown, Pennsylvania

    1 package (1/4 ounce) active dry yeast
1/4 cup warm water (110° to 115°)
3/4 cup warm milk (110° to 115°)
1/4 cup sugar
    1 teaspoon salt
    1 egg, lightly beaten
1/4 cup shortening
    3 to 3-1/2 cups all-purpose flour
FILLING:
1/2 cup butter, softened
    1 cup packed brown sugar
    2 eggs, lightly beaten
    1 teaspoon vanilla extract
    1 teaspoon lemon extract, optional
    4 cups ground *or* finely chopped walnuts

Milk
    1/2 cup confectioners' sugar, optional

In a mixing bowl, dissolve yeast in water. Add milk, sugar, salt, egg, shortening and 1-1/2 cups flour; beat until smooth. Add enough remaining flour to form a soft dough. Turn onto a floured surface; knead until smooth and elastic, about 6-8 minutes. Place in a greased bowl, turning once to grease top. Cover and let rise in a warm place until doubled, about 1 hour.

For filling, combine butter, brown sugar, eggs, vanilla, lemon extract if desired and nuts. Add enough milk until mixture is of spreading consistency, about 1/2 cup; set aside. Punch dough down. Roll into a 30-in. x 20-in. rectangle. Spread filling to within 1 in. of edges. Roll up jelly-roll style, starting with a long side; pinch seams and ends to seal.

Place on a greased baking sheet; shape into a tight spiral. Cover and let rise until nearly doubled, about 1 hour. Bake at 350° for 35 minutes or until golden brown. Cool on a wire rack. If desired, brush with a glaze of confectioners' sugar and milk. **Yield:** 1 coffee cake.

Corn Bread Squares

This simple, economical recipe results in a tall gold-en corn bread. It's a great way to round out a meal.
—Marcia Salisbury, Waukesha, Wisconsin

    1 cup all-purpose flour
    1 cup yellow cornmeal
1/4 cup sugar
    2 teaspoons baking powder
3/4 teaspoon salt
    2 eggs, beaten
    1 cup milk
1/4 cup vegetable oil

In a mixing bowl, combine the flour, cornmeal, sugar, baking powder and salt. Add the eggs, milk and oil. Beat just until moistened. Spoon in-to a greased 8-in. square baking pan.

Bake at 400° for 20-25 minutes or until a toothpick inserted into the center comes out clean. **Yield:** 9 servings.

Nutty Apple Muffins

I teach quick-bread making for 4-H, and I'm always on the lookout for good new recipes. My sister-in-law shared this recipe with me. With apples and coconut, they are moist, chewy and tasty.
—Gloria Kaufmann, Orrville, Ohio

1-1/2 cups all-purpose flour
1-1/2 teaspoons baking soda
3/4 teaspoon salt
1/2 teaspoon ground nutmeg
2 eggs
1 cup plus 2 tablespoons sugar
1/3 cup vegetable oil
2 cups diced peeled apples
1-1/2 cups chopped walnuts
3/4 cup flaked coconut

In a large bowl, combine the flour, baking soda, salt and nutmeg. In another bowl, beat eggs, sugar and oil. Stir in apples, nuts and coconut. Stir into dry ingredients just until moistened. Fill 18 greased muffin cups three-fourths full. Bake at 350° for 25-30 minutes or until a toothpick comes out clean. Cool in pan 10 minutes before removing to a wire rack. **Yield:** 1-1/2 dozen.

Recipe for: Cranberry Nut Bread

Whenever I serve slices of this favorite treat, someone asks for the recipe. It's a moist, dark holiday bread chock-full of old-fashioned, spicy goodness.
—Maxine Smith, Owanka, South Dakota

2-1/2 cups halved fresh *or* frozen
    cranberries, *divided*
2/3 cup sugar
2 teaspoons grated orange peel
2-1/4 cups all-purpose flour
3/4 cup packed light brown sugar
1 tablespoon baking soda
1/2 teaspoon salt
2 teaspoons ground cinnamon
1/4 teaspoon ground cloves
2 eggs, lightly beaten
3/4 cup sour cream
1/4 cup butter, melted
1 cup chopped pecans

In a saucepan, combine 1-1/2 cups cranberries, sugar and orange peel. Bring to a boil; reduce heat and cook for 6-8 minutes or until the cranberries are soft. Remove from the heat; stir in the remaining berries and set aside.

In a bowl, combine flour, brown sugar, baking soda, salt, cinnamon and cloves. Combine eggs, sour cream and butter; stir into dry ingredients until blended. Fold in cranberries and pecans.

Pour into two greased 8-1/2-in. x 4-1/2-in. x 2-1/2-in. loaf pans. Bake at 350° for 55-60 minutes or until a toothpick comes out clean. **Yield:** 2 loaves.

Mexican Corn Bread

This tasty corn bread is easy to mix up. I serve it often with a meal or hearty bowl of soup as an alternative to rolls. Cheddar cheese makes it especially flavorful, and the diced peppers add nice color.
—Esther Shank, Harrisonburg, Virginia

1 cup yellow cornmeal
1/3 cup all-purpose flour
2 tablespoons sugar
1 teaspoon salt
2 teaspoons baking powder
1/2 teaspoon baking soda
2 eggs, beaten
1 cup buttermilk
1/2 cup vegetable oil
1 can (8-3/4 ounces) cream-style corn
1/3 cup chopped onion
2 tablespoons chopped green pepper
1/2 cup shredded cheddar cheese

In a mixing bowl, combine the first six ingredients. Combine the remaining ingredients; add to the dry ingredients and stir just until moistened.

Pour into a greased 9-in. square baking pan or 10-in. ovenproof skillet. Bake at 350° for 30-35 minutes or until bread is golden brown and a toothpick comes out clean. **Yield:** 8-10 servings.

My favorite memory of childhood was visiting my great-grandmother. She cooked on a huge, old wood-burning cookstove. She rose every morning at 4 a.m. no matter the weather. After she got that stove going, she'd start baking hot biscuits for breakfast. I don't think anything was ever as wonderful as waking up to the smell of a batch of her fresh hot biscuits.
—Peggy Nelson, Cambridge, Maryland

Fluffy Whole Wheat Biscuits

These are just scrumptious—light and tasty!
—Ruth Ann Stelfox, Raymond, Alberta

1 cup all-purpose flour
1 cup whole wheat flour
4 teaspoons baking powder
1 tablespoon sugar
3/4 teaspoon salt
1/4 cup butter
1 cup milk

In a medium bowl, combine flours, baking powder, sugar and salt; mix well. Cut in butter until mixture resembles coarse crumbs. Stir in milk just until moistened.

Turn out onto a lightly floured surface; knead gently 8-10 times. Roll to 3/4-in. thickness; cut with a 2-1/2-in. biscuit cutter and place on an ungreased baking sheet. Bake at 450° for 10-12 minutes or until lightly browned. Serve warm. **Yield:** 1 dozen.

Recipe for: *Lemon Bread*

You'll often find me baking this sunshiny-sweet bread when company's due. It has a pound cake-like texture and tangy lemon flavor.
—Kathy Scott, Hemingford, Nebraska

1/2 cup butter, softened
1 cup sugar
2 eggs
2 tablespoons lemon juice
1 tablespoon grated lemon peel
1-1/2 cups all-purpose flour
1 teaspoon baking powder
1/8 teaspoon salt
1/2 cup milk
GLAZE:
2 tablespoons lemon juice
1/2 cup confectioners' sugar

In a mixing bowl, cream butter and sugar. Beat in eggs, lemon juice and peel. Combine flour, baking powder and salt; stir into creamed mixture alternately with milk. Pour into a greased 8-in. x 4-in. x 2-in. loaf pan.

Bake at 350° for 45 minutes or until a toothpick comes out clean. Combine glaze ingredients. Remove bread from pan; immediately drizzle with glaze. Cool on a wire rack. **Yield:** 1 loaf.

Orange Date Bread

I loved visiting my aunt—she was an excellent baker, and her kitchen always smelled great. With her inspiration, I now bake this moist yummy bread every holiday season. Christmas wouldn't be the same without it.
—Joann Wolfe, Sunland, California

1 cup butter, softened
2 cups sugar
3 eggs, beaten
4 cups all-purpose flour
1 teaspoon baking soda
1 teaspoon salt
1-1/3 cups buttermilk
1 cup chopped walnuts
1 cup chopped dates
1 tablespoon grated orange peel
GLAZE:
1/4 cup orange juice
1/2 cup sugar
2 tablespoons grated orange peel

In a mixing bowl, cream butter and sugar. Add eggs; mix well. Combine flour, baking soda and salt; add to creamed mixture alternately with buttermilk. Fold in walnuts, dates and orange peel.

Pour into two greased and floured 8-1/2-in. x 4-1/2-in. x 2-1/2-in. loaf pans. Bake at 350° for 60-65 minutes or until a toothpick comes out clean. Combine glaze ingredients; spoon half over hot bread. Cool for 10 minutes. Remove from pans; spoon remaining glaze over bread. **Yield:** 2 loaves.

Nutty Sweet Potato Biscuits

Back in the 1920s and '30s, Mom always had something good for us to eat when we got home from school. Her wood range had an apron right by the firebox, and Mom often left a plate of these warm wonderful biscuits waiting for us. What a treat!
—Mrs. India Thacker, Clifford, Virginia

2-3/4 cups all-purpose flour
    4 teaspoons baking powder
1-1/4 teaspoons salt
  1/2 teaspoon ground cinnamon
  1/2 teaspoon ground nutmeg
  3/4 cup chopped nuts
    2 cups mashed cooked sweet potatoes

  3/4 cup sugar
  1/2 cup butter, melted
    1 teaspoon vanilla extract

In a large mixing bowl, combine flour, baking powder, salt, cinnamon, nutmeg and nuts. In another bowl, combine sweet potatoes, sugar, butter and vanilla; add to flour mixture and mix well. Turn onto a lightly floured surface; knead slightly. Roll dough to 1/2-in. thickness.

Cut with a 2-1/2-in. biscuit cutter and place on lightly greased baking sheets. Bake at 450° for 12 minutes or until golden brown. **Yield:** 1-1/2 to 2 dozen.

Muenster Bread

My sister and I won blue ribbons in 4-H with this bread many years ago. The recipe makes a beautiful, round golden loaf. With a layer of cheese peeking out of every slice, it's definitely worth the effort.
—Melanie Mero, Ida, Michigan

    2 packages (1/4 ounce *each*) active dry yeast

    1 cup warm milk (110° to 115°)
  1/2 cup butter, softened
    2 tablespoons sugar
    1 teaspoon salt
3-1/4 to 3-3/4 cups all-purpose flour
    1 egg plus 1 egg yolk
    4 cups (1 pound) shredded Muenster cheese
    1 egg white, beaten

In a large mixing bowl, dissolve yeast in milk. Add butter, sugar, salt and 2 cups flour; beat until smooth. Stir in enough remaining flour to form a soft dough. Turn onto a floured surface; knead until smooth and elastic, about 6-8 minutes. Place in a greased bowl, turning once to grease top. Cover and let rise in a warm place until doubled, about 1 hour.

In a large bowl, beat egg and yolk; stir in cheese. Punch dough down; roll into a 16-in. circle. Place in a greased 9-in. round baking pan, letting dough drape over the edges. Spoon the cheese mixture into center of dough. Gather dough up over filling in 1-1/2-in. pleats. Gently squeeze pleats together at top and twist to make a top knot.

Allow to rise 10-15 minutes. Brush loaf with egg white. Bake at 375° for 45-50 minutes. Cool on a wire rack for 20 minutes. Serve warm. **Yield:** 1 loaf.

Buttery Crescents

I learned this recipe many years ago, when I was a new bride and my grandmother taught me how to make these rolls. They're crusty outside and tender inside. —Lynne Peterson, Salt Lake City, Utah

    2 packages (1/4 ounce *each*) active dry
      yeast
    2 cups warm milk (110° to 115°)
6-1/2 to 7 cups all-purpose flour
    2 eggs, lightly beaten
  1/4 cup butter, melted and cooled
    3 tablespoons sugar
    1 teaspoon salt
Additional melted butter, optional

In a large mixing bowl, dissolve yeast in milk. Add 4 cups flour, eggs, butter, sugar and salt; beat until smooth. Add enough remaining flour to form a soft dough. Turn onto a floured surface; knead until smooth and elastic, about 6-8 minutes. Place in a greased bowl, turning once to grease top. Cover and let rise in a warm place until doubled, about 1 hour.

Punch the dough down and divide in thirds. Roll each portion into a 12-in. circle; cut each circle into 12 wedges. Roll up wedges from the wide end and place with pointed end down on greased baking sheets. Cover and let rise until doubled, about 30 minutes. Bake at 400° for 12-14 minutes or until golden brown. Brush with butter if desired. **Yield:** 3 dozen.

Recipe for: Honey Wheat Bread

This recipe produces two beautiful, high loaves that have wonderful texture and slice very well. The tempting aroma of this bread baking can cut the chill from a cool autumn day. It's a tribute to the goodness of wheat. —Dorothy Anderson, Ottawa, Kansas

  2-1/2 to 3 cups all-purpose flour
  3-1/2 cups whole wheat flour, *divided*
      2 packages (1/4 ounce *each*) active dry
        yeast
      1 cup milk
  1-1/4 cups water
    1/4 cup honey
      3 tablespoons butter
      1 tablespoon salt

In a large mixing bowl, combine 2 cups all-purpose flour, 2 cups whole wheat flour and yeast. In a saucepan, heat milk, water, honey, butter and salt to 120°-130°; add to flour mixture. Blend on low speed until moistened; beat on medium for 3 minutes. Gradually stir in remaining whole wheat flour and enough of the remaining all-purpose flour to form a soft dough.

Turn onto a floured surface; knead until smooth and elastic, about 6-8 minutes. Place in a greased bowl, turning once to grease top. Cover and let rise in a warm place until doubled, about 1 hour.

Punch dough down. Shape into two loaves; place in greased 8-in. x 4-in. x 2-in. loaf pans. Cover and let rise until doubled, about 1 hour. Bake at 375° for 40-45 minutes. Remove from pans to cool on wire racks. **Yield:** 2 loaves.

Homemade Egg Bread

People rave about this tender, delicate bread every time I serve it. —June Mullins, Livonia, Missouri

2 packages (1/4 ounce *each*) active dry yeast
1/2 cup warm water (110° to 115°)
1-1/2 cups warm milk (110° to 115°)
1/4 cup sugar
1 tablespoon salt
3 eggs, beaten
1/4 cup butter, softened
7 to 7-1/2 cups all-purpose flour
1 egg yolk
2 tablespoons water
Sesame seeds

Dissolve yeast in water. Add milk, sugar, salt, eggs, butter and 3-1/2 cups flour; mix well. Stir in enough remaining flour to form a soft dough. Turn onto a floured surface; knead until smooth and elastic, 6-8 minutes. Place in greased bowl; turn once to grease top. Cover and let rise in warm place until doubled, 1-1/2 to 2 hours.

Punch down. Cover and let rise until almost doubled, about 30 minutes. Divide into six portions. On a floured surface, shape each into a 14-in.-long rope. For each loaf, braid three ropes together on a greased baking sheet; pinch ends to seal. Cover and let rise until doubled, 50-60 minutes.

Beat egg yolk and water; brush over loaves. Sprinkle with sesame seeds. Bake at 375° for 30-35 minutes. **Yield:** 2 loaves.

Recipe for: Cheese Twists

These impressive loaves take a little time to prepare, but they're well worth the effort. I've used this recipe for several years. I love making bread—there's no better way to work out life's little frustrations and with such yummy results! —Michelle Beran, Claflin, Kansas

3-1/4 cups all-purpose flour
2 packages (1/4 ounce *each*) active dry yeast
1-1/2 cups buttermilk
3/4 cup butter
1/2 cup sugar
1/2 teaspoon salt
5 eggs
3-1/2 to 4 cups whole wheat flour, *divided*
2 cups (8 ounces) shredded cheddar cheese

In a large mixing bowl, combine all-purpose flour and yeast. In a saucepan, heat buttermilk, butter, sugar and salt to 120°-130°; add to flour mixture. Blend on low speed until moistened. Add eggs; beat on low for 30 seconds. Beat on high for 3 minutes. Stir in enough whole wheat flour to make a soft dough. Turn onto a floured surface; knead until smooth and elastic, about 6-8 minutes. Place in a greased bowl, turning once to grease top. Cover and let rise in a warm place until nearly doubled, about 1 hour.

Punch dough down; divide in half. On a lightly floured surface, roll each into a 12-in. x 9-in. rectangle. Cut each into three 12-in. x 3-in. strips. Combine cheese with 2 tablespoons of the remaining whole wheat flour; sprinkle 1/3 cup down center of each strip. Bring long edges together over cheese and pinch to seal. Place three strips seam side down on greased baking sheets. Braid strips together; secure ends. Cover and let rise until doubled, about 45 minutes.

Bake at 375° for 20-25 minutes or until golden. Immediately remove from baking sheets to wire racks; cool. **Yield:** 2 loaves.

Caraway Rye Bread

This delicious round loaf has wonderful old-world goodness. —Connie Moore, Medway, Ohio

> 2 packages (1/4 ounce *each*) active dry yeast
> 1-1/2 cups warm water (110° to 115°), *divided*
> 3 tablespoons molasses
> 3 tablespoons butter, melted
> 1 tablespoon caraway seed
> 1 teaspoon salt
> 1-1/2 to 2 cups all-purpose flour
> 1-1/2 cups whole wheat flour
> 1 cup rye flour

In mixing bowl, dissolve yeast in 1/2 cup water. Add molasses, butter, caraway, salt and remaining water; mix well. Combine flours; add 3 cups to batter. Beat until smooth. Add enough remaining flour to form a firm dough.

Turn onto a floured surface; knead until smooth and elastic, 6-8 minutes. Place in greased bowl, turning once to grease top. Cover and let rise in a warm place until doubled, about 1 hour.

Punch dough down; shape into a round loaf. Place on a greased baking sheet. Cover and let rise until doubled, about 30 minutes. Bake at 375° for 20-25 minutes or until golden brown. **Yield:** 1 loaf (16 slices).

Apple Raisin Bread

I've been making this bread for years. It smells so good in the oven and tastes even better. I make bread almost every Saturday, and it doesn't stay around long. —Perlene Hoekema, Lynden, Washington

> 2 packages (1/4 ounce *each*) active dry yeast
> 1-1/2 cups warm water (110° to 115°), *divided*
> 1 teaspoon sugar
> 3 eggs, beaten
> 1 cup applesauce
> 1/2 cup honey
> 1/2 cup vegetable oil
> 2 teaspoons salt
> 8 to 9 cups all-purpose flour
> 1-1/2 cups diced peeled apples
> 2 tablespoons lemon juice
> 1-1/2 cups raisins
> 2 tablespoons cornmeal
> GLAZE:
> 1 egg, beaten
> Sugar

In a small bowl, combine yeast, 1/2 cup water and sugar; set aside. In a large bowl, combine eggs, applesauce, honey, oil, salt and remaining water; mix well. Stir in yeast mixture. Gradually add enough flour to form a soft dough. Knead on a floured surface until smooth and elastic, about 10 minutes. Place dough in a greased bowl, turning once to grease top. Cover and let rise in a warm place until doubled, about 1 hour.

Punch down and turn over in bowl. Cover and let rise 30 minutes. In a small bowl, combine apples, lemon juice and raisins. Divide dough into three parts; knead one-third of the apple mixture into each part. Shape each into round flat balls. Place each in a greased 8-in. round baking pan that has been sprinkled with cornmeal. Cover and let rise until doubled, about 1 hour.

For glaze, brush each loaf with egg and sprinkle with sugar. Bake at 350° for 30-35 minutes or until golden brown. **Yield:** 3 loaves.

Angel Biscuits

(Pictured on front cover)

I like these light, wonderful biscuits with butter and honey or sausage gravy.
—*Faye Hintz*
Springfield, Missouri

2 packages (1/4 ounce *each*) active dry yeast
1/4 cup warm water (110° to 115°)
2 cups warm buttermilk (110° to 115°)
5 cups all-purpose flour
1/3 cup sugar
2 teaspoons baking powder
1 teaspoon baking soda
2 teaspoons salt

1 cup shortening
Melted butter

Dissolve yeast in warm water. Let stand 5 minutes. Stir in the buttermilk; set aside. In a large mixing bowl, combine flour, sugar, baking powder, baking soda and salt. Cut in shortening with a pastry blender until crumbly. Stir in yeast/buttermilk mixture; mix well.

Turn out onto a lightly floured surface; knead lightly 3-4 times. Roll to a 1/2-in. thickness. Cut with a 2-1/2-in. biscuit cutter. Place on a lightly greased baking sheet. Cover; let rise in a warm place about 1-1/2 hours. Bake at 450° for 8-10 minutes until light brown. Brush tops with melted butter. **Yield:** about 2-1/2 dozen.

Grandma's Orange Rolls

Our grandchildren love these fine-textured sweet rolls.
—*Norma Poole, Auburndale, Florida*

1 package (1/4 ounce) active dry yeast
1/4 cup warm water (110° to 115°)
1 cup warm milk (110° to 115°)
1/4 cup shortening
1/4 cup sugar

1 teaspoon salt
1 egg, lightly beaten
3-1/2 to 3-3/4 cups all-purpose flour
FILLING:
1 cup sugar
1/2 cup butter, softened
2 tablespoons grated orange peel
GLAZE:
1 cup confectioners' sugar
4 teaspoons butter, softened
4 to 5 teaspoons milk
1/2 teaspoon lemon extract

In a small bowl, dissolve yeast in water. In a large mixing bowl, mix milk, shortening, sugar, salt and egg. Add yeast mixture and blend. Stir in enough flour to form a soft dough. Knead on a lightly floured surface until smooth and elastic, about 6-8 minutes. Place in a greased bowl, turning once to grease top. Cover and let rise in a warm place until doubled, about 1 hour.

Punch dough down; divide in half. Roll each half into a 15-in. x 10-in. rectangle. Mix filling ingredients until smooth. Spread half the filling on each rectangle. Roll up jelly-roll style, starting with a long end. Cut each into 15 rolls. Place in two greased 11-in. x 7-in. x 2-in. baking pans. Cover and let rise until doubled, about 45 minutes.

Bake at 375° for 20-25 minutes or until lightly browned. Mix glaze ingredients; spread over warm rolls. **Yield:** 30 rolls.

Country White Bread

Anytime is the right time for a comforting slice of home-made bread. These loaves are especially nice since the crust stays so tender. This recipe is my husband Nick's favorite. He makes most of the bread at our house.
—Joanne Shew Chuk, St. Benedict, Saskatchewan

> 2 packages (1/4 ounce *each*) active dry yeast
> 2 cups warm water (110° to 115°)
> 1/2 cup sugar
> 1 tablespoon salt
> 2 eggs, beaten
> 1/4 cup vegetable oil
> 6-1/2 to 7 cups all-purpose flour

In a large mixing bowl, dissolve yeast in water. Add sugar, salt, eggs, oil and 3 cups of flour; beat until smooth. Stir in enough remaining flour to form a soft dough. Turn onto a floured surface; knead until smooth and elastic, about 6-8 minutes. Place in a greased bowl, turning once to grease top. Cover and let rise in a warm place until doubled, about 1 hour.

Punch dough down. Divide in half and shape into loaves. Place in two greased 9-in. x 5-in. x 3-in. loaf pans. Cover and let rise until doubled, about 1 hour. Bake at 375° for 25-30 minutes or until golden brown. Remove from pans to cool on wire racks. **Yield:** 2 loaves.

Recipe for: Whole Wheat Refrigerator Rolls

This roll recipe is easy and versatile. I like to mix up the dough beforehand and let it rise in the refrigerator. The rolls brown nicely and are wonderful served warm.
—Sharon Mensing, Greenfield, Iowa

> 2 packages (1/4 ounce *each*) active dry yeast
> 2 cups warm water (110° to 115°)
> 1/2 cup sugar
> 2 teaspoons salt
> 4-1/2 to 5 cups all-purpose flour, *divided*
> 1 egg
> 1/4 cup vegetable oil
> 2 cups whole wheat flour

In a mixing bowl, dissolve yeast in water. Let stand 5 minutes. Blend in sugar, salt and 3 cups all-purpose flour at low speed until moistened; beat 2 minutes at medium speed. Beat in egg and oil. By hand, gradually stir in whole wheat flour and enough remaining all-purpose flour to make a soft dough. Turn out onto a lightly floured surface. Knead until smooth and elastic, about 6-8 minutes. Place in a greased bowl, turning once to grease top. Cover and let rise until doubled or cover and refrigerate overnight.

Punch dough down and form into dinner-size rolls. Place on greased baking sheets for plain rolls or knots, or in greased muffin tins for cloverleaf rolls. Cover and let rise until doubled, about 1 hour for dough prepared the same day or 1-2 hours for refrigerated dough.

Bake at 375° for 10-12 minutes or until light golden brown. Serve warm. If desired, dough may be kept up to 4 days in the refrigerator. Punch down daily. **Yield:** 2 dozen.

Lemon Cheese Braid

This recipe came from my mom, who is an excellent cook. It always gets rave reviews. Although fairly simple to make, when you finish you'll feel a sense of accomplishment because it tastes delicious and looks so impressive. —Grace Dickey, Vernonia, Oregon

    1 package (1/4 ounce) active dry yeast
    3 tablespoons warm water (110° to 115°)
1/4 cup sugar
1/3 cup milk
1/4 cup butter, melted
    2 eggs
1/2 teaspoon salt

Butternut Squash Bread

This yeast bread is scrumptious served warm or toasted. A friend shared the recipe years ago.
    —Agnes Miller, Marshall, Illinois

    2 packages (1/4 ounce *each*) active dry
       yeast
1/2 cup warm water (110° to 115°)
1-1/4 cups mashed cooked butternut squash
    1 cup warm milk (110° to 115°)
    2 eggs, beaten
1/3 cup butter, melted
1/3 cup sugar
    1 teaspoon salt
    7 to 7-1/2 cups all-purpose flour

    3 to 3-1/2 cups all-purpose flour
FILLING:
    2 packages (one 8 ounces, one 3 ounces)
      cream cheese, softened
1/2 cup sugar
    1 egg
    1 teaspoon grated lemon peel
ICING:
1/2 cup confectioners' sugar
    2 to 3 teaspoons milk
1/4 teaspoon vanilla extract

In a mixing bowl, dissolve yeast in warm water; let stand for 5 minutes. Add sugar, milk, butter, eggs, salt and 2 cups flour; beat on low speed for 3 minutes. Stir in enough of the remaining flour to form a soft dough. Knead on a floured surface until smooth and elastic, about 6-8 minutes. Place in a greased bowl, turning once to grease top. Cover and let rise in a warm place until doubled, about 1 hour.

Meanwhile, beat filling ingredients in a mixing bowl until fluffy; set aside. Punch dough down. On a floured surface, roll into a 14-in. x 12-in. rectangle. Place on a greased baking sheet. Spread filling down center third of rectangle. On each long side, cut 1-in.-wide strips, 3 in. into center. Starting at one end, fold alternating strips at an angle across filling. Seal end. Cover and let rise for 30 minutes.

Bake at 375° for 25-30 minutes or until golden brown. Cool. Combine icing ingredients; drizzle over bread. **Yield:** 12-14 servings.

In a mixing bowl, dissolve yeast in water; let stand for 5 minutes. Add squash, milk, eggs, butter, sugar and salt; mix well. Gradually add 3-1/2 cups flour; beat until smooth. Add enough remaining flour to form a soft dough. Turn onto a floured surface; knead until smooth and elastic, about 6-8 minutes. Place in a greased bowl, turning once to grease top. Cover and let rise in a warm place until doubled, about 1 hour.

Punch dough down. Shape into three loaves; place in greased 8-in. x 4-in. x 2-in. loaf pans. Cover and let rise until doubled, about 30 minutes. Bake at 375° for 25-30 minutes or until tops are golden. Remove from pans to cool on wire racks. **Yield:** 3 loaves.

Recipe for: *Honey Party Buns*

I use this recipe often for church get-togethers. Finger sandwiches are popular at these events, so I make these golden buns small and add sandwich toppings. They're a big hit with everyone. —Ruth Linscott
Millfield, Ohio

    1 cup butter, cut into pieces
  1/2 cup honey
    2 cups boiling water
    2 packages (1/4 ounce *each*) active dry
      yeast
  1/3 cup warm water (110° to 115°)
    2 eggs, beaten
    1 teaspoon baking powder
    1 teaspoon salt
3-1/2 cups whole wheat flour
    4 to 4-1/2 cups all-purpose flour

Place butter and honey in a large mixing bowl; pour the boiling water over and set aside to cool to 110°-115°. In a small bowl, dissolve yeast in warm water; set aside. To honey mixture, add eggs, baking powder and salt. Add yeast mixture and whole wheat flour; beat until smooth. Stir in enough all-purpose flour to form a soft dough. Turn onto a floured surface; knead until smooth and elastic, about 8-10 minutes. Place in a greased bowl, turning once to grease top. Cover and let rise in a warm place until doubled, about 1 hour.

Punch dough down; divide in half. On a lightly floured surface, roll each half to 1/2-in. thickness; cut with a 2-1/2-in. cutter. Place on greased baking sheets. Cover and let rise in a warm place until doubled, about 1 hour.

Bake at 350° for 15-20 minutes or until golden brown. Remove from pans to cool on wire racks. **Yield:** 4-5 dozen.

Easy Potato Rolls

After I discovered this recipe, it became a mainstay for me. I make the dough ahead of time when company is coming, and I try to keep some in the refrigerator to make for "hay hands" on our cattle ranch. Leftover mashed potatoes are almost sure to go into these rolls. —Jeanette McKinney, Belleview, Missouri

  2/3 cup sugar
  2/3 cup shortening
    1 cup mashed potatoes
2-1/2 teaspoons salt
    2 eggs
    2 packages (1/4 ounce *each*) active dry
      yeast
1-1/3 cups warm water (110° to 115°), *divided*
    6 to 6-1/2 cups all-purpose flour

In a large mixing bowl, cream sugar and shortening. Add potatoes, salt and eggs. In a small bowl, dissolve yeast in 2/3 cup of warm water; add to creamed mixture. Beat in 2 cups flour and remaining water. Add enough remaining flour to form a soft dough. Shape into a ball; do not knead. Place in a greased bowl, turning once to grease top. Cover and let rise in a warm place until doubled, about 1 hour.

Punch dough down; divide into thirds. Shape each portion into 15 balls and arrange in three greased 9-in. round baking pans. Cover and let rise until doubled, about 30 minutes. Bake at 375° for 20-25 minutes. Remove from pans to cool on wire racks. **Yield:** 45 rolls.

Grandma Russell's Bread

I remember as a child always smelling fresh home-made bread and rolls whenever I walked into Grandma's house. The warm slices were delicious and melted in my mouth! —Janet Polito, Nampa, Idaho

     1 package (1/4 ounce) active dry yeast
 1/3 cup warm water (110° to 115°)
 1/2 cup sugar, *divided*
     1 cup milk
 1/2 cup butter
     1 tablespoon salt
     1 cup mashed potatoes
     2 eggs, beaten
     5 to 6 cups all-purpose flour

In a large bowl, combine yeast, warm water and 1 teaspoon sugar; set aside. In a saucepan, heat milk, butter, salt and remaining sugar until butter melts. Remove from the heat; stir in potatoes until smooth. Cool to lukewarm; add eggs and mix well.

To yeast mixture add the potato mixture and 5 cups flour. Stir in enough remaining flour to form a soft dough. Turn out onto a floured surface and knead until smooth and elastic, about 6-8 minutes. Place in a greased bowl, turning once to grease top. Cover and let rise in a warm place until doubled, about 1-1/2 hours.

Punch down and divide in half. Shape two loaves and place in greased 8-1/2-in. x 4-1/2-in. x 2-1/2-in. loaf pans. Cover and let rise until doubled. Bake loaves at 375° for 20 minutes; bake rolls at 375° for 25-30 minutes. Cover with foil if they brown too quickly. **Yield:** 2 loaves or 2 dozen rolls.

Cinnamon Twists

These delightful golden twists are perfect for a spring brunch or lunch. The brown sugar and cinnamon give them a delicate spicy flavor. It's a good thing the recipe makes a big batch, because people can rarely eat just one. —Janet Mooberry, Peoria, Illinois

     1 package (1/4 ounce) active dry yeast
 3/4 cup warm water (110° to 115°), *divided*
     4 to 4-1/2 cups all-purpose flour
 1/4 cup sugar
 1-1/2 teaspoons salt
 1/2 cup warm milk (110° to 115°)
 1/4 cup butter, softened
     1 egg
FILLING:
 1/4 cup butter, melted
 1/2 cup packed brown sugar
     4 teaspoons ground cinnamon

In a large mixing bowl, dissolve yeast in 1/4 cup warm water. Add 2 cups of flour, sugar, salt, milk, butter, egg and remaining water; beat on medium speed for 2 minutes. Stir in enough remaining flour to form a soft dough. Turn onto a floured surface; knead until smooth and elastic, about 6-8 minutes. Place in a greased bowl, turning once to grease top. Cover and let rise in a warm place until doubled, about 1 hour.

Punch down. Roll into a 16-in. x 12-in. rectangle. Brush with butter. Combine brown sugar and cinnamon; sprinkle over butter. Let dough rest for 6 minutes. Cut lengthwise into three 16-in. x 4-in. strips. Cut each strip into sixteen 4-in. x 1-in. pieces. Twist and place on greased baking sheets. Cover and let rise until doubled, about 30 minutes. Bake at 350° for 15 minutes or until golden. **Yield:** 4 dozen.

English Muffin Bread

Many years ago, a good friend gave me her mother's recipe for this delightful bread, and I've made it ever since. It's perfect for a hearty breakfast, especially when smothered with your favorite jam.
—Jane Zielinski, Rotterdam Junction, New York

5 cups all-purpose flour, *divided*
2 packages (1/4 ounce *each*) active dry yeast
1 tablespoon sugar
2 teaspoons salt
1/4 teaspoon baking soda
2 cups warm milk (120° to 130°)
1/2 cup warm water (120° to 130°)
Cornmeal

In a large mixing bowl, combine 2 cups flour, yeast, sugar, salt and baking soda. Add warm milk and water; beat on low speed for 30 seconds, scraping bowl occasionally. Beat on high for 3 minutes. Stir in remaining flour (batter will be stiff). Do not knead. Grease two 8-1/2-in. x 4-1/2- in. x 2-1/2-in. loaf pans. Sprinkle pans with cornmeal. Spoon batter into the pans and sprinkle cornmeal on top. Cover and let rise in a warm place until doubled, about 45 minutes.

Bake at 375° for 35 minutes or until golden brown. Remove from pans immediately and cool on wire racks. Slice and toast. **Yield:** 2 loaves.

Recipe for: Three-Day Yeast Rolls

These rolls are excellent for Thanksgiving, Christmas or most any time you have company or a special occasion to celebrate. I especially like them because I can get the time-consuming steps out of the way days before I serve them.
—Kelly Hardgrave, Hartman, Arkansas

2 packages (1/4 ounce *each*) active dry yeast
2 cups warm water (110° to 115°), *divided*
1 cup butter, softened
3/4 cup sugar
2 eggs
2 teaspoons salt
7-1/2 to 8 cups all-purpose flour
Additional butter, melted, optional

In a mixing bowl, dissolve yeast in 1/4 cup water. Add butter, sugar, eggs, salt and remaining water; mix well. Add 2 cups flour; beat until smooth. Gradually stir in enough remaining flour to form a soft dough (do not knead). Place in a greased bowl. Cover and refrigerate for up to 3 days.

When ready to use, turn out onto a floured surface; knead until smooth and elastic, about 6-8 minutes. Shape into rolls as desired. Place in greased muffin cups or on baking sheets. Cover and let rise until nearly doubled, about 1 hour.

Bake at 375° for 10-15 minutes or until golden brown. Brush with butter if desired. Immediately remove to wire racks to cool. **Yield:** 3-4 dozen.

Beef

At left: Peppered Rib Eye Steaks (p. 98).

At right: Barbecued Beef Sandwiches (p. 100).

Spaghetti 'n' Meatballs

One evening, we had unexpected company. Since I had some of these meatballs left over in the freezer, I warmed them up as appetizers. Everyone raved!
—Mary Lou Koskella, Prescott, Arizona

1-1/2 cups chopped onion
   3 garlic cloves, minced
   2 tablespoons olive oil
   3 cups water

   1 can (29 ounces) tomato sauce
   2 cans (12 ounces *each*) tomato paste
1/3 cup minced fresh parsley
   1 tablespoon dried basil
   1 tablespoon salt
1/2 teaspoon pepper
MEATBALLS:
   4 eggs, lightly beaten
   2 cups soft bread cubes (1/4-inch pieces)
1-1/2 cups milk
   1 cup grated Parmesan cheese
   3 garlic cloves, minced
   1 tablespoon salt
1/2 teaspoon pepper
   3 pounds ground beef
   2 tablespoons vegetable oil
Hot cooked spaghetti

In a Dutch oven over medium heat, saute onion and garlic in oil. Add water, tomato sauce and paste, parsley, basil, salt and pepper; bring to a boil. Reduce heat; cover and simmer for 50 minutes.

In a bowl, combine the first seven meatball ingredients. Crumble beef over mixture and mix well. Shape into 1-1/2-in. balls.

In a skillet over medium heat, cook meatballs in oil; drain. Add to sauce; bring to a boil. Reduce heat; cover and simmer for 1 hour, stirring occasionally. Serve over spaghetti. **Yield:** 12-16 servings.

Peppered Rib Eye Steaks

(Pictured on page 96)

The seasoning rub in this favorite recipe makes a wonderful marinade, and nothing beats the summertime taste of these flavorful grilled steaks!
—Sharon Bickett, Chester, South Carolina

   4 beef rib eye steaks (1-1/2 inches thick)
   1 tablespoon olive oil
   1 tablespoon garlic powder
   1 tablespoon paprika
   2 teaspoons dried thyme
   2 teaspoons dried oregano
1-1/2 teaspoons pepper
   1 teaspoon salt
   1 teaspoon lemon-pepper seasoning

   1 teaspoon crushed red pepper
Orange slices, optional
Parsley sprigs, optional

Brush steaks lightly with oil. In a small bowl, combine all seasonings. Sprinkle seasonings over steaks and press into both sides. Cover and chill for 1 hour.

Grill steaks, turning once, over medium-hot heat 14-18 minutes for rare; 18-22 minutes for medium; 24-28 minutes for well-done.

Place on a warm serving platter; cut across the grain into thick slices. Garnish with orange slices and parsley if desired. **Yield:** 8 servings.

Recipe for: Baked Stuffed Tomatoes

My family loves these tasty garden "containers" filled with a savory mixture of rice and ground beef.
—Bertille Cooper, St. Inigoes, Maryland

6 medium fresh tomatoes
1/2 pound ground beef
1 teaspoon chili powder
1 teaspoon sugar
1/2 teaspoon salt
1/2 teaspoon pepper
1/4 teaspoon dried oregano
2 cups uncooked instant rice
1/2 cup dry bread crumbs
2 tablespoons butter, melted
2 tablespoons water

Cut a thin slice off the top of each tomato. Leaving a 1/2-in.-thick shell, scoop out and reserve pulp. Invert tomatoes onto paper towels to drain.

Meanwhile, in a skillet, cook beef until no longer pink; drain. Add tomato pulp, chili powder, sugar, salt, pepper and oregano; bring to a boil. Reduce heat; simmer 45-50 minutes or until slightly thickened, stirring occasionally.

Add rice; mix well. Simmer 5-6 minutes longer or until rice is tender. Stuff tomatoes and place in a greased 13-in. x 9-in. x 2-in. baking dish. Combine bread crumbs and butter; sprinkle over tomatoes. Add water to baking dish.

Bake, uncovered, at 375° for 20-25 minutes or until crumbs are lightly browned. **Yield:** 6 servings.

Vegetable Beef Casserole

This easy one-dish recipe has been a favorite ever since it was handed down to me over 30 years ago from my husband's family. Add whatever vegetables you have on hand. A simple salad goes nicely with this dish.   —Evangeline Rew, Manassas, Virginia

3 medium unpeeled potatoes, sliced
3 carrots, sliced
3 celery ribs, sliced
2 cups fresh *or* frozen green beans
1 medium onion, chopped
1 pound lean ground beef
1 teaspoon dried thyme
1 teaspoon salt
1 teaspoon pepper
4 medium tomatoes, peeled, seeded and chopped
1 cup (4 ounces) shredded cheddar cheese

In a 3-qt. casserole, layer half of the potatoes, carrots, celery, green beans and onion. Crumble half of the uncooked beef over vegetables. Sprinkle with 1/2 teaspoon each of thyme, salt and pepper. Repeat layers. Top with tomatoes.

Cover and bake at 400° for 15 minutes. Reduce heat to 350°; bake about 1 hour longer or until vegetables are tender and meat is no longer pink. Sprinkle with cheese; cover and let stand until cheese is melted. **Yield:** 6-8 servings.

Barbecued Beef Sandwiches

(Pictured on page 97)

The great thing about this recipe—especially for non-cabbage lovers—is that you can't taste the cabbage in the meat. Yet, at the same time, it adds a nice heartiness and moistness. I credit my mother for my love of cooking. My grandmother, too…I remember how she made barbecued beef on weekends when grandkids visited.
—Denise Marshall
Bagley, Wisconsin

  2 pounds beef stew meat
  2 cups water
  4 cups shredded cabbage
  1/2 cup barbecue sauce
  1/2 cup ketchup

  1/3 cup Worcestershire sauce
  1 tablespoon horseradish
  1 tablespoon prepared mustard
  10 hamburger *or* other sandwich buns, split

In a covered Dutch oven or saucepan, simmer beef in water for 1-1/2 hours or until tender. Drain cooking liquid, reserving 3/4 cup. Cool beef; shred and return to the Dutch oven.

Add the cabbage, barbecue sauce, ketchup, Worcestershire sauce, horseradish, mustard and the reserved cooking liquid. Cover and simmer for 1 hour. Serve warm in buns. **Yield:** 10 servings.

Steak Potpie

When I hear "meat and potatoes", this is the recipe that immediately comes to mind. I've made it for years, and everyone who's tried it has liked it. Most often, friends comment on how tasty and satisfying this dish is.
—Pattie Bonner, Cocoa, Florida

  3/4 cup sliced onions
  4 tablespoons vegetable oil, *divided*
  1/4 cup all-purpose flour
  1 teaspoon salt
  1/2 teaspoon pepper
  1/2 teaspoon paprika
Pinch ground allspice
Pinch ground ginger
  1 pound boneless round steak, cut into 1/2-inch pieces
2-1/2 cups boiling water
  3 medium potatoes, peeled and diced
Pastry for single-crust pie

In a large skillet, saute the onions in 2 tablespoons oil until golden. Drain and set aside. In a plastic bag, combine dry ingredients; add meat and shake to coat. In the same skillet, cook meat in remaining oil until no longer pink. Add water; cover and simmer until meat is tender, about 1 hour.

Add potatoes; simmer, uncovered, for 15-20 minutes or until the potatoes are tender. Pour into a greased 1-1/2-qt. baking dish. Top with onion slices. Roll pastry to fit baking dish. Place over hot filling; seal to edges of dish. Make slits in the crust.

Bake at 450° for 25-30 minutes or until golden brown. If necessary, cover edges of crust with foil to prevent overbrowning. **Yield:** 4-6 servings.

Quick Mushroom Stew

Even with chunky vegetables and tender meat, the mushrooms star in this stick-to-your-ribs main dish.
—Cherie Sechrist, Red Lion, Pennsylvania

1 can (10-3/4 ounces) condensed tomato
   soup, undiluted
1 can (10-3/4 ounces) condensed cream
   of mushroom soup, undiluted
2-1/2 cups water
2 pounds beef stew meat
2 bay leaves
3 medium potatoes, peeled and cut
   into 1-inch chunks
4 carrots, cut into 1/2-inch slices
1 pound medium fresh mushrooms,
   halved
1 tablespoon quick-cooking tapioca

In a Dutch oven, stir the soups and water until smooth. Add meat and bay leaves. Cover and

bake at 325° for 1-1/2 hours.

Stir in potatoes, carrots, mushrooms and tapioca. Cover and bake 1 hour longer or until the meat and vegetables are tender. Remove the bay leaves before serving. **Yield:** 6-8 servings.

Recipe for: "Hearty" Lasagna

Here's a dish that's perfect to share with your sweetie! The heart on top is an easy touch which makes the lasagna extra special. Because you can make it ahead, you won't have to feel rushed when it's time to enjoy your meal.
—Marcy Cella, L'Anse, Michigan

1-1/2 pounds ground beef
1 medium onion, chopped
1 garlic clove, minced
3 tablespoons olive oil
1 can (28 ounces) Italian diced
   tomatoes, undrained
1 can (8 ounces) tomato sauce
1 can (6 ounces) tomato paste
1 teaspoon dried oregano
1 teaspoon sugar
1 teaspoon salt
1/4 teaspoon pepper
2 carrots, halved
2 celery ribs, halved
12 ounces lasagna noodles
1 carton (15 ounces) ricotta cheese
2 cups (8 ounces) shredded mozzarella
   cheese
1/2 cup grated Parmesan cheese

In a large skillet, cook beef, onion and garlic in oil until meat is no longer pink and onion is tender; drain. Stir in tomatoes, tomato sauce, tomato paste, oregano, sugar, salt and pepper. Place carrots and celery in sauce. Simmer, uncovered, for 1-1/2 hours, stirring occasionally.

Meanwhile, cook lasagna noodles according to package directions. Drain; rinse in cold water. Remove and discard carrots and celery from sauce.

In a greased 13-in. x 9-in. x 2-in. baking dish, layer one-third of the noodles, one-third of the meat sauce, one-third of the ricotta, one-third of the mozzarella and one-third of the Parmesan. Repeat layers once. Top with remaining noodles and meat sauce.

Cut a heart out of aluminum foil and center on top of sauce. Dollop and spread remaining ricotta around heart. Sprinkle with remaining mozzarella and Parmesan. Bake, uncovered, at 350° for 45 minutes. Remove and discard foil heart. Let stand 10-15 minutes before cutting. **Yield:** 12 servings.

Mozzarella Meat Loaf

My children were not fond of meat loaf until I dressed up this recipe with pizza flavor. Now the five children are grown and have families of their own, and they still make and serve this hearty, moist meat loaf.
—Darlis Wilfer, Phelps, Wisconsin

2 eggs, lightly beaten
1 cup saltine cracker crumbs
1 cup milk
1/2 cup grated Parmesan cheese
1/2 cup chopped onion
1-1/2 teaspoons salt
1 teaspoon dried oregano
2 pounds lean ground beef
1 can (8 ounces) pizza sauce
3 slices mozzarella cheese, halved
Green pepper rings, optional
Sliced mushrooms, optional
2 tablespoons butter, optional
Chopped fresh parsley, optional

In a bowl, combine the first seven ingredients; crumble beef over mixture and mix well. Shape into a loaf and place in a greased 9-in. x 5-in. x 3-in. loaf pan. Bake at 350° for 1-1/4 hours or until no pink remains; drain.

Spoon pizza sauce over loaf and top with mozzarella cheese slices. Return to the oven for 10 minutes or until the cheese is melted. Meanwhile, if desired, saute green pepper and mushrooms in butter; arrange on top of meat loaf. Sprinkle with parsley if desired. **Yield:** 8-10 servings.

Recipe for: Salisbury Steak Deluxe

Serve the meat patties and gravy over a bed of cooked noodles or mashed potatoes for a satisfying meal. If desired, the patties and gravy can be prepared ahead and reheated.
—Denise Barteet
Shreveport, Louisiana

1 can (10-3/4 ounces) condensed cream of mushroom soup, undiluted
1 tablespoon prepared mustard
2 teaspoons Worcestershire sauce
1 teaspoon horseradish
1 egg
1/4 cup dry bread crumbs
1/4 cup finely chopped onion
1/2 teaspoon salt
Dash pepper
1-1/2 pounds ground beef
1 to 2 tablespoons vegetable oil
1/2 cup water

In a bowl, combine the soup, mustard, Worcestershire sauce and horseradish; blend well. Set aside. In another bowl, lightly beat the egg. Add bread crumbs, onion, salt, pepper and 1/4 cup of the soup mixture. Add beef and mix well. Shape into six patties. In a large skillet, heat oil over medium-high. Brown the patties on both sides; drain.

Combine remaining soup mixture with water; pour over patties. Cover and cook over low heat for 10-15 minutes or until meat is no longer pink. Remove patties to a serving platter; top with sauce. **Yield:** 6 servings.

Savory Pot Roast

My husband and I used to raise cattle, so I prepared a lot of beef. This old-fashioned pot roast is the best. Smooth gravy is a tempting topper for the tender, flavorful meat. —Lee Leuschner, Calgary, Alberta

    1 rolled boneless chuck roast (6 pounds)
    2 tablespoons vegetable oil
    1 large onion, coarsely chopped
    2 medium carrots, coarsely chopped
    1 celery rib, coarsely chopped
    2 cups water
    1 can (14-1/2 ounces) beef broth
    2 bay leaves
GRAVY:
  1/4 cup butter
  1/4 cup all-purpose flour
    1 teaspoon lemon juice
    4 to 5 drops hot pepper sauce

In a large skillet over medium-high heat, brown roast on all sides in oil. Transfer to a large roasting pan; add onion, carrots and celery.

In a saucepan, bring water, broth and bay leaves to a boil. Pour over roast and vegetables. Cover and bake at 350° for 2-1/2 to 3 hours or until meat is tender, turning once. Remove roast to a serving platter and keep warm.

For gravy, strain pan juices, reserving 2 cups. Discard the vegetables and bay leaves. In a saucepan over medium heat, melt butter. Stir in flour until smooth. Gradually stir in pan juices; bring to a boil. Cook and stir for 2 minutes. Add lemon juice and hot pepper sauce; mix well. Serve with the roast. **Yield:** 14-16 servings.

Classic Beef Stew

Here's a good old-fashioned stew with rich beef gravy that lets the flavor of the potatoes and carrots come through. This is the perfect comforting dish for a blustery winter day. I make it often in fall and winter. —Alberta McKay, Bartlesville, Oklahoma

    2 pounds beef stew meat
    1 to 2 tablespoons vegetable oil
1-1/2 cups chopped onion
    1 can (16 ounces) diced tomatoes,
       undrained
    1 can (10-1/2 ounces) condensed beef
       broth, undiluted
    3 tablespoons quick-cooking tapioca
    1 garlic clove, minced
    1 tablespoon dried parsley flakes
    1 teaspoon salt
  1/4 teaspoon pepper
    1 bay leaf
    6 medium carrots, cut into 2-inch pieces
    3 medium potatoes, peeled and cut
       into 2-inch pieces
    1 cup sliced celery (1-inch pieces)

In a Dutch oven, brown the beef, half at a time, in oil. Drain. Return all meat to pan. Add onion, tomatoes, beef broth, tapioca, garlic, parsley, salt, pepper and bay leaf. Bring to a boil; remove from the heat. Cover and bake at 350° for 1-1/2 hours. Stir in carrots, potatoes and celery.

Bake, covered, 1 hour longer or until meat and vegetables are tender. Remove bay leaf before serving. **Yield:** 6-8 servings.

Grandma's Meat Loaf

We love Grandma's version of meat loaf so much that we have it at Thanksgiving, Christmas and Easter—the holidays wouldn't be the same without it! It's just as good the next day as a cold sandwich.
—Joan Frey, Spencer, Ohio

    1 egg, beaten
1/4 cup dry bread crumbs
    3 bacon strips, cut into 1/4-inch pieces
    1 small onion, chopped
    2 ounces cubed cheddar cheese
1/2 teaspoon seasoned salt
1/2 teaspoon pepper
1-1/2 pounds lean ground beef
1/2 pound bulk pork sausage

In a large bowl, combine egg, bread crumbs, bacon, onion, cheese, seasoned salt and pepper. Crumble beef and sausage over mixture and mix well.

    In a shallow baking pan, shape mixture into an 8-1/2-in. x 4-1/2-in. x 2-1/2-in. loaf. Bake at 350° for 1-1/4 hours or until no pink remains. Drain. Let stand a few minutes before serving. **Yield:** 8-10 servings.

Old-Fashioned Cabbage Rolls

It was an abundance of dill in my garden that led me to try this. My family liked the taste so much that, from then on, I made my cabbage rolls with dill.
—Florence Krantz, Bismarck, North Dakota

    1 medium head cabbage (3 pounds)
    1 can (15 ounces) tomato sauce, *divided*
    1 small onion, chopped
1/2 cup uncooked long grain rice
    1 tablespoon dried parsley flakes
1/2 teaspoon salt
1/2 teaspoon dill weed
1/8 teaspoon cayenne pepper
1/2 pound ground beef
1/2 pound ground pork
    1 can (16 ounces) diced tomatoes, undrained
1/2 teaspoon sugar

Remove core from cabbage. In a large kettle or Dutch oven, cook cabbage in boiling salted water for 2-3 minutes. Remove outer leaves when softened; return to boiling water as necessary to obtain 12 leaves. Drain; remove thick center vein from leaves.

    In a bowl, combine 1/2 cup tomato sauce, onion, rice, parsley, salt, dill and cayenne pepper. Crumble beef and pork over mixture and mix well. Place about 1/4 cup meat mixture on each cabbage leaf. Fold in sides; starting at unfolded edge, roll up to completely enclose filling.

    Slice the remaining cabbage; place in a large kettle or Dutch oven. Arrange the cabbage rolls, seam side down, over cabbage. Combine tomatoes, sugar and remaining tomato sauce; pour over the rolls. Cover and bake at 350° for 1-1/2 hours. **Yield:** 6-8 servings.

Barbecued Short Ribs

The meat on these ribs is fork-tender, and the sauce is wonderfully tangy. We raised beef for many years, and we still put this recipe to good use.
—Margery Bryan, Royal City, Washington

3-1/2 to 4 pounds beef short ribs
1-1/2 cups water
   1 medium onion, sliced
   1 tablespoon white vinegar
SAUCE:
 1/2 cup ketchup
 1/4 cup chopped onion
   2 tablespoons lemon juice
   2 garlic cloves, minced
   1 teaspoon sugar
 1/2 teaspoon salt
 1/8 teaspoon pepper

In a Dutch oven, combine ribs, water, onion and vinegar; bring to a boil. Reduce heat; cover and simmer for 1 hour, turning ribs occasionally.

Drain. Place ribs in a single layer in an ungreased 13-in. x 9-in. x 2-in. baking dish.

   Combine sauce ingredients; spoon over ribs. Cover and bake at 325° for 1-1/4 hours or until the meat is tender. **Yield:** 4-6 servings.

Recipe for: Swedish Meatballs

The allspice and nutmeg—plus a hint of dill—are what give these tender meatballs their special old-world flavor.
—Kathy Ringel, Saline, Michigan

   2 eggs, beaten
1/2 cup milk

   1 cup dry bread crumbs
   2 teaspoons salt

1/2 teaspoon pepper
1-1/2 teaspoons dill weed

1/4 teaspoon ground allspice
1/4 teaspoon ground nutmeg

   1 cup chopped onion
   2 tablespoons butter

   2 pounds ground beef
1/2 pound ground pork
SAUCE:
  1/4 cup butter

  1/2 cup all-purpose flour
   2 cans (14-1/2 ounces *each*) beef broth

   1 pint heavy whipping cream
  1/2 teaspoon dill weed
  1/2 teaspoon salt

1/4 teaspoon pepper
Fresh dill sprigs, optional

In a large mixing bowl, combine eggs, milk, bread crumbs and seasonings; set aside. In a skillet, saute onion in butter until soft; add to egg mixture. Crumble beef and ground pork over mixture; mix well. Cover; refrigerate for 1 hour.

   Shape meat mixture into 1-1/4- to 1-1/2-in. balls. Place on a jelly roll pan. Bake, uncovered, at 350° for 20-25 minutes. Remove from oven and place in a 3-qt. casserole.

   For sauce, melt butter in a saucepan; stir in flour to form a smooth paste. Gradually stir in broth; bring to a boil, stirring constantly. Reduce heat; stir in cream, dill, salt and pepper. If a thicker sauce is desired, continue cooking 10-15 minutes longer, stirring occasionally. Pour sauce over meatballs.

   Bake, uncovered, at 350° for 40-45 minutes or until heated through and bubbly. Garnish with fresh dill if desired. **Yield:** 10-12 servings.

Baked Spaghetti

Every time that I make this cheesy dish, I get requests for the recipe. It puts a different spin on spaghetti and is great for any meal. The leftovers, if there are any, also freeze well for a quick meal later on in the week.
—Ruth Koberna, Brecksville, Ohio

1 cup chopped onion
1 cup chopped green pepper

1 tablespoon butter
1 can (28 ounces) diced tomatoes, undrained
1 can (4 ounces) mushroom stems and pieces, drained
1 can (2-1/4 ounces) sliced ripe olives, drained
2 teaspoons dried oregano
1 pound cooked ground beef
12 ounces spaghetti, cooked and drained
2 cups (8 ounces) shredded cheddar cheese
1 can (10-3/4 ounces) condensed cream of mushroom soup, undiluted
1/4 cup water
1/4 cup grated Parmesan cheese

In a large skillet, saute onion and green pepper in butter until tender. Add tomatoes, mushrooms, olives and oregano. Add ground beef. Simmer, uncovered, for 10 minutes. Place half of the spaghetti in a greased 13-in. x 9-in. x 2-in. baking dish. Top with half of the vegetable mixture. Sprinkle with 1 cup of cheddar cheese. Repeat layers.

Mix the soup and water until smooth; pour over casserole. Sprinkle with Parmesan cheese. Bake, uncovered, at 350° for 30-35 minutes or until heated through. **Yield:** 12 servings.

When I was in grade school, I often went to see my granny and granddad at lunchtime. Granny, who thought a cold sandwich wasn't "fitting for a growing child," always served me a hot meal with a glass of cold buttermilk from the old wooden icebox.
—Dale Smith, West Worthington, Ohio

All-American Barbecue Sandwiches

I came up with this delicious recipe on my own. It's my husband's favorite and is a big hit with family and friends who enjoy it at our Fourth of July picnic.
—Sue Gronholz, Columbus, Wisconsin

4-1/2 pounds ground beef
1-1/2 cups chopped onion
2-1/4 cups ketchup
3 tablespoons prepared mustard
3 tablespoons Worcestershire sauce
2 tablespoons cider vinegar

2 tablespoons sugar
1 tablespoon salt
1 tablespoon pepper
18 hamburger buns, split

In a Dutch oven, cook beef and onion until meat is no longer pink and onion is tender; drain. Combine ketchup, mustard, Worcestershire, vinegar, sugar, salt and pepper; stir into beef mixture. Heat through. Serve on buns. **Yield:** 18 servings.

Grandma's Favorites

Recipe for: *Cornish Pasties*

Years ago, when bakeries in my Midwestern hometown made pasties, people scrambled to get there before they were all gone. Now I make my own…filled with meat, potatoes and vegetables. These meat pies make a complete meal and are great for picnics or potlucks. —Gayle Lewis, Yucaipa, California

FILLING:
- 1 pound boneless top round steak, cut into 1/2-inch pieces
- 2 to 3 medium potatoes, peeled and cut into 1/2-inch cubes
- 1 cup chopped carrots
- 1/2 cup finely chopped onion
- 2 tablespoons chopped fresh parsley
- 1 teaspoon salt
- 1/2 teaspoon pepper
- 1/4 cup butter, melted

PASTRY:
- 3 cups all-purpose flour
- 1 teaspoon salt
- 1 cup shortening
- 8 to 9 tablespoons ice water
- 1 egg, beaten, optional

In a bowl, combine round steak, potatoes, carrots, onion, parsley, salt and pepper; mix well. Add butter and toss to coat; set aside.

For pastry, combine flour and salt in a mixing bowl. Cut in shortening until crumbly. Sprinkle with water, 1 tablespoon at a time. Toss lightly with a fork until dough forms a ball. Do not overmix.

Divide dough into fourths. Roll out one portion into a 9-in. circle; transfer to a greased baking sheet. Mound about 1-1/4 cups of meat filling on half of circle. Moisten edges with water; fold dough over mixture and press edges with fork to seal. Repeat with remaining pastry and filling.

Cut slits in the top of each pasty. Brush with beaten egg if desired. Bake at 375° for 50-60 minutes or until golden brown. **Yield:** 4 servings.

Corned Beef and Mixed Vegetables

For St. Patrick's Day, prepare a traditional corned beef dinner and add a special twist—a colorful medley of cooked fresh vegetables. It's a festive combination to serve family or guests. —Gloria Warczak, Cedarburg, Wisconsin

- 1 corned beef brisket (3 to 4 pounds), trimmed
- 6 to 8 small red potatoes
- 3 medium carrots, cut into 2-inch pieces
- 3 celery ribs, cut into 2-inch pieces
- 2 tablespoons chopped celery leaves
- 2 turnips, peeled and cut into wedges
- 1 medium head cabbage, cut into 6 to 8 wedges
- 1/2 pound fresh green beans
- 3 to 4 ears fresh corn, halved

Place corned beef and enclosed seasoning packet in an 8-qt. Dutch oven. Cover with water and bring to a boil. Reduce heat; cover and simmer for 2 hours or until meat is tender.

Add potatoes, carrots, celery, celery leaves and turnips; return to a boil. Reduce heat; cover and simmer for 20 minutes. Add cabbage, beans and corn; return to a boil. Reduce heat; cover and simmer 15-20 minutes or until vegetables are tender. **Yield:** 6-8 servings.

Vegetable Beef Chili

This chili is big on fresh tomato taste and works well in a slow cooker. —Marlene Muckenhirn
Delano, Minnesota

1 pound ground beef
6 medium tomatoes, cubed
2 medium green peppers, chopped
2 medium onions, chopped
3 garlic cloves, minced
1 can (15-1/2 ounces) kidney beans,
  rinsed and drained
1 can (15-1/2 ounces) chili beans,
  undrained
3 tablespoons chili powder
1-1/2 teaspoons salt
1/2 teaspoon ground turmeric
1/2 teaspoon Italian seasoning
1/2 teaspoon ground cumin

In a 5-qt. Dutch oven or saucepan, cook beef until no longer pink; drain. Add tomatoes, green peppers, onions and garlic. Cook over medium-low heat, stirring occasionally, for 20-30 minutes or until vegetables are tender.

Add beans and seasonings; mix well. Simmer, uncovered, for 45-50 minutes or until thickened, stirring occasionally. **Yield:** 8-10 servings.

Perfect Pot Roast

Cooking meats, I have to confess, isn't my specialty. But everyone who tastes this main-course dish wants more! I'm a mostly at-home mom. I like to sew and read. I also enjoy gardening—we grow a good-sized patch, and it's so nice to have fresh-picked vegetables to go along with the meat.
—Melody Sroufe, Wichita, Kansas

1 teaspoon seasoned salt
1/2 teaspoon onion powder
1/4 teaspoon pepper
1/8 teaspoon garlic powder
1 beef chuck pot roast (3 to 4 pounds)
1 tablespoon olive oil
3/4 cup water
1 large onion, chopped
1/4 cup chopped green pepper
2 garlic cloves, minced
2 bay leaves
2 teaspoons dried parsley flakes
1/4 teaspoon dried thyme
All-purpose flour

Combine first four ingredients; rub onto roast. In a skillet, brown roast in oil. Place in a roasting pan. Add water, onion, green pepper and seasonings. Cover and bake at 325° for 2-1/2 to 3 hours or until roast is tender. Remove and keep warm.

Discard bay leaf. Skim fat from pan juices. Measure juices and return juices to pan. For each cup of juices, combine 1 tablespoon flour with 2 tablespoons water; mix well. Stir flour mixture into pan; cook over medium heat, stirring constantly, until thickened and bubbly. Serve gravy with roast. **Yield:** 8-10 servings.

Stuffed Zucchini

An abundance of squash from my garden inspired me to make up this recipe, which is now a favorite.
—Marjorie Roberts, West Chazy, New York

1 large onion, chopped
1 large green pepper, chopped
1 jalapeno pepper, minced
1-1/4 cups soft bread crumbs
1 egg, beaten
1 tablespoon dried parsley flakes
1 teaspoon dried basil
1 teaspoon Italian seasoning
1 teaspoon salt
1/8 teaspoon pepper
1-1/2 pounds lean ground beef
2 cans (8 ounces *each*) tomato sauce, *divided*
2 medium tomatoes, coarsely chopped
4 to 5 medium zucchini
2 cups (8 ounces) shredded mozzarella
    cheese

In a large bowl, combine the first 10 ingredients. Crumble beef over mixture; mix well. Add one can of tomato sauce; mix well. Stir in tomatoes.

Halve zucchini lengthwise; scoop out seeds. Fill with meat mixture; place in two 13-in. x 9-in. x 2-in. baking dishes. Spoon remaining tomato sauce over each. Bake, uncovered, at 375° for 45 minutes or until the zucchini is tender. Sprinkle with cheese during the last few minutes of baking. **Yield:** 8-10 servings.

Editor's Note: When cutting or seeding hot peppers, use rubber or plastic gloves to protect your hands. Avoid touching your face.

Recipe for: **Herbed Beef Stew**

(Pictured on cover)

This stew looks as terrific as it tastes! Flavored with a variety of herbs and chock-full of vegetables, this recipe lists salt as an option, making it ideal for family members and friends who must restrict sodium.
—Marlene Severson, Everson, Washington

2 pounds beef stew meat, cut
    into 1-inch cubes
2 tablespoons vegetable oil
3 cups water
1 large onion, chopped
2 teaspoons pepper
1 to 2 teaspoons salt, optional
1-1/2 teaspoons garlic powder
1 teaspoon dried rosemary, crushed
1 teaspoon dried oregano
1 teaspoon dried basil
1 teaspoon ground marjoram
2 bay leaves
1 can (6 ounces) tomato paste
2 cups cubed peeled potatoes
2 cups sliced carrots
1 large green pepper, chopped
1 package (10 ounces) frozen green
    beans
1 package (10 ounces) frozen peas
1 package (10 ounces) frozen kernel
    corn
1/4 pound mushrooms, sliced
3 medium tomatoes, chopped

In a Dutch oven, brown meat in oil. Add water, onion, seasonings and tomato paste. Cover and simmer for 1-1/2 hours or until meat is tender. Stir in potatoes, carrots and green pepper; simmer 30 minutes. Add additional water if necessary. Stir in remaining ingredients; cover and simmer 20 minutes. **Yield:** 10-12 servings.

Spicy Tomato Steak

My family loves this spicy tomato dish. I came up with the recipe more than 25 years ago, after eating a similar dish on vacation in New Mexico. I came home and tried to duplicate it from memory, with delicious results! —Anne Landers, Louisville, Kentucky

2 tablespoons white vinegar
1 teaspoon salt
1 teaspoon pepper
1 pound round steak, trimmed and cut into 1/4-inch strips
1/4 cup all-purpose flour
2 tablespoons olive oil
3 medium tomatoes, peeled, seeded and cut into wedges
2 medium potatoes, peeled and thinly sliced
2 cans (4 ounces *each*) chopped green chilies
1 garlic clove, minced
1 teaspoon dried basil

In a mixing bowl, combine vinegar, salt and pepper; toss with beef. Cover and marinate for 30 minutes; drain. Place flour in a bowl; add beef and toss to coat.

In a skillet, cook beef in oil over medium heat for 15-20 minutes or until tender. Add remaining ingredients. Cover and simmer for 20-30 minutes or until the potatoes are tender, stirring occasionally. **Yield:** 6 servings.

Recipe for: Barbecued Brisket

For a mouth-watering main dish to star in a summer meal, this brisket can't be beat. Baked slowly, the meat gets tender and picks up the sweet and tangy flavor of the barbecue sauce.
—Page Alexander, Baldwin City, Kansas

1 beef brisket (3 to 4 pounds)
1-1/4 cups water, *divided*
1/2 cup chopped onion
3 garlic cloves, minced
1 tablespoon vegetable oil
1 cup ketchup
3 tablespoons red wine vinegar
2 tablespoons lemon juice
2 tablespoons brown sugar
1 tablespoon Worcestershire sauce
2 teaspoons cornstarch
1 teaspoon paprika
1 teaspoon chili powder
1/4 teaspoon salt
1/4 teaspoon pepper
1/4 teaspoon Liquid Smoke, optional

Place brisket in a large Dutch oven. Add 1/2 cup water. Cover and bake at 325° for 2 hours.

Meanwhile, in a medium saucepan, saute onion and garlic in oil until tender. Add ketchup, vinegar, lemon juice, brown sugar, Worcestershire sauce, cornstarch, paprika, chili powder, salt, pepper and remaining water. Simmer, uncovered, for 1 hour, stirring occasionally.

Add Liquid Smoke if desired; mix well. Drain drippings from Dutch oven. Pour sauce over meat. Cover and bake 1-2 hours longer or until meat is tender. **Yield:** 6-8 servings.

Editor's Note: This is a fresh beef brisket, not corned beef.

Savory Spaghetti Sauce

This fresh-tasting spaghetti sauce is a real crowd-pleaser. With a husband and 12 kids to feed every day, I rely on this flavorful recipe often. It tastes especially good in the summer made with fresh garden herbs. —Anne Heinonen, Howell, Michigan

1 pound ground beef
1 large onion, chopped
2 cans (15 ounces *each*) tomato sauce
1 garlic clove, minced
1 bay leaf
1 tablespoon minced fresh basil *or* 1 teaspoon dried basil
2 teaspoons minced fresh oregano *or* 3/4 teaspoon dried oregano
2 teaspoons sugar
1/2 to 1 teaspoon salt
1/2 teaspoon pepper
Hot cooked spaghetti

In a Dutch oven, cook ground beef and onion until meat is no longer pink and onion is tender; drain. Add the next eight ingredients; bring to a boil.

Reduce heat; cover and simmer for 1 hour, stirring occasionally. Remove the bay leaf. Serve over spaghetti. **Yield:** 4-6 servings (about 1 quart).

Standing Rib Roast

Treat your family to tender slices of standing rib roast or use the seasoning blend on a different beef roast for a hearty, delicious main dish. I love to prepare this recipe for special occasions. —Lucy Meyring Walden, Colorado

1 tablespoon lemon-pepper seasoning
1 tablespoon paprika
1-1/2 teaspoons garlic salt
1 teaspoon dried rosemary, crushed
1/2 teaspoon cayenne pepper
1 standing beef rib roast (6 to 7 pounds)
2 cups boiling water
1 teaspoon instant beef bouillon granules

Combine lemon-pepper, paprika, garlic salt, rosemary and cayenne pepper; rub over roast. Place roast with fat side up in a large roasting pan. Bake, uncovered, at 325° until roast reaches desired doneness. Allow 23-25 minutes per pound for rare (140° on thermometer), 27-30 minutes for medium (160°) and 32-35 minutes for well-done (170°).

Remove to serving platter and keep warm. Let stand 15 minutes before carving. Pour meat juices from roasting pan into a glass measuring cup; skim off fat. Add boiling water and bouillon to roasting pan and stir to remove drippings. Add meat juices; stir. Serve with the roast. **Yield:** 10-12 servings.

Poultry

At left: Nutty Oven-Fried Chicken (p. 114) and Artichoke Chicken (p. 116).

At right: Roasted Duck with Apple-Raisin Dressing (p. 119).

Turkey with Country Ham Stuffing

As delicious as this is right out of the oven, the bird and stuffing both taste great as leftovers, too. I am careful, though, not to overcook the turkey.
—Bobbie Love, Kapaa, Hawaii

3 cups cubed crustless day-old white
   bread
3 cups cubed crustless day-old whole
   wheat bread

1-1/2 cups cubed fully cooked ham
1/2 cup butter
   3 cups chopped onion
   2 cups chopped celery
1-1/2 teaspoons rubbed sage
1-1/2 teaspoons dried thyme
1/2 teaspoon pepper
   1 to 1-1/2 cups chicken broth
   1 turkey (12 to 14 pounds)

Place bread cubes in a single layer in a 13-in. x 9-in. x 2-in. baking pan. Bake at 325° for 20-25 minutes or until golden, stirring occasionally. Place in a large bowl; set aside.

In a large skillet, cook ham in butter for 5-10 minutes or until edges are crisp. Remove with a slotted spoon and place over bread cubes. In the same skillet, saute the onion, celery, sage, thyme and pepper until vegetables are tender; toss with bread and ham. Stir in enough broth to moisten.

Just before baking, stuff the turkey. Skewer openings; tie drumsticks together. Place on a rack in a roasting pan. Bake at 325° for 4-1/2 to 5 hours or until a meat thermometer reads 180° for the turkey and 165° for the stuffing. When the turkey begins to brown, cover lightly with a tent of aluminum foil and baste if needed. Remove all stuffing. **Yield:** 10-12 servings.

Editor's Note: Stuffing may be baked in a greased 3-qt. covered baking dish at 325° for 70 minutes (uncover for the last 10 minutes). Stuffing yields about 10 cups.

Nutty Oven-Fried Chicken

(Pictured on page 112)

The pecans that give this dish its unique nutty flavor are plentiful in the South, and so is chicken. I love to make and serve this easy dish because the chicken comes out moist, tasty and crispy.
—Diane Hixon, Niceville, Florida

1 cup biscuit/baking mix
1/3 cup finely chopped pecans
2 teaspoons paprika
1/2 teaspoon salt
1/2 teaspoon poultry seasoning

1/2 teaspoon rubbed sage
   1 broiler-fryer chicken (2 to 3 pounds),
   cut up
1/2 cup evaporated milk
1/3 cup butter, melted

In a shallow dish, combine biscuit mix, pecans and seasonings; mix well. Dip chicken pieces in milk; coat generously with pecan mixture. Place in a lightly greased 13-in. x 9-in. x 2-in. baking dish. Drizzle butter over chicken.

Bake, uncovered, at 350° for 1 hour or until juices run clear. **Yield:** 6-8 servings.

Recipe for: Barbecued Picnic Chicken

When we entertain friends for a picnic at our cabin, I like to serve this savory chicken. Cooked on a covered grill, the poultry stays so tender and juicy. Everyone loves the zesty, slightly sweet homemade barbecue sauce—and it's so easy to make.
—Priscilla Weaver, Hagerstown, Maryland

2 garlic cloves, minced
2 teaspoons butter
1 cup ketchup
1/4 cup packed brown sugar
1/4 cup chili sauce
2 tablespoons Worcestershire sauce
1 tablespoon celery seed
1 tablespoon prepared mustard
1/2 teaspoon salt
2 dashes hot pepper sauce
2 broiler-fryer chickens (3-1/2 to 4 pounds *each*), quartered

In a saucepan, saute the garlic in butter until tender. Add the next eight ingredients. Bring to a boil, stirring constantly. Remove from the heat and set aside.

Grill the chicken, covered, over medium heat for 30 minutes, turning occasionally. Baste with sauce. Grill 15 minutes longer or until juices run clear, basting and turning several times. **Yield:** 8 servings.

Cranberry Chicken

My husband loves chicken when it's nice and moist, like it is in this delicious recipe. I serve it over hot fluffy rice with a salad and warm rolls on the side. The ruby-red sauce has a tart cinnamony flavor.
—Dorothy Bateman, Carver, Massachusetts

1/2 cup all-purpose flour
1/2 teaspoon salt
1/4 teaspoon pepper
6 boneless skinless chicken breast halves
1/4 cup butter
1 cup fresh *or* frozen cranberries
1 cup water
1/2 cup packed brown sugar
Dash ground nutmeg
1 tablespoon red wine vinegar, optional
Hot cooked rice

In a large resealable plastic bag, combine flour, salt and pepper. Add chicken a few pieces at a time and shake to coat.

In a skillet, melt butter over medium heat. Brown the chicken on both sides. Remove and keep warm. In the same skillet, add cranberries, water, brown sugar, nutmeg and vinegar if desired. Cook and stir until the cranberries burst, about 5 minutes. Return chicken to skillet. Cover and simmer for 20-30 minutes or until chicken is tender, basting occasionally with the sauce. Serve over rice. **Yield:** 4-6 servings.

Artichoke Chicken

(Pictured on page 112)

Rosemary, mushrooms and artichokes combine to give chicken a wonderful, savory flavor in this dish. I've served it for a large group by doubling the recipe. It's always a big hit with everyone—especially my family! —Ruth Stenson, Santa Ana, California

8 boneless skinless chicken breast halves
2 tablespoons butter
2 jars (6 ounces *each*) marinated
    artichoke hearts, drained
1 jar (4-1/2 ounces) whole mushrooms,
    drained
1/2 cup chopped onion
1/3 cup all-purpose flour
1-1/2 teaspoons dried rosemary
1 teaspoon salt
1/4 teaspoon pepper
2 cups chicken broth *or* 1 cup broth
    and 1 cup dry white wine
Hot cooked noodles
Chopped fresh parsley

In a skillet, brown chicken in butter. Remove chicken to an ungreased 13-in. x 9-in. x 2-in. baking dish; do not drain pan juices. Cut the artichokes into quarters. Arrange artichokes and mushrooms on top of chicken; set aside.

Saute onion in pan juices; blend in flour, rosemary, salt and pepper. Add chicken broth; cook until thickened and bubbly. Remove from the heat and spoon over chicken.

Cover and bake at 350° for 50-60 minutes or until chicken is tender. Place noodles on serving platter; top with chicken and sauce. Sprinkle with parsley. **Yield:** 8 servings.

Turkey Stir-Fry

Here's a tasty way to prepare turkey any time of year. My family loves the tender turkey strips, colorful vegetables and crunchy cashews. You don't always have to fix the whole bird to enjoy the wonderful taste of turkey. —Julianne Johnson, Grove City, Minnesota

1-1/2 pounds uncooked boneless turkey, cut
    into strips
1 tablespoon vegetable oil
1 small onion, chopped
1 carrot, julienned
1/2 medium green pepper, sliced
2 cups fresh mushrooms, sliced
1 cup chicken broth
3 tablespoons cornstarch
3 tablespoons soy sauce
1/2 teaspoon ground ginger
2 cups pea pods, trimmed
Hot cooked rice, optional
1/3 cup cashews, optional

In a large skillet or wok, stir-fry turkey in oil over medium-high heat until no longer pink, about 5-6 minutes. Remove turkey and keep warm. Stir-fry onion, carrot, green pepper and mushrooms until crisp-tender, about 5 minutes.

In a small bowl, combine chicken broth, cornstarch, soy sauce and ginger. Add to the skillet; cook and stir until thickened and bubbly. Return turkey to skillet with pea pods; cook and stir until heated through. If desired, serve over rice and top with cashews. **Yield:** 6 servings.

Tropical Chicken Salad

Over the years my husband and I have moved to different areas, and I've collected recipes from all over the United States. This flavorful salad recipe comes from New York. I've served it for luncheons for many years, and it's one of my husband's very favorites.
—Linda Wheatley, Garland, Texas

    2 cups cubed cooked chicken
    1 cup chopped celery
    1 cup mayonnaise
    1/2 to 1 teaspoon curry powder
    1 can (20 ounces) chunk pineapple,
        drained
    2 large firm bananas, sliced
    1 can (11 ounces) mandarin oranges,
        drained
    1/2 cup flaked coconut
Salad greens, optional
    3/4 cup salted peanuts *or* cashew halves

In a large bowl, place chicken and celery. Combine mayonnaise and curry powder; add to chicken mixture and mix well. Cover and chill for at least 30 minutes.

Before serving, add the pineapple, bananas, oranges and coconut; toss gently. Serve on salad greens if desired. Sprinkle with nuts. **Yield:** 4-6 servings.

Recipe for: Turkey with Corn Bread Dressing

Nothing gets family hanging around the kitchen like the aroma of a turkey stuffed with savory dressing roasting in the oven. Drizzled with hot gravy, it tastes even better than it smells!
—Norma Poole
Auburndale, Florida

    2 cups chopped celery
    1 cup chopped onion
    1/2 cup butter
    6 cups cubed day-old corn bread
    2 cups soft bread crumbs
    1 tablespoon rubbed sage
    1 tablespoon poultry seasoning
    1/2 cup egg substitute
    1 cup chicken broth
    1 turkey (10 to 12 pounds)
Melted butter

In a skillet, saute celery and onion in butter until tender. Place in a large bowl with corn bread, crumbs, sage and poultry seasoning. Combine egg substitute and chicken broth; add to corn bread mixture, stirring gently to mix.

Just before baking, stuff the turkey body cavity and inside of the neck with dressing. Skewer or fasten openings. Tie the drumsticks together. Place on a rack in a roasting pan. Brush with melted butter.

Bake at 325° for 3-1/2 to 4 hours or until a meat thermometer reads 180° for the turkey and 165° for the dressing. When turkey begins to brown, cover lightly with a tent of aluminum foil. When turkey is done, allow to stand for 20 minutes. Remove all dressing to a serving bowl. **Yield:** 8-10 servings.

Editor's Note: Dressing may be prepared as above and baked in a greased 2-qt. casserole dish. Cover and bake at 400° for 20 minutes. Uncover and bake 10 minutes longer or until lightly browned. Dressing yields 8 cups.

Chicken Rice Dinner

With chicken and rice, this casserole is comforting and delicious. It's an appealing and economical dish to serve company.
—Judith Anglen
Riverton, Wyoming

1/2 cup all-purpose flour
1 teaspoon salt
1/2 teaspoon pepper
10 chicken thighs (about 3 pounds)
3 tablespoons vegetable oil
1 cup uncooked long grain rice
1/4 cup chopped onion
2 garlic cloves, minced
1 can (4 ounces) mushroom stems and pieces, undrained
2 chicken bouillon cubes
2 cups boiling water
Minced fresh parsley, optional

In a large resealable plastic bag, combine flour, salt and pepper. Add chicken a few pieces at a time and shake to coat. In a large skillet over medium heat, brown the chicken in oil. Place rice in an ungreased 13-in. x 9-in. x 2-in. baking dish. Sprinkle with onion and garlic; top with mushrooms.

Dissolve bouillon in boiling water; pour over all. Place chicken pieces on top. Cover and bake at 350° for 1 hour or until chicken juices run clear and rice is tender. Sprinkle with parsley if desired. **Yield:** 5 servings.

Recipe for: Chicken Cheese Lasagna

This creamy pasta dish gives an old favorite a new twist! Three cheeses and chicken blended with the fresh taste of spinach make it a real crowd-pleaser.
—Mary Ann Kosmas, Minneapolis, Minnesota

1 medium onion, chopped
1 garlic clove, minced
1/2 cup butter
1/2 cup all-purpose flour
1 teaspoon salt
2 cups chicken broth
1-1/2 cups milk
4 cups (16 ounces) shredded mozzarella cheese, *divided*
1 cup grated Parmesan cheese, *divided*
1 teaspoon dried basil
1 teaspoon dried oregano
1/2 teaspoon white pepper
2 cups (15 to 16 ounces) ricotta cheese
1 tablespoon minced fresh parsley
9 lasagna noodles (8 ounces), cooked and drained
2 packages (10 ounces *each*) frozen spinach, thawed and well drained
2 cups cubed cooked chicken

In a saucepan, saute onion and garlic in butter until tender. Stir in flour and salt; cook until bubbly. Gradually stir in broth and milk. Bring to a boil, stirring constantly. Boil 1 minute. Stir in 2 cups mozzarella, 1/2 cup Parmesan cheese, basil, oregano and pepper; set aside.

In a bowl, combine ricotta cheese, parsley and remaining mozzarella; set aside. Spread one-quarter of the cheese sauce into a greased 13-in. x 9-in. x 2-in. baking dish; cover with one-third of the noodles. Top with half of ricotta mixture, half of spinach and half of chicken. Cover with one-quarter of cheese sauce and one-third of noodles.

Repeat layers of ricotta mixture, spinach, chicken and one-quarter cheese sauce. Cover with remaining noodles and cheese sauce. Sprinkle remaining Parmesan cheese over all. Bake at 350°, uncovered, for 35-40 minutes. Let stand 15 minutes. **Yield:** 12 servings.

Roasted Duck with Apple-Raisin Dressing

(Pictured on page 113)

As a boy growing up on the farm, my husband had "duck every Sunday." I tried to maintain that tradition after we married—more than 50 years ago now!   —Fran Kirchhoff, Harvard, Illinois

  2 domestic ducklings (4 to 5 pounds *each*)
Salt
DRESSING:
  3/4 pound bulk pork sausage
  1/2 cup chopped onion
  1/2 cup chopped celery
    1 cup chopped peeled apple
    1 cup golden raisins
  1/2 cup water
1-1/2 teaspoons salt
    1 teaspoon rubbed sage
  1/4 teaspoon pepper
    2 tablespoons chopped fresh parsley

  8 cups cubed crustless day-old white bread
  3/4 cup egg substitute
  1/2 cup chicken broth

Sprinkle the inside of ducklings with salt; prick skin well all over and set aside. In a large skillet, cook sausage with onion and celery until sausage is no longer pink and vegetables are tender. Add apple and simmer for 3 minutes, stirring occasionally; drain.

Meanwhile, simmer raisins in water for 8 minutes; do not drain. In a large bowl, combine sausage mixture, raisins, salt, sage, pepper and parsley; mix well. Add the bread cubes, egg substitute and broth; mix lightly. Divide and spoon into ducklings. Place with breast side up on a rack in a large shallow roasting pan.

Bake, uncovered, at 375° for 1-3/4 to 2-1/4 hours or until a meat thermometer reads 180° for the duck and 165° for the dressing. Drain fat from pan as it accumulates. Remove all dressing. **Yield:** 4 servings.

Honey-Glazed Chicken

My family raves over this nicely browned chicken. The rich honey glaze gives each luscious piece a spicy tang. This dish is simple enough to prepare for a family dinner and delightful enough to serve to guests.
    —Ruth Andrewson, Leavenworth, Washington

  1/2 cup all-purpose flour
    1 teaspoon salt
  1/2 teaspoon cayenne pepper
    1 broiler/fryer chicken (about 3 pounds),
      cut up
  1/2 cup butter, melted, *divided*
  1/4 cup packed brown sugar
  1/4 cup honey
  1/4 cup lemon juice
    1 tablespoon soy sauce
1-1/2 teaspoons curry powder

In a bowl or resealable plastic bag, combine flour, salt and cayenne pepper; add chicken pieces and dredge or shake to coat. Pour 4 tablespoons butter into a 13-in. x 9-in. x 2-in. baking pan; place chicken in pan, turning pieces once to coat. Bake, uncovered, at 350° for 30 minutes.

Combine brown sugar, honey, lemon juice, soy sauce, curry powder and remaining butter; pour over chicken. Bake 45 minutes more or until chicken is tender, basting several times with pan drippings. **Yield:** 4-6 servings.

Mom's Chicken 'n' Buttermilk Dumplings

I serve this—with a tossed or cucumber salad—to friends dining with us or on visits by our two sons and their families. —Ellen Proefrock, Brodhead, Wisconsin

  1 stewing chicken (about 5 pounds), cut up
10 cups water
  1 large onion, chopped
  2 medium carrots, sliced
  3 celery ribs, chopped
  4 garlic cloves, minced
  1 teaspoon salt

1/4 cup butter
  6 tablespoons all-purpose flour
1/8 teaspoon paprika
1/8 teaspoon pepper
1/2 cup half-and-half cream
DUMPLINGS:
  2 cups all-purpose flour
  4 teaspoons baking powder
  4 teaspoons sugar
  1 teaspoon salt
  2 eggs
1/2 cup buttermilk
1/4 cup butter, melted

In a soup kettle or Dutch oven, combine the first seven ingredients. Bring to a boil; skim foam from broth. Reduce heat; cover and simmer for 1-1/2 hours or until chicken is tender. Remove chicken; when cool enough to handle, debone and dice. Strain broth, reserving the broth and vegetables.

In the same kettle, melt butter. Stir in flour, paprika and pepper until smooth. Gradually stir in 6 cups reserved broth (save remaining broth for another use). Bring to a boil; boil and stir for 2 minutes. Reduce heat; stir in the cream, reserved vegetables and chicken. Cover and bring to a boil; reduce the heat to simmer.

For dumplings, combine flour, baking powder, sugar and salt in a bowl. Combine eggs, buttermilk and butter; stir into dry ingredients to form a stiff batter. Drop by tablespoonfuls onto simmering mixture. Cover and simmer for 20 minutes or until a toothpick inserted in a dumpling comes out clean (do not lift cover while simmering). Serve immediately. **Yield:** 6-8 servings.

Teriyaki Chicken

This moist, tasty chicken is an economical yet satisfying supper. —Jean Clark, Albion, Maine

3/4 cup soy sauce
1/4 cup vegetable oil
  3 tablespoons brown sugar
  2 tablespoons cooking sherry, optional
1/2 teaspoon ground ginger
1/2 teaspoon garlic powder
 12 chicken drumsticks (about 2-1/2
    pounds)

In a large glass dish, combine the soy sauce, oil, brown sugar, cooking sherry if desired, ginger and garlic powder; mix well. Add drumsticks; turn to coat. Cover and refrigerate for 1 hour or overnight, turning occasionally.

Drain and discard marinade. Place chicken in a single layer on a foil-lined baking sheet. Bake at 375° for 35-45 minutes or until chicken is no longer pink. **Yield:** 6 servings.

Recipe for: Turkey with Herbed Rice Dressing

Our children and grandchildren enjoy this special turkey for Sunday dinner or for the holidays.
—Melanie Habener, Lompoc, California

1/2 pound bulk pork sausage
1/2 pound ground beef
1/2 cup chopped onion
1/2 cup egg substitute
  1 tablespoon poultry seasoning
  2 tablespoons chopped fresh parsley
  2 tablespoons chopped celery leaves
  2 teaspoons salt, *divided*
  2 teaspoons pepper, *divided*
3/4 teaspoon garlic powder, *divided*
  4 cups cooked white rice, cooled
  3 garlic cloves, minced
  1 teaspoon *each* dried thyme, tarragon
    and marjoram
  1 turkey (10 to 12 pounds)
  2 cans (14-1/2 ounces *each*) chicken broth
  3 tablespoons butter

In a large skillet, cook pork, beef and onion until the meat is no longer pink; drain. In a large bowl, combine egg substitute, poultry seasoning, parsley, celery leaves, 1 teaspoon salt, 1 teaspoon pepper and 1/2 teaspoon garlic powder; mix well. Add meat mixture and rice. Just before baking, stuff turkey. Skewer openings; tie drumsticks together. Place on a rack in a roasting pan.

Combine garlic, thyme, tarragon, marjoram and remaining salt, pepper and garlic powder; rub over turkey. Add broth and butter to pan. Bake at 325° for 4 to 4-1/2 hours or until a meat thermometer reads 180° for the turkey and 165° for the dressing, basting frequently. When turkey begins to brown, cover lightly with a tent of aluminum foil. Remove all dressing. **Yield:** 8-10 servings.

Editor's Note: Dressing may be baked in a greased 2-1/2-qt. covered baking dish at 325° for 70 minutes (uncover during the last 10 minutes). Dressing yields about 8 cups.

Wild Goose with Giblet Stuffing

This recipe is one of our favorite ways to prepare goose and it's especially nice for the holidays. My husband does a lot of hunting, so I'm always looking for new ways to fix game. —Louise Laginess
East Jordan, Michigan

1 wild goose (6 to 8 pounds dressed)
Lemon wedges
Salt
STUFFING:
Goose giblets
   2 cups water
  10 cups crumbled corn bread
   2 large tart apples, chopped
   1 large onion, chopped
 1/3 cup minced fresh parsley
   1 to 2 tablespoons rubbed sage
   1 teaspoon salt
 1/4 teaspoon pepper
 1/4 teaspoon garlic powder
Butter, softened

Rub inside goose cavity with lemon and salt; set aside. In a saucepan, cook giblets in water until tender, about 20-30 minutes. Remove giblets with a slotted spoon and reserve liquid. Chop giblets and place in a large bowl with the corn bread, apples, onion, parsley, sage, salt, pepper and garlic powder. Add enough of the reserved cooking liquid to make a moist stuffing; toss gently. Stuff the body and neck cavity; truss openings.

Place goose, breast side up, on a rack in a shallow roasting pan. Spread with softened butter. Bake, uncovered, at 325° for 25 minutes per pound or until tender and a meat thermometer reads 180° for the goose and 165° for the stuffing. **Yield:** 6-8 servings.

Sour Cream Apple Chicken

I've found that apples and chicken go well together because they both have subtle flavors. I developed this recipe myself. I think it's not only a great-tasting main course, it also looks nice on the table.
—Carolyn Popwell, Lacey, Washington

  4 boneless skinless chicken breast halves
  1 tablespoon vegetable oil
  2 medium baking apples, peeled and
    thinly sliced
1/2 cup apple juice *or* cider
1/3 cup chopped onion
  1 teaspoon dried basil
1/2 teaspoon salt
  1 cup (8 ounces) sour cream
  1 tablespoon all-purpose flour
Hot cooked spinach noodles
Paprika

In a large skillet, cook chicken in oil over medium heat until browned and no longer pink inside, about 6-8 minutes per side. Remove from skillet and keep warm. Add apples, juice, onion, basil and salt to the skillet; bring to a boil. Reduce heat; cover and simmer until apples are tender.

Combine sour cream and flour; add to skillet. Stir and cook until sauce is warm (do not boil). Arrange noodles on a serving platter. Top with chicken. Spoon the apple sauce over all. Sprinkle with paprika. **Yield:** 4 servings.

Recipe for: Roasted Chicken with Rosemary

This is a lot like pot roast, only it uses chicken instead of beef. The rosemary gives it a sweet taste and blends well with the garlic, butter and parsley.
—Isabel Zienkosky, Salt Lake City, Utah

1/2 cup butter
2 tablespoons dried rosemary
2 tablespoons chopped fresh parsley
3 garlic cloves, minced
1 teaspoon salt
1/2 teaspoon pepper
1 whole roasting chicken (5 to 6 pounds)
8 small red potatoes, halved
6 carrots, cut into 2-inch pieces and halved lengthwise
2 medium onions, quartered

In a small saucepan, melt butter. Add rosemary, parsley, garlic, salt and pepper. Place chicken on a rack in a roasting pan; tie drumsticks together. Spoon half of the butter mixture over chicken.

Place the potatoes, carrots and onions around chicken. Drizzle remaining butter mixture over vegetables. Cover and bake at 350° for 1-1/2 hours, basting every 30 minutes. Uncover; bake 1 hour longer or until juices run clear, basting occasionally. **Yield:** 6 servings.

Oven Barbecued Chicken

Chicken and Sunday dinner go together in my mind. During my 20 years of married life on a dairy farm, I'd often brown the chicken and mix up the sauce while my husband milked, then pop it in the oven when we left for church. It was ready when we came home.
—Esther Shank, Harrisonburg, Virginia

Vegetable oil
3 to 4 pounds chicken pieces
1/3 cup chopped onion
3 tablespoons butter
3/4 cup ketchup
1/3 cup cider vinegar
3 tablespoons brown sugar
1/2 cup water
2 teaspoons prepared mustard
1 tablespoon Worcestershire sauce
1/4 teaspoon salt
1/8 teaspoon pepper

In a large skillet, heat a small amount of oil; cook chicken until browned. Drain; place chicken in a 13-in. x 9-in. x 2-in. baking dish.

In a saucepan, saute onion in butter until tender; stir in remaining ingredients. Simmer, uncovered, for 15 minutes. Pour over chicken. Bake at 350° for 1 hour or until meat juices run clear, basting occasionally. **Yield:** 6-8 servings.

Saucy Chicken and Asparagus

You won't believe how delicious and easy this dish is. We tasted it for the first time when our son's godparents made it for us. Even my grandmother—who's 95 years old—likes to serve this creamy dish for luncheons with friends! —Vicki Schlechter
Davis, California

1-1/2 pounds fresh asparagus spears, halved
  4 boneless skinless chicken breast halves
  2 tablespoons vegetable oil
1/2 teaspoon salt
1/4 teaspoon pepper
  1 can (10-3/4 ounces) condensed cream
    of chicken soup, undiluted
1/2 cup mayonnaise

  1 teaspoon lemon juice
1/2 teaspoon curry powder
  1 cup (4 ounces) shredded cheddar cheese

If desired, partially cook asparagus; drain. Place the asparagus in a greased 9-in. square baking dish. In a skillet over medium heat, brown the chicken in oil on both sides. Season with salt and pepper. Arrange chicken over asparagus.

In a bowl, mix soup, mayonnaise, lemon juice and curry powder; pour over chicken. Cover and bake at 375° for 40 minutes or until the chicken is tender and juices run clear. Sprinkle with cheese. Let stand 5 minutes before serving. **Yield:** 4 servings.

Marinated Turkey

When I first fixed this, we were living on a ranch along a river with lots of game. Wild turkey can be dry, but not prepared this way! Of course, it's just as tasty with store-bought turkey. And the gravy it makes is out of this world. —Wilma Lovejoy
Hastings, Nebraska

1/2 cup soy sauce
1/2 cup vegetable oil

  2 tablespoons honey
  1 teaspoon ground ginger
  1 teaspoon ground mustard
  1 teaspoon lemon juice
  2 teaspoons Worcestershire sauce
  2 garlic cloves, minced
  6 to 7 pounds fresh turkey parts
1/4 cup all-purpose flour, optional
Salt and pepper, optional

In a small bowl, combine the soy sauce, oil, honey, ginger, mustard, lemon juice, Worcestershire sauce and garlic. Place turkey parts in a large resealable plastic bag; add marinade. Seal bag; refrigerate overnight, turning bag occasionally.

Arrange turkey parts in a single layer in a large shallow roasting pan. Pour marinade over turkey. Bake, uncovered, at 325° for 1-1/2 to 2 hours or until a meat thermometer inserted in a piece of dark meat reads 180°. Baste occasionally if desired. Remove turkey to serving platter and keep warm.

If desired, make gravy: Strain pan juices into a large measuring cup. Skim fat and reserve 1/4 cup in a medium saucepan; discard remaining fat. Blend flour into saucepan. Add water to pan juices to make 2 cups. Add to saucepan; cook and stir until thickened and bubbly. Cook and stir 1 minute longer. Season with salt and pepper. Serve with turkey. **Yield:** 8-10 servings.

Grandma's Favorites

Smoked Turkey and Apple Salad

An eye-catching dish, this refreshing salad is a great main course for a summer lunch or light dinner. The dressing's Dijon flavor goes nicely with the turkey, and the apples add crunch.
—Carolyn Popwell, Lacey, Washington

DRESSING:
- 2 tablespoons cider vinegar
- 5 tablespoons olive oil
- 1 tablespoon Dijon mustard
- 1 teaspoon lemon-pepper seasoning
- 1/2 teaspoon salt, optional

SALAD:
- 1 bunch watercress *or* romaine, torn into bite-size pieces
- 1 carrot, julienned
- 10 cherry tomatoes, halved
- 8 ounces smoked turkey, julienned
- 4 unpeeled apples, sliced
- 1/3 cup chopped walnuts, toasted

Whisk together dressing ingredients and set aside. Just before serving, arrange salad greens on a platter or individual plates. Top with carrot, tomatoes, turkey and apples. Drizzle dressing over salad and sprinkle with walnuts. **Yield:** 8 servings.

Recipe for: Three-Cheese Chicken Bake

This is a hearty, comforting casserole that's always a crowd-pleaser. The combination of flavors and interesting colors ensure I come home with an empty dish!
—Vicky Raatz, Waterloo, Wisconsin

- 1/2 cup chopped onion
- 1/2 cup chopped green pepper
- 4 tablespoons butter, *divided*
- 1 can (10-3/4 ounces) condensed cream of chicken soup, undiluted
- 1 can (8 ounces) sliced mushrooms, drained
- 1 jar (2 ounces) chopped pimientos, drained
- 1/2 teaspoon dried basil
- 1 package (8 ounces) noodles, cooked and drained
- 3 cups diced cooked chicken
- 2 cups Ricotta *or* cottage cheese
- 2 cups (8 ounces) shredded cheddar cheese
- 1/2 cup grated Parmesan cheese
- 1/4 cup dry bread crumbs

In a skillet, saute onion and green pepper in 3 tablespoons butter until tender. Remove from the heat. Stir in the soup, mushrooms, pimientos and basil; set aside.

In a large bowl, combine noodles, chicken and cheeses; add mushroom sauce and mix well. Transfer to a greased 13-in. x 9-in. x 2-in. baking dish. Bake, uncovered, at 350° for 40-45 minutes or until bubbly.

Melt remaining butter; mix with bread crumbs. Sprinkle crumbs over casserole. Bake 15 minutes longer. **Yield:** 12-15 servings.

Parmesan Chicken

The savory coating on this chicken has the satisfying flavor of Parmesan cheese. It's easy enough to be a family weekday meal yet impressive enough to serve to guests. When I make this chicken for dinner, we never have leftovers. —Schelby Thompson Winter Haven, Florida

1/2 cup butter, melted
2 teaspoons Dijon mustard
1 teaspoon Worcestershire sauce
1/2 teaspoon salt
1 cup dry bread crumbs
1/2 cup grated Parmesan cheese
6 to 8 boneless skinless chicken breast halves

In a pie plate or shallow bowl, combine butter, mustard, Worcestershire sauce and salt. In a plastic bag, combine crumbs and Parmesan cheese. Dip chicken in butter mixture, then shake in crumb mixture.

Place in an ungreased 13-in. x 9-in. x 2-in. baking pan. Drizzle with any remaining butter mixture. Bake at 350° for 40-45 minutes or until chicken is no longer pink and juices run clear. **Yield:** 6-8 servings.

Recipe for: Chicken and Dumpling Casserole

This savory casserole is one of my husband's favorites. He loves the fluffy dumplings with plenty of gravy poured over them. The basil adds just the right touch of flavor and makes the whole house smell so good.
—Sue Mackey, Galesburg, Illinois

1/2 cup chopped onion
1/2 cup chopped celery
2 garlic cloves, minced
1/4 cup butter
1/2 cup all-purpose flour
2 teaspoons sugar
1 teaspoon salt
1 teaspoon dried basil
1/2 teaspoon pepper
4 cups chicken broth
1 package (10 ounces) frozen green peas
4 cups cubed cooked chicken
DUMPLINGS:
2 cups biscuit/baking mix
2 teaspoons dried basil
2/3 cup milk

In a large saucepan, saute onion, celery and garlic in butter until tender. Add flour, sugar, salt, basil, pepper and broth; bring to a boil. Cook and stir for 1 minute; reduce heat. Add peas and cook for 5 minutes, stirring constantly. Stir in chicken. Pour into a greased 13-in. x 9-in. x 2-in. baking dish.

For dumplings, combine biscuit mix and basil in a bowl. Stir in milk with a fork until moistened. Drop by tablespoonfuls onto casserole (12 dumplings). Bake, uncovered, at 350° for 30 minutes. Cover and bake 10 minutes more or until a toothpick inserted into a dumpling comes out clean. **Yield:** 6-8 servings.

Cheddary Chicken Potpie

This is a comforting chicken dish that features a medley of flavorful cheeses. Some days I make it in the morning so I can just pop it in the oven for dinner or have my husband bake it if I'm not home.
—Vicki Raatz, Waterloo, Wisconsin

1 can (10-3/4 ounces) condensed cream
   of chicken soup, undiluted
1 cup milk, *divided*
1/2 cup chopped onion
1 package (3 ounces) cream cheese,
   softened
1/4 cup chopped celery
1/4 cup shredded carrots
1/4 cup grated Parmesan cheese
1/2 teaspoon salt
3 cups cubed cooked chicken
1 package (10 ounces) frozen chopped
   broccoli, cooked and drained

1 egg
1 tablespoon vegetable oil
1 cup buttermilk pancake mix
1 cup (4 ounces) shredded sharp cheddar
   cheese
1/4 cup sliced almonds, optional

In a large saucepan, combine soup, 1/2 cup of milk, onion, cream cheese, celery, carrots, Parmesan cheese and salt. Cook and stir until the mixture is hot and cream cheese is melted. Stir in the chicken and broccoli; heat through. Pour into an ungreased 2-qt. baking dish.

In a medium bowl, combine the egg, oil and remaining milk. Add the pancake mix and cheddar cheese; blend well. Spoon over hot chicken mixture. Sprinkle with almonds if desired. Bake, uncovered, at 375° for 20-25 minutes or until golden brown. **Yield:** 6 servings.

Turkey with Sausage Stuffing

Here's a super way to savor roast turkey and stuffing without having to cook the big holiday bird. The stuffing is hearty, and the meat is juicy and tender.
—Aura Lee Johnson, Vermilion, Ohio

1 whole bone-in turkey breast (5 to 7
   pounds)
1/4 cup butter, melted
1-1/2 pounds bulk pork sausage
2 cups sliced celery
2 medium onions, chopped
4 cups dry bread cubes
2 cups pecan halves
1 cup raisins
2/3 cup chicken broth
2 eggs, beaten
1 teaspoon salt
1/2 teaspoon rubbed sage
1/4 teaspoon pepper

Place turkey breast with breast side up in a shallow baking dish. Brush with butter. Bake, uncovered, at 325° for 2 to 2-1/2 hours or until a meat thermometer reads 180°. Cover loosely with foil to prevent excess browning if necessary.

Meanwhile, in a skillet, cook sausage, celery and onions until the sausage is no longer pink

and vegetables are tender; drain. Remove from the heat; add all remaining ingredients and mix well. Spoon into a greased 3-qt. casserole. Cover and bake at 325° for 1 hour or until a meat thermometer reads 165°. Serve with sliced turkey. **Yield:** 15-20 servings.

Chicken 'n' Hash Brown Bake

The first time I served this dish for company was to a family with five children. The kids and the adults loved it! This is one recipe I often make for potlucks —it goes a long way, and all ages enjoy it.
—Ruth Andrewson, Leavenworth, Washington

1 package (32 ounces) frozen
  Southern-style hash brown potatoes
1 teaspoon salt
1/4 teaspoon pepper
4 cups diced cooked chicken
1 can (4 ounces) sliced mushrooms,
  drained
1 cup (8 ounces) sour cream
2 cups chicken broth *or* stock
1 can (10-3/4 ounces) condensed cream
  of chicken soup, undiluted
2 teaspoons instant chicken bouillon
  granules
2 tablespoons finely chopped onion
2 tablespoons finely chopped sweet red
  pepper
1 garlic clove, minced
Paprika
1/4 cup sliced almonds

Thaw hash browns overnight in refrigerator. Layer in an ungreased 13-in. x 9-in. x 2-in. baking dish. Sprinkle with salt and pepper. Place chicken and mushrooms over hash browns.

Stir together sour cream, broth, soup, bouillon, onion, red pepper and garlic; pour over all. Sprinkle with paprika and almonds. Bake, uncovered, at 350° for 50-60 minutes or until heated through. **Yield:** 8-10 servings.

Cordon Bleu Casserole

Whenever I'm invited to attend a potluck, people usually ask me to bring this tempting casserole. The turkey, ham and cheese are delectable combined with the crunchy topping. When I bake a turkey, I prepare the leftovers for this dish, knowing I'll be making it again soon.
—Joyce Paul
Moose Jaw, Saskatchewan

4 cups cubed cooked turkey
3 cups cubed fully cooked ham
1 cup (4 ounces) shredded cheddar cheese
1 cup chopped onion
1/4 cup butter
1/3 cup all-purpose flour
2 cups half-and-half cream
1 teaspoon dill weed
1/8 teaspoon ground mustard
1/8 teaspoon ground nutmeg
TOPPING:
1 cup dry bread crumbs
2 tablespoons butter, melted
1/4 teaspoon dill weed
1/4 cup shredded cheddar cheese
1/4 cup chopped walnuts

In a large bowl, combine turkey, ham and cheese; set aside. In a saucepan, saute onion in butter until tender. Add flour; stir to form a paste. Gradually add cream, stirring constantly. Bring to a boil; boil 1 minute or until thick. Add dill, mustard and nutmeg; mix well. Remove from the heat and pour over meat mixture. Spoon into a greased 13-in. x 9-in. x 2-in. baking dish.

Toss bread crumbs, butter and dill; stir in cheese and walnuts. Sprinkle over the casserole. Bake, uncovered, at 350° for 30 minutes or until heated through. **Yield:** 8-10 servings.

Chicken Provencale

When I serve this entree at a dinner party, people always comment on the tender chicken and flavorfully seasoned beans. I sometimes fix it a day ahead—it's as good as it is the first day it's made.
—*Barbara Zeilinger, Columbus, Indiana*

1 broiler/fryer chicken (3 to 4 pounds), cut up
1 tablespoon vegetable oil
1-1/2 cups chopped onion
3 garlic cloves, minced
2 cans (15-1/2 ounces *each*) great northern beans, rinsed and drained
1 can (29 ounces) diced tomatoes, undrained
3 medium carrots, sliced 1/4 inch thick
1 tablespoon chicken bouillon granules
1 teaspoon dried thyme
1/2 teaspoon dried oregano
1/2 teaspoon pepper

In a skillet, brown the chicken in oil; remove and set aside. Saute onion and garlic in drippings until tender. Stir in remaining ingredients. Spoon into a 3-qt. baking dish; arrange chicken pieces on top. Cover and bake at 350° for 65-75 minutes or until chicken juices run clear. **Yield:** 4 servings.

Recipe for: Turkey Tetrazzini

This recipe comes from a cookbook our church compiled. It's convenient because it can be made ahead and frozen. After the holidays, we use leftover turkey to prepare a meal for university students. They clean their plates!
—*Gladys Waldrop, Calvert City, Kentucky*

1 package (7 ounces) spaghetti, broken into 2-inch pieces
2 cups cubed cooked turkey
1 cup (4 ounces) shredded cheddar cheese
1 can (10-3/4 ounces) condensed cream of mushroom soup, undiluted
1 medium onion, chopped
2 cans (4 ounces *each*) sliced mushrooms, drained
1/3 cup milk
1/4 cup chopped green pepper
1 jar (2 ounces) chopped pimientos, drained
1/4 teaspoon salt
1/8 teaspoon pepper

Additional shredded cheddar cheese, optional

Cook spaghetti according to package directions; drain. Transfer to a large bowl; add the next 10 ingredients and mix well.

Spoon into a greased 2-1/2-qt. casserole; sprinkle with cheese if desired. Bake, uncovered, at 375° for 40-45 minutes or until heated through. **Yield:** 6-8 servings.

Pork, Ham & Sausage

At left: Herbed Pork and Apples (p. 132).

At right: Sweet-and-Sour Pork (p. 135).

Apricot Baked Ham

Ham is a super choice for a holiday meal because once you put it in the oven, it practically takes care of itself until dinnertime. I serve it because everyone in my family loves it! The sugary crust makes the ham beautiful to serve.
—Marge Clark
West Lebanon, Indiana

1/2 fully cooked ham with bone (5 to 7 pounds)
20 whole cloves
1/2 cup apricot preserves
3 tablespoons ground mustard
1/2 cup packed light brown sugar

Score the surface of ham with shallow diamond-shaped cuts. Insert cloves in cuts. Combine preserves and mustard; spread over ham. Pat brown sugar over apricot mixture.

Place ham on a rack in a roasting pan. Bake at 325° for 20 minutes per pound or until ham is heated through and a meat thermometer reads 140°. **Yield:** 10-14 servings.

Herbed Pork and Apples

(Pictured on page 130)

Whenever I make this dish for friends and family, I'm reminded of the wonderful scent of the Maine orchards where we picked our own apples every fall before we moved to Missouri. The aroma of the pork and apples certainly takes the chill out of crisp autumn air. —Louise Keithley, Columbia, Missouri

1 teaspoon rubbed sage
1 teaspoon *each* dried thyme, rosemary and marjoram, crushed
1 teaspoon salt
1 teaspoon pepper
1 pork loin roast with bone (about 6 pounds)
4 medium tart apples, cut into 1-inch chunks
1 large red onion, cut into 1-inch chunks

3 tablespoons brown sugar
1 cup apple juice
2/3 cup maple syrup

Combine herbs, salt and pepper; rub over roast. Cover and refrigerate for several hours or overnight. Bake, uncovered, at 325° for 1-1/2 hours. Drain fat. Mix apples and onion with brown sugar; spoon around roast. Continue to roast 1 hour or until internal temperature reaches 160°-170°.

Transfer the roast, apples and onion to a serving platter and keep warm. Skim excess fat from meat juices; pour into a heavy skillet (or leave in the roasting pan if it can be heated on stovetop). Add apple juice and syrup. Cook and stir over medium-high heat until liquid has been reduced by half, about 1 cup. Slice roast and serve with gravy. **Yield:** about 12 servings.

Recipe for: Country Pork 'n' Sauerkraut

The secret ingredient in this recipe is the applesauce. When everything's cooked up, you wouldn't know it's in there...yet the taste is just a bit sweeter. My mother and grandmother once ran a beanery for a train crew. That inspired a lot of my cooking. In fact, I adapted this recipe from one of theirs.

—Donna Hellendrung, Minneapolis, Minnesota

2 pounds country-style pork ribs
1 medium onion, chopped
1 tablespoon vegetable oil
1 can (14 ounces) sauerkraut, undrained
1 cup applesauce
2 tablespoons brown sugar
2 teaspoons caraway seed
1 teaspoon garlic powder
1/2 teaspoon pepper

In a Dutch oven, cook ribs and onion in oil until ribs are browned and onion is tender. Remove from the heat. Combine remaining ingredients and pour over ribs. Cover and bake at 350° for 1-1/2 to 2 hours or until ribs are tender. **Yield: 4 servings.**

Garlic Pork Roast

Mom cooked for 11 children, so her menus usually featured simple foods. But on New Year's Day, she always treated us to this special pork roast. All of us kids agree this was our mom's best meal!

—Ruby Williams, Bogalusa, Louisiana

1 pork loin roast, backbone loosened
   (about 5 pounds)
1/2 medium green pepper, finely chopped
1/2 cup thinly sliced green onions
1/2 cup chopped celery
8 garlic cloves, minced
1 teaspoon salt
1/4 teaspoon cayenne pepper

With a sharp knife, cut a deep pocket between each rib on meaty side of roast. Combine green pepper, green onions, celery and garlic; stuff deeply into pockets. Season roast with salt and cayenne pepper. Place roast, rib side down, in a shallow roasting pan.

Bake, uncovered, at 325° for 2-3 hours or until a meat thermometer reads 170°. Let stand for 15 minutes before carving. **Yield: 6-8 servings.**

Sauerkraut 'n' Sausage

I've fixed this satisfying stovetop supper for dozens of group gatherings, and everyone seems to enjoy the wonderful blend of flavors. Sweet and tart ingredients balance nicely, complemented with bacon and spices.
—Edna Hoffman, Hebron, Indiana

1 small onion, chopped
1 tablespoon butter
1 jar (32 ounces) sauerkraut, rinsed and drained
1 pound fully cooked Polish sausage, cut into 1/2-inch chunks
3-1/2 cups diced cooked peeled potatoes
1 cup apple juice
1 medium unpeeled apple, diced
2 tablespoons brown sugar
2 tablespoons all-purpose flour
1 tablespoon caraway seed
3 bacon strips, cooked and crumbled

In a large saucepan, saute onion in butter until tender. Add sauerkraut, sausage, potatoes, apple juice and apple.

In a small bowl, combine brown sugar, flour and caraway; stir into saucepan. Simmer for 35 minutes, stirring occasionally. Garnish with bacon. **Yield:** 10-12 servings.

Ham-Stuffed Manicotti

Here's a fun and different use for ham. It's unexpected combined with the manicotti, yet delicious. The creamy cheese sauce makes this casserole perfect for chilly days. I'm always asked for the recipe whenever I serve it.
—Dorothy Anderson
Ottawa, Kansas

8 manicotti shells
1/2 cup chopped onion
1 tablespoon vegetable oil
3 cups (1 pound) ground fully cooked ham
1 can (4 ounces) sliced mushrooms, drained
1 cup (4 ounces) shredded Swiss cheese, *divided*
3 tablespoons grated Parmesan cheese
1/4 to 1/2 cup chopped green pepper
3 tablespoons butter
3 tablespoons all-purpose flour
2 cups milk
Paprika
Chopped fresh parsley

Cook manicotti according to package directions; set aside. In a large skillet, saute onion in oil until tender. Remove from the heat. Add ham, mushrooms, half of the Swiss cheese and Parmesan; set aside.

In a saucepan, saute green pepper in butter until tender. Stir in flour until thoroughly combined. Add milk; cook, stirring constantly, until thickened and bubbly. Mix 1/4 of the sauce into ham mixture. Stuff each shell with about 1/3 cup of filling.

Place in a greased 11-in. x 7-in. x 2-in. baking dish. Top with remaining sauce; sprinkle with paprika. Cover and bake at 350° for 30 minutes or until heated through. Sprinkle with parsley and remaining Swiss cheese before serving. **Yield:** 8 servings.

Kielbasa Skillet Stew

I grew up on a Montana ranch, and this dish reminds me of the kind we used to prepare for the hay and harvest crews. The bacon and sausage provide rich flavor to this comforting stew. When I make this dish, I share a taste of my country memories with my family. —Machelle Lewis, Henderson, Nevada

5 bacon strips
1 medium onion, chopped
1 to 1-1/2 pounds smoked fully cooked
    kielbasa, thinly sliced
2 cans (15-1/2 ounces *each*) great
    northern beans, undrained
2 cans (8 ounces each) tomato sauce
1 can (4 ounces) chopped green chilies
2 medium carrots, thinly sliced
1/2 medium green pepper, chopped
1/2 teaspoon Italian seasoning
1/2 teaspoon dried thyme
1/8 teaspoon pepper

In a 12-in. skillet, cook bacon until crisp; remove to paper towel to drain. In drippings, cook onion and sausage until the onion is tender; drain.

Stir in remaining ingredients; bring to a boil. Reduce heat; cover and simmer for 45 minutes or until vegetables are tender, stirring occasionally. Crumble bacon and sprinkle on top. **Yield:** 6-8 servings.

Recipe for: Sweet-and-Sour Pork

(Pictured on page 131)

Sweet-and-Sour Pork always proves to be a perfect quick main course. It's a hearty stir-fry, yet it's light enough to leave room for a side dish and dessert. —Doris Sokolotosky, Smoky Lake, Alberta

1 can (20 ounces) pineapple chunks
2 tablespoons cornstarch
1/4 cup soy sauce
1 tablespoon honey
1/2 teaspoon chicken bouillon granules
1 garlic clove, minced
1/8 teaspoon pepper
2 tablespoons vegetable oil
3/4 pound pork tenderloin, cut into
    bite-size pieces
1 medium green pepper, thinly sliced
Hot cooked rice

Drain pineapple, reserving the juice; set pineapple aside. Add enough water to juice to equal 3/4 cup. Add cornstarch, soy sauce, honey, bouillon, garlic and pepper; set aside.

Heat oil in a large skillet; cook and stir pork and green pepper for 6-8 minutes or until pork is no longer pink and green pepper is crisp-tender. Stir pineapple juice mixture into skillet with pineapple. Cook until thickened and bubbly. Serve over rice. **Yield:** 4 servings.

Asparagus Ham Rolls

I love this delicious recipe because it includes three of my favorite locally produced foods—ham, asparagus and cheese. Prepared with leftover Easter ham and fresh asparagus, these rolls make an excellent spring-time meal.   —Laurie Timm, Minneiska, Minnesota

2 tablespoons butter
1/4 cup all-purpose flour
2 cups milk
1/2 cup shredded cheddar cheese
1/4 teaspoon salt
1/4 teaspoon white pepper
24 fresh *or* frozen asparagus spears
8 thin slices fully cooked ham (about 1/2 pound)
1/4 cup dry bread crumbs

In a saucepan, melt butter; stir in flour and cook until thick. Gradually stir in milk and cook until bubbly and thickened. Stir in cheese, salt and pepper. Remove from the heat.

Place three asparagus spears on each ham slice. Roll up; fasten with toothpicks if necessary. Place in a 13-in. x 9-in. x 2-in. baking pan; cover with cheese sauce. Sprinkle with crumbs. Bake at 375° for 20 minutes. **Yield: 8 servings.**

Recipe for: ## Ham Loaves

These mini ham loaves are a deliciously different way to serve ham, and they also freeze well.
—Carol Van Sickle, Versailles, Kentucky

2 pounds ground pork
2 pounds ground fully cooked ham
4 cups dry bread crumbs
4 eggs, lightly beaten
1 cup milk
1-1/2 cups packed brown sugar
3/4 cup water
1/2 cup cider vinegar
1 teaspoon ground mustard

In a bowl, combine pork, ham, crumbs, eggs and milk. Shape into 12 ovals, using 1 cup of mixture for each. Place in an ungreased 15-in. x 10-in. x 1-in. baking pan. Combine brown sugar, water, vinegar and mustard; pour over the loaves.

Bake, uncovered, at 350° for 1 hour and 15 minutes, basting every 15-20 minutes. Place the loaves on a platter and spoon some of the sauce over them. **Yield: 12 servings.**

Grilled Ham Steak

I love to grill this ham steak all year-round. It's an impressive meat dish to make for company or family. So quick to prepare, the ham tastes great with the smoky flavor from the grill and the tangy sweetness of the sauce. —Sharon Mensing, Greenfield, Iowa

    1/4 cup apricot *or* plum preserves
    1 tablespoon prepared mustard
    1 teaspoon lemon juice
    1/8 teaspoon ground cinnamon

    1 ham steak (1 inch thick and about 2
      pounds)

In a small saucepan, combine the preserves, mustard, lemon juice and cinnamon. Cook and stir over low heat until thoroughly combined, about 2-3 minutes.

Score fat edges of ham. Grill over medium heat for 8-10 minutes per side, brushing with glaze during the last few minutes of grilling. **Yield:** 6 servings.

Once in a while we would travel to Kansas to visit my grandparents. One thing I especially remember is going down the steps into the dark, damp cellar. After adjusting to the darkness, I could distinguish the rows of canned fruit on the shelves and the bins of potatoes and other vegetables. My grandmother would uncover a wooden barrel and dig out a ham which had been placed in there to cure. It smelled so good—and tasted even better.

    —Mrs. Zane Frasier, Cortez, Colorado

Scalloped Potatoes and Pork Chops

I truly enjoy trying new recipes and baking hearty casseroles like this one for my family. This dish is easy to prepare, and baking the chops with the potatoes gives the whole meal great flavor. —Susan Chavez, Vancouver, Washington

    5 cups thinly sliced peeled potatoes
    1 cup chopped onion
Salt and pepper to taste
    1 can (10-3/4 ounces) condensed cream
      of mushroom soup, undiluted
    1/2 cup sour cream
    6 pork loin chops (1 inch thick)
Chopped fresh parsley

In a greased 13-in. x 9-in. x 2-in. baking dish, layer half of the potatoes and onion; sprinkle with salt and pepper. Repeat layers. Combine the soup and sour cream; pour over potato mixture. Cover and bake at 375° for 30 minutes.

Meanwhile, in a skillet, brown pork chops on both sides. Place chops on top of casserole. Cover and return to the oven for 45 minutes or until chops are tender, uncovering during the last 15 minutes of baking. Sprinkle with parsley. **Yield:** 6 servings.

Maple Country Ribs

I brought this recipe with me from Quebec when my husband, Russ, and I were first married. The rich maple flavor impressed my in-laws the first time I made dinner for them. —Anne-Marie Fortin
Swanton, Vermont

     3 pounds country-style pork ribs
     1 cup maple syrup
     1/2 cup applesauce
     1/4 cup ketchup
     3 tablespoons lemon juice
     1/4 teaspoon *each* salt, pepper, paprika,
         garlic powder and ground cinnamon

Place ribs in a large kettle or Dutch oven. Cover with water; bring to a boil. Reduce heat and simmer for 10 minutes. Drain.

Place ribs in a greased 13-in. x 9-in. x 2-in. baking pan. Combine remaining ingredients; pour half over the ribs.

Bake, uncovered, at 325° for 1-1/2 hours or until the meat is tender, basting often with remaining sauce. **Yield:** 4 servings.

Skillet Pork Chops With Zucchini

My husband and I are always blessed with plenty of zucchini from our garden in summer, so I try lots of different zucchini recipes. This is one of my family's favorites. —Diane Banaszak, West Bend, Wisconsin

     3 tablespoons all-purpose flour
     5 tablespoons grated Parmesan cheese,
         divided

 1-1/2 teaspoons salt
     1/2 teaspoon dill weed
     1/4 teaspoon pepper
         6 pork chops (about 3/4 inch thick)
         1 tablespoon vegetable oil
         2 medium onions, sliced
     1/3 cup water
         3 medium zucchini (about 1 pound),
             sliced
     1/2 teaspoon paprika

In a large plastic bag, combine flour, 2 tablespoons Parmesan cheese, salt, dill weed and pepper. Place pork chops in bag and shake to coat; shake off excess flour and reserve.

Heat oil in a large skillet over medium-high; brown pork chops on both sides. Reduce heat. Place onion slices on chops. Add water to skillet; cover and simmer for 15 minutes. Place zucchini slices over the onion.

Mix remaining Parmesan cheese with reserved flour mixture; sprinkle over zucchini. Sprinkle paprika on top. Cover and simmer for 25 minutes or until pork chops are tender. **Yield:** 6 servings.

Sugar-Glazed Ham

This old-fashioned sugar glaze gives ham a pretty, golden-brown coating just like Grandma used to make. The mustard and vinegar complement the brown sugar and add tangy flavor. Be prepared to serve seconds!
—Carol Strong Battle
Heathsville, Virginia

1 fully cooked bone-in ham (5 to 7 pounds)
1 cup packed brown sugar
2 teaspoons prepared mustard
1 to 2 tablespoons cider vinegar

Score ham about 1/2 in. deep with a sharp knife. Place ham on a rack in a shallow baking pan. Bake at 325° for 2 to 2-1/2 hours (20 minutes per pound).

Combine brown sugar, mustard and enough vinegar to make a thick paste. During the last hour of baking, brush glaze on ham every 15 minutes. **Yield:** 10-14 servings.

Recipe for: Potato Pork Pie

A true comfort food that's impossible to resist, this main dish is hearty and saucy with flavors that blend nicely together. Many shepherd's pie recipes call for beef, so this pork version is a tasty change of pace.
—Michelle Ross, Stanwood, Washington

2 pounds potatoes, peeled and cubed
1/3 cup heavy whipping cream
4 tablespoons butter, *divided*
3/4 teaspoon salt
1/8 teaspoon pepper
1 medium onion, chopped
1 garlic clove, minced
1/4 cup all-purpose flour
1 can (14-1/2 ounces) beef broth
1 tablespoon Dijon mustard
1 teaspoon dried thyme
4 tablespoons minced fresh parsley, *divided*
2-1/2 cups cubed cooked pork

Place potatoes in a saucepan and cover with water; bring to a boil. Cover and cook for 20-25 minutes or until very tender. Drain well. Mash potatoes with cream, 2 tablespoons butter, salt and pepper. Spread 1-1/2 cups of mashed potatoes into a greased shallow 1-1/2-qt. baking dish.

In a skillet, saute onion and garlic in remaining butter until tender. Stir in flour until blended. Gradually stir in broth, mustard, thyme and 2 tablespoons parsley. Bring to a boil; cook and stir for 2 minutes or until thickened. Stir in pork; heat through.

Pour over the potato crust. Pipe or spoon remaining mashed potatoes over top. Bake, uncovered, at 375° for 35-40 minutes or until the potatoes are lightly browned. Sprinkle with remaining parsley. **Yield:** 6 servings.

Broccoli-Ham Hot Dish

One of my best friends shared this recipe with me. My family loves it because it includes one of our favorite vegetables—broccoli. It's a delicious and colorful way to use up leftover ham. —Margaret Wagner Allen
Abingdon, Virginia

2 packages (10 ounces *each*) frozen cut broccoli
2 cups cooked rice
6 tablespoons butter
2 cups soft bread crumbs (about 2-1/2 slices)
1 medium onion, chopped
3 tablespoons all-purpose flour
1 teaspoon salt
1/4 teaspoon pepper
3 cups milk
1-1/2 pounds fully cooked ham, cubed
Shredded cheddar *or* Swiss cheese

Cook broccoli according to package directions; drain. Spoon rice into a 13-in. x 9-in. x 2-in. baking pan. Place broccoli over rice. Melt butter in a large skillet. Sprinkle 2 tablespoons of melted butter over the bread crumbs and set aside.

In remaining butter, saute onion until soft. Add flour, salt and pepper, stirring constantly until bubbly. Stir in milk and continue cooking until sauce thickens and bubbles. Cook and stir for 1 minute; add ham and heat through. Pour over rice and broccoli. Sprinkle the crumbs over all.

Bake at 350° for 30 minutes or until heated through. Sprinkle with cheese; let stand 5 minutes before serving. **Yield:** 8 servings.

Pork Chops with Caraway Cabbage

This quick and easy stovetop recipe has all the flavor of an old-world pork and cabbage dinner. It tastes like you fussed. —David Frame, Waxahachie, Texas

4 pork loin chops (3/4 inch thick)
2 tablespoons vegetable oil
1/2 teaspoon pepper
1-1/2 cups finely chopped onion
3 tablespoons butter
6 cups shredded cabbage
2 garlic cloves, minced
3 tablespoons red wine vinegar
1 teaspoon caraway seed
1/2 teaspoon salt

In skillet over high heat, brown the pork chops in oil; drain. Sprinkle with pepper; remove. Set aside. In same skillet, saute onion in butter for 1-2 minutes or until tender.

Add cabbage, garlic, vinegar, caraway and salt; cook, stirring occasionally, until cabbage wilts. Place chops on top of cabbage. Cover and simmer for 15-17 minutes or until meat is tender. Serve immediately. **Yield:** 4 servings.

Cranberry-Glazed Pork Roast

My family loves pork prepared in this festive way. You'll find that this succulent roast, with its tangy ruby glaze, is an entree that you, too, will be proud to serve on holidays and for other special dinners year after year.
—Theresa Pearson, Ogilvie, Minnesota

1 boneless pork loin roast (3-1/2 to 4 pounds)
12 small whole onions
1 can (16 ounces) whole-berry cranberry sauce
1/4 cup orange juice
2 teaspoons cornstarch
1/2 to 1 teaspoon grated orange peel
1/4 teaspoon ground cinnamon
1/8 teaspoon salt

Place roast, fat side up, in a greased roasting pan. Bake, uncovered, at 325° for 45 minutes. Place onions around roast; cover and bake for 30 minutes.

Meanwhile, in a saucepan, combine cranberry sauce, orange juice, cornstarch, orange peel, cinnamon and salt; mix well. Bring to a boil over medium heat; boil and stir for 2 minutes or until thickened. Spoon 3/4 cup over roast and onions; set remaining sauce aside.

Bake, basting occasionally, 30-45 minutes longer or until a meat thermometer reads 160° and onions are tender. Let stand 15 minutes before slicing. Heat reserved sauce; serve with roast and onions. **Yield:** 12-14 servings.

Pork and Spinach Salad

My family enjoys picnics any time of year—especially in the spring. To get in the mood for warmer weather, I serve this hearty main-dish salad. You just can't beat a salad that tastes great and is good for you, too.   *—Marian Pratt, Sequim, Washington*

10 ounces fresh spinach, washed and stems removed
1 can (16 ounces) black-eyed peas, rinsed and drained
1/3 cup Italian dressing
1/4 cup sliced green onions
1/2 cup sliced fresh mushrooms
1/4 cup sliced celery
1 jar (2 ounces) sliced pimiento, drained
2 to 3 tablespoons sliced ripe olives
2 garlic cloves, minced
1 tablespoon olive oil
1/2 pound pork tenderloin, cut into thin strips

Line four plates with spinach leaves; set aside. In a bowl, combine peas, Italian dressing, green onions, mushrooms, celery, pimiento and olives; set aside.

In a medium skillet, saute garlic in oil for 30 seconds. Add pork and stir-fry for 2-3 minutes or until no pink remains. Remove from the heat; add vegetable mixture and mix well. Divide among spinach-lined plates. Serve immediately. **Yield:** 4 servings.

Ham Buns

These tasty sandwiches are a great way to use left-over ham. Friends with whom I've shared the recipe tell me that ham buns disappear quickly at potlucks or parties. Make mini-buns ahead for an easy meal or snack. —Esther Shank, Harrisonburg, Virginia

1/2 cup butter, softened
1 small onion, grated
1 tablespoon poppy seeds
2 teaspoons Worcestershire sauce
2 teaspoons prepared mustard
1-1/4 cups finely chopped fully cooked ham
(about 8 ounces)

1 cup (4 ounces) shredded Swiss cheese
6 to 8 hamburger buns *or* 16 to 20 mini buns

In a bowl, mix butter, onion, poppy seeds, Worcestershire sauce and mustard until well blended. Add ham and cheese; mix well.

Divide evenly among buns. Place in a shallow baking pan and cover with foil. Bake at 350° for 15-20 minutes or until hot. **Yield:** 6-8 main dish or 16-20 appetizer servings.

Pork Chow Mein

I give all the credit for my love of cooking and baking to my mother, grandmother and mother-in-law. That trio inspired delicious dishes like this hearty skillet dinner. When we get a taste for stir-fry, this dish really hits the spot. —Helen Carpenter
Marble Falls, Texas

1 pound boneless pork loin
2 garlic cloves, minced
4 tablespoons soy sauce, *divided*
1 cup chicken broth
2 tablespoons cornstarch
1/2 to 1 teaspoon ground ginger
1 tablespoon vegetable oil
1 cup thinly sliced carrots
1 cup thinly sliced celery
1 cup chopped onion
1 cup coarsely chopped cabbage
1 cup coarsely chopped fresh spinach
Hot cooked rice, optional

Cut pork into 4-in. x 1/2-in. x 1/4-in. strips; place in a bowl. Add garlic and 2 tablespoons soy sauce. Cover and refrigerate 2-4 hours.

Meanwhile, combine broth, cornstarch, ginger and remaining soy sauce; mix well and set aside. Heat oil in a large skillet or wok on high; stir-fry pork until no longer pink. Remove and keep warm. Add carrots and celery; stir-fry 3-4 minutes. Add onion, cabbage and spinach; stir-fry 2-3 minutes.

Stir broth mixture and add to skillet along with pork. Cook and stir until broth thickens, about 3-4 minutes. Serve immediately over rice if desired. **Yield:** 6 servings.

Festive Ham Glaze

As long as I can remember, my favorite room's been the kitchen. My glaze dates way back to shortly after my husband and I were married. My parents were visiting, and I cooked a Sunday ham with this glaze—I've done it that same way all the years since.

—Becky Magee, Chandler, Arizona

1 bone-in fully cooked ham (5 to 8 pounds)
1-1/2 cups orange juice
1-1/4 cups packed brown sugar
1 tablespoon grated orange peel
1 teaspoon ground mustard
1/4 teaspoon ground cloves

Score surface of ham, making diamond shapes 1/2 in. deep. Place in a large baking dish. In a bowl, mix remaining ingredients; pour over ham. Cover and refrigerate overnight, turning ham occasionally.

Reserving glaze, remove ham to a rack in a shallow roasting pan. Bake, uncovered, at 325° until a meat thermometer reads 140°, about 2-4 hours, brushing occasionally with glaze. **Yield:** 10-16 servings.

Recipe for: Barbecued Spareribs

My husband is a meat cutter at a supermarket and likes to find new ways to smoke or barbecue meat. Several years ago, he discovered this recipe for pork ribs covered in a rich tangy sauce. It was an instant success with our family and friends.

—Bette Brotzel, Billings, Montana

4 pounds pork spareribs, cut into serving-size pieces
1 medium onion, quartered
2 teaspoons salt
1/4 teaspoon pepper
SAUCE:
1/2 cup cider vinegar
1/2 cup packed brown sugar
1/2 cup ketchup
1/4 cup chili sauce
1/4 cup Worcestershire sauce
2 tablespoons chopped onion
1 tablespoon lemon juice
1/2 teaspoon ground mustard
1 garlic clove, minced
Dash cayenne pepper

In a large kettle or Dutch oven, place ribs and onion; sprinkle with salt and pepper. Add enough water to cover ribs; bring to a boil. Reduce heat; cover and simmer for 1-1/2 hours or until tender; drain.

Combine all of the sauce ingredients in a saucepan. Simmer, uncovered, for 1 hour or until slightly thickened, stirring occasionally.

Arrange ribs on a rack in a broiler pan. Brush with sauce. Broil 5 in. from the heat for 5 minutes on each side, brushing frequently with sauce. **Yield:** 4 servings.

Tuscan Pork Roast

Everyone's eager to eat after the wonderful aroma of this roast tempts us all afternoon. This is a great Sunday dinner with little fuss. Since I found this recipe a few years ago, it's become a favorite with our seven grown children and their families.

—Elinor Stabile, Canmore, Alberta

  5 to 8 garlic cloves, peeled
  1 tablespoon dried rosemary
  1 tablespoon olive oil
1/2 teaspoon salt
  1 boneless pork loin roast (3 to 4 pounds)

In a blender or food processor, combine garlic, rosemary, olive oil and salt; blend until mixture turns to paste. Rub over the roast; cover and let stand for 30 minutes.

Place on a greased baking rack, fat side up, in a roasting pan. Bake, uncovered, at 325° for 2 to 2-1/2 hours or until the internal temperature reaches 160°. Let stand for 15 minutes before slicing. **Yield:** 10-12 servings.

Recipe for: Sausage and Mushroom Stew

The perfect dish for a hungry hardworking bunch, this savory stew has a hearty sausage flavor and a delicious creamy sauce. Lots of vegetables add color and interest to each ladleful.

—Ann Nace
Perkasie, Pennsylvania

  2 cans (10-3/4 ounces *each*) cream of
    mushroom soup, undiluted
1-1/2 pounds smoked kielbasa, cut
    into 1-inch rounds
  5 medium potatoes, peeled and cut
    into 1-inch chunks
  4 carrots, peeled and cut into 1 inch
    pieces
  3 medium onions, coarsely chopped
  1 cup fresh green beans, halved
3/4 pound fresh mushrooms, halved
1/2 medium head cabbage, coarsely
    chopped

In an ovenproof 5-qt. Dutch oven or casserole, combine all ingredients except cabbage. Cover and bake at 350° for 1-1/4 hours.

Uncover and stir. Add the cabbage. Cover and bake 30 minutes longer or until vegetables are tender. Stir again before serving. **Yield:** 6-8 servings.

Dandy Ham Sandwiches

These sandwiches are a delicious alternative to cold ham salad. Caraway adds nice flavor.
—Mrs. Wallace Carlson, Two Harbors, Minnesota

  2 cups (8 ounces) shredded cheddar
     cheese
1-1/2 cups ground fully cooked ham
  1/2 cup finely chopped onion
  1/3 cup French salad dressing
  2 tablespoons prepared mustard
  4 teaspoons caraway seed
  5 hamburger buns, split

In a bowl, combine the first six ingredients; mix well. Spread over cut side of buns. Place on a greased baking sheet.

Bake at 350° for 15-20 minutes or until the cheese is melted. **Yield:** 10 sandwiches.

One-Dish Pork Chop Dinner

When I had to make a dinner with a Mennonite theme, I came up with this meaty main dish. Most often, I serve it with salad, soup and bread. The apple juice gives the pork a wonderful flavor, and the cabbage taste isn't too strong. —Pat Waymire
Yellow Springs, Ohio

  8 pork chops (1/2 inch thick)
  1/3 cup all-purpose flour
  1/4 cup butter
Salt and pepper to taste
  2 cups apple juice, *divided*
  2 pounds small red potatoes
  1 pound *or* 1 jar (16 ounces) small whole
     onions, drained
  1 pound carrots, peeled and cut
     into 3-inch pieces
  6 to 8 cups shredded cabbage

Coat pork chops in flour; reserve excess flour. In a large Dutch oven, melt butter over medium-high heat. Brown chops on both sides. Season with pepper and salt if desired. Remove and set aside.

Stir reserved flour into pan; cook and stir until a paste forms. Gradually whisk in 1-1/2 cups apple juice; blend until smooth. Return chops to Dutch oven; cover and bake at 350° for 30 minutes.

Add potatoes, onions, carrots and remaining apple juice. Cover and bake 30 minutes longer. Top with cabbage; cover and bake for 1 to 1-1/2 hours or until the pork chops are tender, basting occasionally with juices. **Yield:** 8 servings.

Seafood & Meatless Main Dishes

At left: Lime Broiled Catfish (p. 149).

At right: Florida Seafood Casserole (p. 150).

Red Beans and Rice

This savory, filling recipe originated with my sister-in-law. I changed it around a bit to suit the tastes of my family.
                              —Marcia Salisbury
                              Waukesha, Wisconsin

1/2 pound dry kidney beans, rinsed
1/2 pound dry pinto beans, rinsed
  4 cups water
  4 cups chicken broth

2 garlic cloves, minced
2 bay leaves
1 can (14-1/2 ounces) diced tomatoes, undrained
1 jar (4 ounces) diced pimientos, drained
1 large green pepper, chopped
1 large sweet red pepper, chopped
1 large onion, chopped
1 cup chopped celery
1 can (4 ounces) diced green chilies
1 teaspoon paprika
1 teaspoon salt
1 tablespoon cider vinegar
1/4 cup snipped fresh parsley
1/4 to 1/2 teaspoon crushed red pepper flakes
1/4 to 1/2 teaspoon ground cumin
1/4 to 1/2 teaspoon hot pepper sauce
Hot cooked rice

Place beans in a Dutch oven with water. Bring to a boil; simmer 2 minutes. Remove from the heat. Cover and let stand 1 hour. Drain and rinse beans. Return to Dutch oven with broth, garlic and bay leaves; bring to a boil. Reduce heat; cover and simmer for 1-1/4 hours.

Stir in the next 14 ingredients. Cover and simmer for 1 hour or until beans and vegetables are tender and gravy is thick. Remove bay leaves. Serve over hot cooked rice. **Yield:** 12 servings.

Broiled Fish

Mother's secret in preparing this recipe was to butter the fish first before dusting it with flour. That seals in the moisture of the fish, which makes it succulent and absolutely delicious.
                              —Ann Berg
                              Chesapeake, Virginia

4 orange roughy, red snapper, catfish *or* trout fillets (1-1/2 to 2 pounds)
6 tablespoons butter, melted, *divided*
1 tablespoon all-purpose flour
Paprika
Juice of 1 lemon
  1 tablespoon minced fresh parsley
  2 teaspoons Worcestershire sauce

Place fish on a broiler rack coated with nonstick cooking spray. Brush tops of fish with 3 tablespoons of the butter; dust with flour and sprinkle with paprika.

Broil 5-6 in. from the heat for 5 minutes or until fish just begins to brown. Combine lemon juice, parsley, Worcestershire sauce and remaining butter; pour over the fish. Broil 5 minutes longer or until fish flakes easily with a fork. **Yield:** 4 servings.

Recipe for: Lime Broiled Catfish

(Pictured on page 146)

To serve a reduced-calorie dish that is ready in about 15 minutes, I turn to this fast, simple recipe. I think the lime juice adds a different, fresh flavor to the mild taste of the fish.
—Nick Nicholson
Clarksdale, Mississippi

1 tablespoon butter
2 tablespoons lime juice
1/2 teaspoon salt, optional
1/4 teaspoon pepper
1/4 teaspoon garlic powder
2 catfish fillets (6 ounces *each*)
Lime slices *or* wedges, optional
Fresh parsley, optional

In a saucepan, melt butter. Stir in lime juice, salt if desired, pepper and garlic powder; mix well. Remove from the heat and set aside.

Place fillets in a shallow baking dish. Brush each fillet generously with lime-butter sauce. Broil for 5-8 minutes or until fish flakes easily with a fork. Remove to a warm serving dish; spoon pan juices over each fillet. Garnish with lime and parsley if desired. **Yield:** 2 servings.

Budget Macaroni and Cheese

This is a quick, creamy and comforting main dish. I've tried many macaroni and cheese recipes, but this is my favorite.—Debbie Carlson, San Diego, California

1 package (7 ounces) elbow macaroni
3 tablespoons butter
3 tablespoons all-purpose flour
1/4 teaspoon salt
Dash pepper
1 cup milk
1 cup (4 ounces) shredded cheddar
cheese

Cook the macaroni according to package directions. Drain; set aside and keep warm. In a saucepan over medium-low heat, melt butter. Add flour, salt and pepper; stir to make a smooth paste.

Gradually add milk, stirring constantly. Heat and stir until thickened. Remove from the heat; stir in cheese until melted. Pour over macaroni and mix well. **Yield:** 4 servings.

Seafood & Meatless Main Dishes

Florida Seafood Casserole

(Pictured on page 147)

We have lots of friends from up North who come down here to Florida each winter to be out of the snow and in the sun. They love to be served fresh seafood, so we always try to accommodate them.
—Lucille Pennington, Ormond Beach, Florida

1/3 cup minced onion
1/4 cup butter
1/4 cup all-purpose flour
1 cup milk
1 cup half-and-half cream
3 cups cooked rice
1 cup (4 ounces) shredded cheddar cheese, *divided*
1 cup flaked cooked crabmeat
1 cup peeled cooked shrimp
1 can (8 ounces) sliced water chestnuts, drained
2 tablespoons lemon juice
1 tablespoon chopped pimiento
1 tablespoon minced fresh parsley
1/2 teaspoon salt
1/2 teaspoon pepper

In a saucepan, saute the onion in butter until tender; blend in flour. Add milk and cream; cook and stir until thick and bubbly. Remove from the heat. Stir in the rice, half of the cheese, crabmeat, shrimp, water chestnuts, lemon juice, pimiento, parsley, salt and pepper.

Spoon into a greased 2-1/2-qt. casserole. Bake, uncovered, at 350° for 25 minutes or until heated through. Sprinkle with remaining cheese just before serving. **Yield:** 6 servings.

Tomato Quiche

I first tried this recipe at a family gathering and loved it. It is a great meatless lunch or dinner for a warm day, served hot or cold. This is my most-requested dish for parties and a fairly simple one to make. Enjoy!
—Heidi Anne Quinn, West Kingston, Rhode Island

1 cup chopped onion
2 tablespoons butter
4 large tomatoes, peeled, seeded, chopped and drained
1 teaspoon salt
1/4 teaspoon pepper
1/4 teaspoon dried thyme
2 cups (8 ounces) shredded Monterey Jack cheese, *divided*
1 unbaked pie pastry (10 inches)
4 eggs
1-1/2 cups half-and-half cream

In a skillet, saute onion in butter until tender. Add tomatoes, salt, pepper and thyme. Cook over medium-high heat until liquid is almost evaporated, about 10-15 minutes.

Remove from heat. Sprinkle 1 cup cheese into bottom of pie shell. Cover with tomato mixture; sprinkle with remaining cheese. In a mixing bowl, beat eggs until foamy. Stir in cream; mix well. Pour into pie shell. Bake at 425° for 10 minutes.

Reduce heat to 325°; bake 40 minutes more or until top begins to brown and a knife inserted near the center comes out clean. Let stand 10 minutes before cutting. **Yield:** 6-8 servings.

Honey Walleye

Our state is known as the "Land of 10,000 Lakes," so fishing is a favorite recreation here. This recipe is a quick way to prepare all the fresh walleye that's hooked by the anglers in our family. —Kitty McCue
St. Louis Park, Minnesota

      1 egg
      2 teaspoons honey
      2 cups crushed butter-flavored crackers
         (about 45 to 50)
  1/2 teaspoon salt
      4 to 6 walleye fillets (1-1/2 to 2 pounds)
  1/3 to 1/2 cup vegetable oil
Lemon wedges, optional

In a shallow bowl, beat egg; add honey. In a plastic bag, combine crackers and salt. Dip fish in egg mixture, then shake in bag until coated.

In a skillet, cook fillets in oil for 3-5 minutes on each side or until golden and fish flakes easily with a fork. Serve with lemon wedges if desired. **Yield:** 4-6 servings.

Recipe for: *Lemon Herbed Salmon*

We sometimes send our delicious Washington salmon all the way to Michigan for my sister to use in this family-favorite dish! The tasty topping can be used on other types of fish, too. Fresh thyme from your garden really sparks the flavor.
—Perlene Hoekema, Lynden, Washington

  2-1/2 cups fresh bread crumbs
      4 garlic cloves, minced
  1/2 cup chopped fresh parsley
      6 tablespoons grated Parmesan cheese
  1/4 cup chopped fresh thyme *or* 1
         tablespoon dried thyme
      2 teaspoons grated lemon peel
  1/2 teaspoon salt
      6 tablespoons butter, melted, *divided*
      1 salmon fillet (3 to 4 pounds)

In a bowl, combine bread crumbs, garlic, parsley, cheese, thyme, lemon peel and salt; mix well. Add 4 tablespoons butter and toss lightly to coat; set aside.

Pat salmon dry. Place skin side down in a greased baking dish. Brush with remaining butter; cover with crumb mixture. Bake at 350° for 20-25 minutes or until salmon flakes easily with a fork. **Yield:** 8 servings.

Catfish Cakes

These cakes are crispy on the outside and moist and flavorful on the inside—a real treat! I like to serve them with hush puppies and coleslaw. I developed the recipe to use all the catfish we catch at our lake cabin. —Jan Campbell, Purvis, Mississippi

1-1/2 pounds catfish fillets
2 eggs, beaten
1 large potato, peeled, cooked and mashed
1 large onion, finely chopped
1 to 2 tablespoons chopped fresh parsley
2 to 3 drops hot pepper sauce
1 garlic clove, minced
1 teaspoon salt
1/2 teaspoon pepper
1/2 teaspoon dried basil
2 cups finely crushed butter-flavored crackers
Oil for cooking
Tartar sauce, optional

Poach or bake catfish fillets. Drain and refrigerate. Flake cooled fish into a large mixing bowl. Add eggs, potato, onion, parsley, hot pepper sauce, garlic, salt, pepper and basil; mix well. Shape into eight patties; coat with cracker crumbs.

Heat a small amount of oil in a large skillet. Cook patties, a few at a time, until browned on both sides and heated through. Serve with tartar sauce if desired. **Yield:** 8 servings.

Recipe for: North Carolina Shrimp Saute

It takes longer to cook the pasta than it does the shrimp in this recipe, so cook the shrimp only until they turn pink and immediately remove the pan from the heat. —Teresa Hildreth, Stoneville, North Carolina

8 ounces linguini *or* spaghetti
1/4 cup butter
1 pound raw shrimp, peeled and deveined
1/2 pound fresh mushrooms, sliced
1 small green pepper, chopped
3 garlic cloves, minced
1/2 cup grated Romano cheese
1/2 teaspoon salt
1/4 teaspoon pepper
Chopped fresh parsley
Lemon slices

Cook pasta according to package directions. Meanwhile, in a skillet, melt butter over medium heat. Add shrimp, mushrooms, green pepper and garlic. Saute until shrimp turn pink, about 3-5 minutes.

Drain pasta; place in a serving dish. Top with shrimp mixture. Sprinkle with cheese, salt, pepper and parsley; toss. Garnish with lemon. **Yield:** 4 servings.

Stuffed Trout

We raise trout on our New England farm, so I'm always happy to use that fresh fish in this delicious recipe. —Shirley Coleman, Monkton, Vermont

2 bacon strips, cooked and crumbled
1/2 cup fresh coarse bread crumbs
1/4 cup chopped onion
2 tablespoons chopped fresh parsley
1/8 teaspoon salt
1/8 teaspoon pepper
4 dressed trout (1/2 pound *each*)

In a medium bowl, combine the first six ingredients; mix well. Stuff 1/4 cup into cavity of each trout. Place on a lightly greased rack in a shallow roasting pan.

Bake at 350° for 35-40 minutes or until fish flakes easily with a fork. **Yield:** 4 servings.

Tuna Mushroom Casserole

I love to serve this dressed-up version of a tuna casserole. The green beans add nice texture, color and flavor. The first time I made this dish, my uncle asked for seconds even though tuna casseroles are not usually his favorite. —Jone Furlong
Santa Rosa, California

1/2 cup water
1 teaspoon chicken bouillon granules
1 package (10 ounces) frozen green beans
1 cup chopped onion
1 cup sliced fresh mushrooms
1/4 cup chopped celery
1 garlic clove, minced
1/2 teaspoon dill weed
1/2 teaspoon salt
1/8 teaspoon pepper
4 teaspoons cornstarch
1-1/2 cups milk
1/2 cup shredded Swiss cheese
1/4 cup mayonnaise
2-1/2 cups medium egg noodles, cooked and drained
1 can (12-1/4 ounces) tuna, drained and flaked
1/3 cup dry bread crumbs
1 tablespoon butter

In a large saucepan, bring water and bouillon to a boil, stirring to dissolve. Add the next eight ingredients; bring to a boil. Reduce heat; cover and simmer 5 minutes or until vegetables are tender.

Dissolve cornstarch in milk; add to vegetable mixture, stirring constantly. Bring to a boil; boil 2 minutes or until thickened. Remove from the heat; stir in cheese and mayonnaise until cheese is melted.

Fold in noodles and tuna. Pour into a greased 2-1/2-qt. baking dish. Brown bread crumbs in butter; sprinkle on top of casserole. Bake, uncovered, at 350° for 25-30 minutes or until heated through. **Yield:** 4-6 servings.

Mock Lobster

Mock Lobster goes well with macaroni and cheese or coleslaw. For a change of taste, you can substitute your favorite seafood sauce for the melted butter and lemon. —Gloria Jarrett, Loveland, Ohio

1-1/2 to 2 pounds frozen cod *or* haddock
    fillets, partially thawed
1-1/2 teaspoons salt
    2 teaspoons seafood seasoning *or* paprika
    3 tablespoons vinegar
Melted butter
Lemon wedges

Cut fillets into 2-in. x 2-in. pieces; place in a skillet. Cover with water. Add salt and seafood seasoning; bring to a boil. Reduce heat; simmer, uncovered, for 10 minutes. Drain.

Cover with cold water. Add vinegar and bring to a boil. Reduce heat; simmer, uncovered, for 10 minutes. Drain. Serve with melted butter and lemon. **Yield:** 4-6 servings.

Stuffed Sole

Seafood was a staple for my large family when I was growing up. Inspired by my mother's delicious meals, I developed this recipe. The fish is moist and flavorful, and the sauce is so good over rice. As I do when serving this dish, you'll get many compliments and recipe requests. —Winnie Higgins
Salisbury, Maryland

1 cup chopped onion
2 cans (4-1/4 ounces *each*) shrimp, rinsed
    and drained
1 jar (4-1/2 ounces) sliced mushrooms,
    drained
2 tablespoons butter
1/2 pound fresh cooked *or* canned crabmeat,
    drained and cartilage removed
8 sole *or* flounder fillets (2 to 2-1/2
    pounds)
1/2 teaspoon salt
1/4 teaspoon pepper
1/4 teaspoon paprika
    2 cans (10-3/4 ounces *each*) condensed
    cream of mushroom soup, undiluted
1/3 cup chicken broth
    2 tablespoons water
2/3 cup shredded cheddar cheese
    2 tablespoons minced fresh parsley
Cooked wild, brown *or* white rice *or* a
    mixture, optional

In a saucepan, saute onion, shrimp and mushrooms in butter until onion is tender. Add crabmeat; heat through. Sprinkle fillets with salt, pepper and paprika. Spoon crabmeat mixture on fillets; roll up and fasten with a toothpick. Place in a greased 13-in. x 9-in. x 2-in. baking dish.

Combine the soup, broth and water; blend until smooth. Pour over fillets. Sprinkle with cheese. Cover and bake at 400° for 30 minutes. Sprinkle with parsley; return to the oven, uncovered, for 5 minutes or until the fish flakes easily with a fork. Serve over rice if desired. **Yield:** 8 servings.

Tomato Pizza

My children liked to eat pizza with a lot of toppings, so I developed this recipe. With fresh tomatoes available year-round here, we still make it often, even though the kids are grown. It's a delightful change from the usual meat-topped pizza. —Lois McAtee
Oceanside, California

6 medium firm tomatoes, thinly sliced
1 large baked pizza crust (13 to 16 inches)
2 tablespoons olive oil
1 teaspoon salt
1 teaspoon pepper
1 can (2-1/4 ounces) sliced ripe olives, drained, optional
1/2 cup diced green pepper
1/2 cup diced onion
1 tablespoon chopped fresh basil
1 cup (4 ounces) shredded mozzarella cheese
1 cup (4 ounces) shredded cheddar cheese

Place tomato slices in a circle on crust, overlapping slightly until crust is completely covered. Drizzle with olive oil. Season with salt and pepper. Cover with olives if desired, green pepper and onion. Sprinkle basil over all. Cover with mozzarella and cheddar cheeses. Bake at 400° for 15 minutes or until cheese is melted. Serve immediately. **Yield:** 8 servings.

Recipe for: Meatless Spaghetti Sauce

When my tomatoes ripen, the first things I make are BLT's and this delicious homemade spaghetti sauce.
—Sondra Bergy, Lowell, Michigan

4 medium onions, chopped
1-1/4 teaspoons pepper
1/2 cup vegetable oil
4 garlic cloves, minced
12 cups chopped peeled fresh tomatoes
3 bay leaves
4 teaspoons salt
2 teaspoons dried oregano
1/2 teaspoon dried basil
2 cans (6 ounces *each*) tomato paste
1/3 cup packed brown sugar
Hot cooked pasta

In a large Dutch oven, saute the onions and pepper in oil until onions are tender. Add garlic, tomatoes, bay leaves, salt, oregano and basil. Simmer for 2 hours, stirring occasionally. Add tomato paste and brown sugar; simmer 1 hour longer. Remove bay leaves. Serve over pasta. **Yield:** 2 quarts.

Editor's Note: Browned ground beef or Italian sausage can be added to the cooked sauce if desired. The sauce also freezes well.

Tuna Burgers

These savory burgers are tasty inside and cook up golden brown and crispy on the outside. They're also simple and quick to make. Pair these burgers with a great-tasting, colorful salad that contains a mixture of crunchy, fresh ingredients. Not only is this sandwich inexpensive, it's also impressive to serve.
—Kim Stoller, Smithville, Ohio

    1 can (6 to 7 ounces) tuna, drained and flaked
  1/2 cup dry bread crumbs
  1/2 cup finely chopped celery
  1/3 cup mayonnaise
  1/4 cup finely chopped onion
    2 tablespoons chili sauce
    1 egg, beaten
    2 tablespoons butter
    4 hamburger buns, split and toasted
Lettuce, optional
Sliced tomatoes, optional

In a bowl, combine tuna, bread crumbs, celery, mayonnaise, onion, chili sauce and egg. Shape into four patties.

    Melt butter in a skillet; cook patties for about 4-5 minutes per side or until lightly browned. Serve on buns with lettuce and tomatoes if desired. **Yield:** 4 servings.

To me, nothing tasted as good as the cool water that came from the well on my grandparents' farm. A wooden bucket was lowered by a rope on a pulley, and when we pulled that bucket back up, we'd drink from a tin dipper.
      —Dorothy Elliott
      Orange, Texas

Sole in Herbed Butter

I often rely on seafood recipes for quick meals. This flavorful fish is easy to make and ready in minutes.
—Marilyn Paradis, Woodburn, Oregon

    4 tablespoons butter, softened
    1 teaspoon dill weed
  1/2 teaspoon onion powder
  1/2 teaspoon garlic powder
  1/2 teaspoon salt, optional
  1/4 teaspoon white pepper
    2 pounds sole fillets
Fresh dill and lemon wedges, optional

In a bowl, mix butter, dill, onion powder, garlic powder, salt if desired and pepper. Transfer to a skillet; heat on medium until melted.

    Add the sole and saute for several minutes on each side or until it flakes easily with a fork. Garnish with dill and lemon if desired. **Yield:** 6 servings.

Baked Lemon Haddock

Baked Lemon Haddock is my husband's favorite dish. I enjoy making it since it comes together quickly and is ready in 30 minutes.
—Jean Ann Perkins, Newburyport, Maryland

2 pounds haddock fillets
1 cup seasoned bread crumbs
1/4 cup butter, melted
2 tablespoons dried parsley flakes
2 teaspoons grated lemon peel
1/2 teaspoon garlic powder

Cut fish into serving-size pieces. Place in a greased 11-in. x 7-in. x 2-in. baking dish. Combine remaining ingredients; sprinkle over fish. Bake at 350° for 25 minutes or until fish flakes easily with a fork. **Yield:** 6 servings.

Grilled Salmon

We love to cook on the grill at our house. I've used this flavorful salmon recipe several times and we always enjoy it. The parsley, rosemary and green onions help make the tender fillets a tempting main dish that looks special.
—Monell Nuckols
Carpinteria, California

2 salmon fillets (about 1 pound *each*)
1/2 cup vegetable oil
1/2 cup lemon juice
4 green onions, thinly sliced
3 tablespoons minced fresh parsley
1-1/2 teaspoons minced fresh rosemary
or 1/2 teaspoon dried rosemary
1/2 teaspoon salt
1/8 teaspoon pepper

Place salmon in a shallow dish. Combine remaining ingredients and mix well. Set aside 1/4 cup for basting; pour the rest over the salmon. Cover and refrigerate for 30 minutes. Drain, discarding marinade.

Grill salmon over medium heat, skin side down, for 15-20 minutes or until fish flakes easily with a fork. Baste occasionally with reserved marinade. **Yield:** 4 servings.

Pan-Fried Trout

Nothing could be more easy or delicious than this wonderful trout.
—*Shirley Coleman*
Monkton, Vermont

2 eggs
8 trout fillets
2/3 cup grated Parmesan cheese
2 tablespoons vegetable oil

In a shallow bowl, beat eggs. Dip fillets in eggs, then dredge in the Parmesan cheese. Shake off excess. Heat oil in a large skillet over high heat; brown fillets lightly on both sides until fish flakes easily with a fork, about 5-7 minutes. **Yield: 4 servings.**

Grandmothers cook like artists paint, using what looks or feels right, instead of following exact directions. Learning to cook the "old way" is more than just passing family recipes from one generation to the next...it's like solder in a link of chain, connecting each new link to the last.
—*Loretta Baughan, Comstock Park, Michigan*

Catfish with Lemon-Butter Sauce

I created this recipe for a catfish cooking contest by modifying a recipe for shrimp and spaghetti, which I also developed.
—*Rita Futral*
Ocean Springs, Mississippi

3/4 cup butter
8 ounces fresh mushrooms, sliced
1 garlic clove, minced
1/2 cup chicken broth *or* dry white wine
2 tablespoons lemon juice
1/4 to 1/3 cup chopped fresh parsley
1 teaspoon salt
1/2 teaspoon pepper
1-1/2 pounds catfish fillets, cut into bite-size pieces
16 ounces spaghetti, cooked and drained
1/2 cup grated Parmesan cheese
Lemon slices *or* wedges, optional
Additional parsley, optional

In a large skillet, melt butter over medium heat. Cook mushrooms and garlic, stirring occasionally, for 5 minutes. Add broth or wine, lemon juice, parsley, salt and pepper; cook 3 minutes, stirring occasionally.

Add catfish; simmer, uncovered, for 6-8 minutes or until fish flakes easily with a fork. (Butter sauce will be thin.) Serve over spaghetti. Sprinkle with Parmesan cheese. Garnish with lemon and parsley if desired. **Yield: 6-8 servings.**

Curried Egg Salad

These hearty sandwiches make a satisfying and nutritious meal. They're also easy and quick to assemble for my family's supper when I get home after a full day of work. —Joyce McDowell, Winchester, Ohio

  1/2 cup mayonnaise
  1/2 teaspoon honey
  1/2 teaspoon ground curry
Dash ground ginger
    6 hard-cooked eggs, coarsely chopped
    3 green onions, sliced
    6 lettuce leaves
    6 slices whole wheat bread
Sliced tomato, optional

In a bowl, blend mayonnaise, honey, curry and ginger. Stir in eggs and green onions. Put one lettuce leaf on each slice of bread. Divide egg salad among bread slices and spread over lettuce to cover. Top with a tomato slice if desired. **Yield:** 6 servings.

Recipe for: **Tuna Dill Spread**

Dill adds spark to this creamy tuna spread. It's a nice alternative to traditional tuna salad.
—Geraldine Grisdale, Mt. Pleasant, Michigan

  1 can (6-1/8 ounces) tuna, drained and
    flaked
  1 package (3 ounces) cream cheese,
    softened
1/3 cup finely chopped seeded cucumber
  2 tablespoons lemon juice
  1 to 2 tablespoons minced fresh dill

1/2 teaspoon salt
1/4 teaspoon pepper

In a bowl, combine all ingredients; mix well. Use as sandwich filling or spread on crackers. **Yield:** 1-1/4 cups.

Cakes & Cheesecakes

At left: Luscious Almond Cheesecake (p. 165).

At right: Sandy's Chocolate Cake (p. 162).

Apple Walnut Cake

This moist cake is perfect for brunch. It gets its appeal from chunks of sweet apples, nutty flavor and creamy frosting. —Renae Moncur, Burley, Idaho

1-2/3 cups sugar
2 eggs
1/2 cup vegetable oil

2 teaspoons vanilla extract
2 cups all-purpose flour
2 teaspoons baking soda
1-1/2 teaspoons ground cinnamon
1 teaspoon salt
1/2 teaspoon ground nutmeg
4 cups chopped unpeeled apples
1 cup chopped walnuts
FROSTING:
2 packages (3 ounces *each*) cream cheese, softened
3 tablespoons butter, softened
1 teaspoon vanilla extract
1-1/2 cups confectioners' sugar

In a mixing bowl, beat sugar and eggs. Add oil and vanilla; mix well. Combine flour, baking soda, cinnamon, salt and nutmeg; gradually add to sugar mixture, mixing well. Stir in apples and walnuts. Pour into a greased and floured 13-in. x 9-in. x 2-in. baking pan. Bake at 350° for 50-55 minutes or until a toothpick inserted near the center comes out clean. Cool on a wire rack.

For frosting, beat cream cheese, butter and vanilla in a mixing bowl. Gradually add confectioners' sugar until the frosting has reached desired spreading consistency. Frost cooled cake. **Yield:** 16-20 servings.

Sandy's Chocolate Cake

(Pictured on page 161)

This velvety, rich cake won first place in the Greatest Cocoa Cake Contest at our state farm show.
—Sandy Johnson, Tioga, Pennsylvania

1 cup butter, softened
3 cups packed brown sugar
4 eggs
2 teaspoons vanilla extract
2-2/3 cups all-purpose flour
3/4 cup baking cocoa
1 tablespoon baking soda
1/2 teaspoon salt
1-1/3 cups sour cream
1-1/3 cups boiling water
FROSTING:
1/2 cup butter
3 squares (1 ounce *each*) unsweetened chocolate
3 squares (1 ounce *each*) semisweet chocolate

5 cups confectioners' sugar
1 cup (8 ounces) sour cream
2 teaspoons vanilla extract

In a mixing bowl, cream butter and brown sugar. Add eggs, one at a time, beating well after each addition. Beat on high speed until light and fluffy. Blend in vanilla.

Combine flour, cocoa, baking soda and salt; add alternately with sour cream to creamed mixture. Mix on low just until combined. Stir in water until blended. Pour into three greased and floured 9-in. round baking pans. Bake at 350° for 35 minutes or until a toothpick comes out clean. Cool in pans 10 minutes; remove to wire racks to cool completely.

For frosting, in a medium saucepan, melt butter and chocolate over low heat. Cool several minutes. In a mixing bowl, combine sugar, sour cream and vanilla. Add chocolate mixture and beat until smooth. Frost cooled cake. **Yield:** 12-14 servings.

Grandma's Favorites

Recipe for: Creamy Chocolate Cupcakes

The "surprise" inside these rich chocolate cupcakes is the smooth cream cheese filling.

—Mrs. Walter Jacobson, Ashland, Ohio

1-1/2 cups all-purpose flour
1 cup sugar
1/4 cup baking cocoa
1 teaspoon baking soda
1/2 teaspoon salt
2 eggs, lightly beaten
3/4 cup water
1/3 cup vegetable oil
1 tablespoon vinegar
1 teaspoon vanilla extract
FILLING:
1 package (8 ounces) cream cheese, softened
1/3 cup sugar
1 egg, lightly beaten
1/8 teaspoon salt
1 cup (6 ounces) semisweet chocolate chips
1 cup chopped walnuts

In a large mixing bowl, combine the dry ingredients. Add the eggs, water, oil, vinegar and vanilla; mix well. Pour into 18 greased or paper-lined muffin cups.

For filling, beat cream cheese and sugar in another mixing bowl. Add egg and salt; mix well. Fold in chocolate chips. Drop by tablespoonfuls into center of each cupcake. Sprinkle with nuts. Bake at 350° for 25-30 minutes. **Yield:** 1-1/2 dozen.

Pumpkin Raisin Cake

This nutty, golden cake is one of my mom's best. It's a wonderfully different use for pumpkin and looks beautiful dusted with sugar. —*Ruby Williams Bogalusa, Louisiana*

2 cups all-purpose flour
2 cups sugar
2 teaspoons pumpkin pie spice
2 teaspoons baking powder
1 teaspoon baking soda
1/2 teaspoon salt
4 eggs
1 can (16 ounces) pumpkin
3/4 cup vegetable oil
2 cups bran cereal (not flakes)
1 cup chopped pecans
1 cup raisins
Confectioners' sugar, optional

Combine flour, sugar, pumpkin pie spice, baking powder, baking soda and salt; set aside. In a large bowl, beat eggs. Add pumpkin and oil; stir in cereal just until moistened. Add dry ingredients and stir just until combined. Fold in pecans and raisins.

Pour into a greased 10-in. tube pan. Bake at 350° for 60-65 minutes or until a toothpick comes out clean. Cool in pan for 10 minutes before removing to a wire rack to cool completely. Dust with confectioners' sugar before serving if desired. **Yield:** 12-16 servings.

Pineapple Bundt Cake

Drizzled with a pretty lemon glaze, this firm-textured and fruity cake quickly gets noticed when I set it on the table. —Fayne Lutz, Taos, New Mexico

    1 cup butter, softened
1-1/2 cups sugar
    2 eggs, lightly beaten
    2 egg whites
    2 teaspoons lemon extract
2-2/3 cups all-purpose flour
    1 teaspoon baking powder
    1 can (8 ounces) crushed pineapple,
      undrained
GLAZE:
    1 cup confectioners' sugar

    1 to 2 tablespoons milk
1/2 teaspoon lemon extract

In a mixing bowl, cream butter and sugar. Add eggs, egg whites and extract; beat until fluffy, about 2 minutes. Combine flour and baking powder; gradually add to the creamed mixture. Stir in pineapple. Pour into a greased 10-in. fluted tube pan.

Bake at 350° for 55-60 minutes or until a toothpick inserted near the center comes out clean. Cool in pan 10 minutes before removing to a wire rack. Cool. In a small bowl, combine glaze ingredients until smooth. Drizzle over cake. **Yield:** 12-16 servings.

White Texas Sheet Cake

This cake gets better the longer it sits, so I try to make it a day ahead. My mother-in-law introduced this deliciously rich cake to me. With its creamy frosting and light almond flavor, no one can stop at just one piece! —Joanie Ward, Brownsburg, Indiana

    1 cup butter
    1 cup water
    2 cups all-purpose flour
    2 cups sugar
    2 eggs, beaten
1/2 cup sour cream
    1 teaspoon almond extract
    1 teaspoon salt
    1 teaspoon baking soda
FROSTING:
1/2 cup butter
1/4 cup milk
4-1/2 cups confectioners' sugar
1/2 teaspoon almond extract
    1 cup chopped walnuts

In a large saucepan, bring butter and water to a boil. Remove from the heat; stir in flour, sugar, eggs, sour cream, almond extract, salt and baking soda until smooth. Pour into a greased 15-in. x 10-in. x 1-in. baking pan. Bake at 375° for 20-22 minutes or until cake is golden brown and a toothpick inserted near the center comes out clean. Cool for 20 minutes.

Meanwhile, for frosting, combine butter and milk in a saucepan. Bring to a boil. Remove from the heat; add sugar and extract and mix well. Stir in walnuts; spread over warm cake. **Yield:** 16-20 servings.

Great-Grandma's Ginger Cake

This spicy, old-fashioned cake is wonderful with just about any meal. For the perfect finish, simply add a dollop of whipped topping. —Teresa Pelkey
Cherry Valley, Massachusetts

2-1/4 cups all-purpose flour
1 teaspoon baking soda
1 teaspoon ground ginger
1 teaspoon ground cinnamon
1/2 teaspoon salt
Dash ground cloves
1/2 cup sugar
1/2 cup shortening
2/3 cup molasses
1 egg, beaten
3/4 cup boiling water
Whipped topping

Combine flour, baking soda, ginger, cinnamon, salt and cloves; set aside. In a mixing bowl, cream sugar and shortening. Add molasses and egg; mix well. Stir in the dry ingredients alternately with water; mix well. Pour into a greased 9-in. square baking pan. Bake at 350° for 35-40 minutes or until a toothpick comes out clean. Cool completely. Cut into squares; top with a dollop of whipped topping. Leftovers will keep several days in an airtight container. **Yield:** 9 servings.

Recipe for: Luscious Almond Cheesecake

(Pictured on page 160)

I received this recipe along with a set of springform pans from a cousin at my wedding shower. It makes a heavenly cheesecake. —Brenda Clifford, Overland Park, Kansas

CRUST:
1-1/4 cups crushed vanilla wafers
3/4 cup finely chopped almonds
1/4 cup sugar
1/3 cup butter, melted
FILLING:
4 packages (8 ounces *each*) cream cheese, softened
1-1/4 cups sugar
4 eggs
1-1/2 teaspoons almond extract
1 teaspoon vanilla extract
TOPPING:
2 cups (16 ounces) sour cream
1/4 cup sugar
1 teaspoon vanilla extract
2 tablespoons toasted sliced almonds

In a bowl, combine wafers, almonds and sugar; add the butter and mix well. Press into the bottom of an ungreased 10-in. springform pan; set aside.

In a large mixing bowl, beat cream cheese and sugar until creamy. Add eggs, one at a time, beating well after each addition. Add extracts; beat just until blended. Pour into crust. Bake at 350° for 55 minutes or until center is almost set. Remove from the oven; let stand for 5 minutes.

Combine sour cream, sugar and vanilla; spread over filling. Return to the oven for 5 minutes. Cool on a wire rack; chill overnight. Just before serving, sprinkle with almonds and remove sides of pan. Store in the refrigerator. **Yield:** 14-16 servings.

Saucy Apple Cake

I found this recipe in a Midwestern cookbook. My friends and family consider it one of their favorite desserts. I like it because it's so easy to make. One delectable slice calls for another! —DeEtta Twedt
Mesa, Arizona

1 cup sugar
1/4 cup shortening
1 egg, lightly beaten
1 cup all-purpose flour
1 teaspoon baking soda
1/2 teaspoon ground cinnamon
1/4 teaspoon salt
2 cups shredded peeled tart apples
1/4 cup chopped walnuts
VANILLA SAUCE:
1 cup sugar
2 tablespoons cornstarch
1/2 cup half-and-half cream
1/2 cup butter
1-1/2 teaspoons vanilla extract

In a mixing bowl, cream sugar and shortening. Add egg and mix well. Add the dry ingredients; mix well. Fold in the apples and walnuts. Spread in a greased 8-in. square baking pan. Bake at 350° for 35-40 minutes or until a toothpick inserted near the center of cake comes out clean.

For sauce, combine sugar, cornstarch and cream in a saucepan. Bring to a boil over medium heat; boil for 2 minutes. Remove from the heat. Add butter and vanilla; stir until butter is melted. Serve warm over warm cake. **Yield:** 9 servings.

Recipe for: Pumpkin Sheet Cake

The pastor at our church usually cuts his message short on carry-in dinner days when he knows this sheet cake is waiting in the fellowship hall. (I think he prays for leftovers since he gets to take them home!) This moist cake travels well and is also easy to prepare. —Nancy Baker, Boonville, Missouri

1 can (16 ounces) pumpkin
2 cups sugar
1 cup vegetable oil
4 eggs, lightly beaten
2 cups all-purpose flour
2 teaspoons baking soda
1 teaspoon ground cinnamon
1/2 teaspoon salt
FROSTING:
1 package (3 ounces) cream cheese, softened
5 tablespoons butter, softened
1 teaspoon vanilla extract
1-3/4 cups confectioners' sugar
3 to 4 teaspoons milk
Chopped nuts

In a mixing bowl, beat pumpkin, sugar and oil. Add eggs; mix well. Combine flour, baking soda, cinnamon and salt; add to pumpkin mixture and beat until well blended. Pour into a greased 15-in. x 10-in. x 1-in. baking pan. Bake at 350° for 25-30 minutes or until a toothpick inserted near the center comes out clean. Cool.

For frosting, beat the cream cheese, butter and vanilla in a mixing bowl until smooth. Gradually add sugar; mix well. Add milk until frosting reaches desired spreading consistency. Frost cake. Sprinkle with nuts. **Yield:** 20-24 servings.

Grandma's Favorites

Chocolate Potato Cake

Potatoes are the secret ingredient in this moist, rich chocolate cake. —Jill Kinder, Richlands, Virginia

3/4 cup butter, softened
1-1/2 cups sugar, *divided*
4 eggs, *separated*
1 cup hot mashed *or* riced potatoes (no milk, butter or seasoning added)
1-1/2 cups all-purpose flour
1/2 cup baking cocoa
2 teaspoons baking powder
1 teaspoon ground cinnamon
1/2 teaspoon salt
1/2 teaspoon ground nutmeg
1/4 teaspoon ground cloves
1 cup milk
1 teaspoon vanilla extract
1 cup chopped nuts
FLUFFY WHITE FROSTING:
2 egg whites
1-1/2 cups sugar
1/3 cup water
2 teaspoons light corn syrup
1/8 teaspoon salt
1 teaspoon vanilla extract

In a mixing bowl, cream butter and 1 cup sugar. Add egg yolks; beat well. Set the egg whites aside. Add potatoes and mix thoroughly. Combine flour, cocoa, baking powder, cinnamon, salt, nutmeg and cloves; add to the creamed mixture alternately with milk, beating until smooth. Stir in vanilla and nuts.

In a mixing bowl, beat the reserved egg whites until foamy. Gradually add remaining sugar; beat until stiff peaks form. Fold into batter. Pour into a greased and floured 13-in. x 9-in. x 2-in. baking pan. Bake at 350° for 40-45 minutes or until a toothpick inserted near the center of cake comes out clean. Cool.

Combine first five frosting ingredients in top of a double boiler. Beat with electric mixer for 1 minute. Place over boiling water; beat constantly for 7 minutes, scraping sides of pan occasionally. Remove from heat. Add vanilla; beat 1 minute. Frost cake. **Yield:** 16-20 servings.

Editor's Note: Cake is moist and has a firm texture.

Citrus Cheesecake

Here's the perfect cheesecake for spring or for a special gathering any time of year. The rich, cookie-like crust and creamy filling make the zesty, citrus taste a wonderful surprise.
—Marcy Cella
L'Anse, Michigan

1 cup sifted all-purpose flour
1/4 cup sugar
1 teaspoon grated lemon peel
1/2 teaspoon vanilla extract
1 egg yolk
1/4 cup butter, softened
FILLING:
   5 packages (8 ounces *each*) cream cheese, softened
1-3/4 cups sugar

3 tablespoons all-purpose flour
1-1/2 teaspoons grated lemon peel
1-1/2 teaspoons grated orange peel
1/4 teaspoon vanilla extract
5 eggs
2 egg yolks
1/4 cup heavy whipping cream
TOPPING:
1-1/2 cups (12 ounces) sour cream
3 tablespoons sugar
1 teaspoon vanilla extract

In a bowl, combine flour, sugar, peel and vanilla. Make well; add yolk and butter. Mix with hands until ball is formed. Wrap with plastic wrap; chill at least 1 hour. Grease bottom and sides of a 9-in. springform pan. Remove sides. Divide dough in half. Between waxed paper, roll half of dough to fit bottom of pan. Peel off top paper; invert dough onto bottom of pan. Remove paper; trim dough to fit pan. Bake at 400° for 6-8 minutes or until lightly browned. Cool.

Divide remaining dough into thirds. Fold a piece of waxed paper in half; place one-third inside folded paper. Roll dough into 9-1/2- x 2-1/2-in. strip. Trim and patch as needed. Repeat with remaining dough to make two more strips. Tear away top layer of paper from strips. Put together pan with crust on bottom. Fit dough strips to side of pan, overlapping ends. Press ends of dough together; press sides of dough to bottom crust to seal. Chill.

Beat cream cheese, sugar, flour, peels and vanilla until mixed. Beat in eggs and yolks. Add cream; beat just until mixed. Pour into crust. Bake at 500° for 10 minutes. Reduce heat to 250°; bake 1 hour or until center is almost set. Cool slightly. Combine topping ingredients; spread over cake. Chill overnight. **Yield:** 12-16 servings.

Chocolate Almond Cake

The first time I baked this cake, I took it to a friend. She raved about it so much that I made one for us.
—Sherri Gentry, Dallas, Oregon

3/4 cup butter, softened
1-2/3 cups sugar
2 eggs
3/4 cup sour cream
1 teaspoon vanilla extract
1 teaspoon almond extract
2 cups all-purpose flour
2/3 cup baking cocoa
2 teaspoons baking soda
1/2 teaspoon salt
1 cup buttermilk
FROSTING:
5 tablespoons butter, softened
2-1/2 cups confectioners' sugar
1 teaspoon vanilla extract
1/2 teaspoon almond extract
3 to 4 tablespoons milk
Sliced almonds, toasted

In a large mixing bowl, cream butter and sugar. Add eggs, one at a time, beating well after each addition. Add sour cream and extracts; mix well. Combine flour, cocoa, baking soda and salt; add to the creamed mixture alternately with buttermilk. Pour into a greased 10-in. fluted tube pan. Bake at 350° for 50-55 minutes or until a toothpick comes out clean. Cool in pan for 10 minutes before removing to a wire rack.

For frosting, cream butter, sugar and extracts in a small mixing bowl until smooth. Add milk until frosting reaches desired spreading consistency. Frost cooled cake. Decorate with almonds. **Yield:** 12-16 servings.

Recipe for: Turtle Cheesecake

Our guests love this rich, delicious dessert. I like the fact that I can make it the day before and chill it overnight. Then I just add a garnish of nuts and whipped cream. —Jo Groth, Plainfield, Iowa

2 cups vanilla wafer crumbs
1/2 cup butter, melted
1 package (14 ounces) caramels
1 can (5 ounces) evaporated milk
2 cups chopped pecans, toasted, *divided*
4 packages (8 ounces *each*) cream cheese, softened
1 cup sugar
2 teaspoons vanilla extract
4 eggs
1 cup (6 ounces) semisweet chocolate chips, melted and slightly cooled
Whipped cream, optional

Combine crumbs and butter; blend well. Press into the bottom and 2 in. up the sides of a 10-in. springform pan. Bake at 350° for 8-10 minutes or until set; cool.

In a saucepan over low heat, melt caramels in milk, stirring until smooth. Cool 5 minutes. Pour into crust; top with 1-1/2 cups of pecans. In a mixing bowl, beat cream cheese until smooth. Add sugar and vanilla; mix well. Add eggs, one at a time, beating well after each addition. Add chocolate; mix just until blended. Carefully spread over pecans.

Bake at 350° for 55-65 minutes or until center is almost set. Cool to room temperature. Chill overnight. Garnish with remaining pecans and whipped cream if desired. **Yield:** 16 servings.

Golden Chocolate Cake

In our family, dessert is just as important as the main course. —*Kay Hansen, Escondido, California*

    1 package (18-1/4 ounces) yellow cake
      mix without pudding
    1 package (3.4 ounces) instant vanilla
      pudding mix

1/2 cup vegetable oil
1/2 cup water
  4 eggs
  1 cup (8 ounces) sour cream
  3 milk chocolate candy bars (1.55 ounces
    each), chopped
  1 cup (6 ounces) semisweet chocolate
    chips
  1 cup chopped pecans
  1 cup flaked coconut
Confectioners' sugar, optional

In a mixing bowl, combine cake and pudding mixes, oil, water and eggs; beat on low speed for about 30 seconds or until moistened. Beat 2 minutes on high. Blend in sour cream. Stir in candy bars, chocolate chips, nuts and coconut. Pour into a greased and floured 12-cup fluted tube pan.

Bake at 350° for 60-65 minutes or until a toothpick inserted near the center comes out clean. Cool in pan 15 minutes before removing to a wire rack. Cool completely. Chill before slicing. Dust with confectioners' sugar if desired. **Yield:** 12-16 servings.

Snowflake Cake

The coconut on this fluffy cake gives the impression of snow. —*Lynne Peterson, Salt Lake City, Utah*

    2 eggs plus 4 egg yolks
1-1/2 cups sugar
    1 cup milk
    1/2 cup butter
2-1/2 cups all-purpose flour
    1 tablespoon baking powder
    1 teaspoon vanilla extract
    1/2 cup chopped nuts, optional
FROSTING:
1-3/4 cups sugar
    1/2 cup water
      4 egg whites
    1/2 teaspoon cream of tartar
      1 teaspoon vanilla extract
      2 cups flaked coconut

In a mixing bowl, beat eggs, yolks and sugar until light and fluffy, about 5 minutes. In a saucepan, heat milk and butter until butter melts. Combine flour and baking powder; add to egg mixture alternately with milk mixture. Beat until well mixed. Add vanilla. Fold in chopped nuts if desired.

Pour into three greased 9-in. round baking pans. Bake at 350° for 15-18 minutes or until a toothpick comes out clean. Cool in pans 10 minutes before removing to a wire rack to cool completely.

For frosting, in a saucepan, bring sugar and water to a boil. Boil 3-4 minutes or until a candy thermometer reads 242° (firm-ball stage).

Meanwhile, beat egg whites and cream of tartar in a mixing bowl until foamy. Slowly pour in the hot sugar mixture and continue to beat on high for 6-8 minutes or until stiff peaks form. Add vanilla.

Frost the tops of two cake layers and sprinkle with coconut; stack on a cake plate with plain layer on top. Frost sides and top of cake; sprinkle with coconut. Refrigerate for several hours. **Yield:** 12-16 servings.

Recipe for: Decadent Fudge Cake

I don't know anyone who can resist the rich chocolate flavor of this attractive cake. Drizzled with white chocolate, it truly is a decadent dessert.
—Anna Hogge, Yorktown, Virginia

1 cup butter, softened
1-1/2 cups sugar
4 eggs
1 cup buttermilk
1/2 teaspoon baking soda
2-1/2 cups all-purpose flour
2 bars (4 ounces *each*) German sweet chocolate, melted
1 cup chocolate syrup
2 teaspoons vanilla extract
1-1/4 cups semisweet chocolate mini-morsels, *divided*
4 ounces white chocolate, chopped
2 tablespoons plus 1 teaspoon shortening, *divided*

Cream butter in a large mixing bowl. Gradually mix in sugar. Add eggs, one at a time, beating well after each addition. Combine buttermilk and baking soda; add to creamed mixture alternately with flour, beginning and ending with flour. Add melted chocolate, chocolate syrup and vanilla. Stir in 1 cup mini-morsels. Pour batter into a greased and floured 10-in. fluted tube pan.

Bake at 325° for 1 hour and 15 minutes or until a toothpick comes out clean. Immediately invert cake onto plate; cool completely. Meanwhile, combine white chocolate and 2 tablespoons shortening in top of double boiler. Bring water to a boil; reduce heat to low and cook until mixture is melted and smooth. Remove from heat and cool slightly; drizzle over cake.

Melt remaining mini-morsels and shortening in a small saucepan over low heat, stirring until smooth. Remove from heat; cool slightly. Drizzle over white chocolate. **Yield:** 12-16 servings.

Rhubarb Upside-Down Cake

I've baked this cake every spring for many years, and my family loves it! At potluck dinners it disappears quickly, drawing compliments even from those who normally don't care for rhubarb. —*Helen Breman Mattydale, New York*

TOPPING:
3 cups fresh rhubarb, cut into 1/2-inch slices
1 cup sugar
2 tablespoons all-purpose flour
1/4 teaspoon ground nutmeg
1/4 cup butter, melted
BATTER:
1-1/2 cups all-purpose flour
3/4 cup sugar
2 teaspoons baking powder
1/4 teaspoon salt
1/2 teaspoon ground nutmeg
1/4 cup butter, melted
2/3 cup milk
1 egg
Sweetened whipped cream, optional

Sprinkle rhubarb in a greased 10-in. heavy skillet. Combine sugar, flour and nutmeg; sprinkle over rhubarb. Drizzle with butter. For batter, combine flour, sugar, baking powder, salt and nutmeg in a mixing bowl. Add butter, milk and egg; beat until smooth. Spread over rhubarb mixture.

Bake at 350° for 35 minutes or until a toothpick inserted near the center comes out clean. Loosen edges immediately and invert onto serving dish. Serve warm, topped with whipped cream if desired. **Yield:** 8-10 servings.

Carrot Cake

(Pictured on front cover)

This wonderful recipe dates back to my great-grand-mother. —Debbie Jones, California, Maryland

2 cups all-purpose flour
2 cups sugar
1/2 teaspoon salt
1 teaspoon baking soda
2 teaspoons ground cinnamon
3 eggs
1-1/2 cups vegetable oil
2 cups finely grated carrots
1 teaspoon vanilla extract
1 cup well-drained crushed pineapple
1 cup flaked coconut
1 cup chopped nuts, *divided*

CREAM CHEESE FROSTING:
2 packages (3 ounces *each*) cream cheese, softened
3 cups confectioners' sugar
6 tablespoons butter, softened
1 teaspoon vanilla extract

In a mixing bowl, combine dry ingredients. Add eggs, oil, carrots and vanilla; beat until combined. Stir in pineapple, coconut and 1/2 cup nuts. Pour into a greased 13-in. x 9-in. x 2-in. baking pan. Bake at 350° for 50-60 minutes or until a toothpick comes out clean. Cool.

Combine frosting ingredients in a small bowl; mix until well blended. Frost cooled cake. Sprinkle with remaining nuts. Store in refrigerator. **Yield:** 12-16 servings.

Mocha Cupcakes

This recipe is one that I have called on over the years for numerous occasions—birthdays, PTA meetings, etc. Everyone likes it. —Lorna Smith
New Hazelton, British Columbia

1 cup boiling water
1 cup mayonnaise
1 teaspoon vanilla extract
2 cups all-purpose flour
1 cup sugar
1/2 cup baking cocoa
2 teaspoons baking soda
MOCHA FROSTING:
3/4 cup confectioners' sugar
1/4 cup baking cocoa
1/2 to 1 teaspoon instant coffee granules
Pinch salt
1-1/2 cups heavy whipping cream

In a mixing bowl, combine water, mayonnaise and vanilla. Combine flour, sugar, cocoa and baking soda; add to the mayonnaise mixture and beat until well mixed. Fill greased or paper-lined muffin cups two-thirds full. Bake at 350° for 20-25 minutes or until a toothpick inserted near the center comes out clean. Cool in tins 10 minutes; remove to wire racks and cool completely.

For frosting, combine sugar, cocoa, coffee and salt in a mixing bowl. Stir in cream; cover and chill with beaters for 30 minutes. Beat frosting until stiff peaks form. Frost the cupcakes. **Yield:** about 1-1/2 dozen.

To make a cake: Prepare batter and bake as directed for cupcakes, except use two greased 8-in. round baking pans. Frost between layers and sides and top of cake. Serves 12.

Editor's Note: Do not substitute reduced-fat or fat-free mayonnaise for regular mayonnaise.

Lemon Custard Pudding Cake

With its creamy lemon bottom layer topped by a light white cake, this recipe makes an excellent company dessert. It's a perfect finale to a big meal for family and guests, and it's not hard to make.
—Alberta McKay, Bartlesville, Oklahoma

    4 eggs, *separated*
1/3 cup lemon juice
    1 teaspoon grated lemon peel
    1 tablespoon butter, melted
1-1/2 cups sugar
    1/2 cup all-purpose flour
    1/2 teaspoon salt
1-1/2 cups milk
Whipped cream

In a mixing bowl, beat egg yolks until thick and lemon colored, about 5-8 minutes. Blend in lemon juice, peel and butter. Combine sugar, flour and salt; add alternately with milk, beating well after each addition. Beat egg whites until stiff; fold into batter. Pour into a 1-1/2-qt. baking dish; set in a pan of hot water. Bake at 350° about 50 minutes or until lightly browned. Serve warm topped with whipped cream. **Yield:** 8 servings.

Recipe for: Banana Nut Layer Cake

In our family, this cake is often requested as a birthday cake. Everyone loves the yummy banana flavor combined with a filling of crunchy nuts.
—Patsy Howard, Bakersfield, California

    1/2 cup shortening
    2 cups sugar
    1 egg plus 1 egg white
    1 cup buttermilk
    1 cup mashed ripe bananas
    2 cups all-purpose flour
    1 teaspoon baking soda
    1 teaspoon salt
    1 teaspoon vanilla extract
    1/2 cup chopped walnuts
FILLING:
    1/4 cup butter
    1/2 cup packed brown sugar
    1/4 cup all-purpose flour
Pinch salt
    3/4 cup milk
    1 egg yolk
    1 teaspoon vanilla extract
    1/2 cup chopped walnuts
Confectioners' sugar

In a mixing bowl, cream shortening and sugar. Beat in egg and egg white. Add buttermilk and bananas; mix well. Combine flour, baking soda and salt; stir into the creamed mixture. Add vanilla and nuts. Pour into two greased and floured 9-in. round baking pans. Bake at 350° for 35 minutes or until a toothpick comes out clean. Cool in pans 10 minutes before removing to a wire rack.

For filling, melt butter and brown sugar in a saucepan over medium heat. In a small bowl, combine flour and salt with a small amount of milk; stir until smooth. Add the remaining milk gradually. Add egg yolk and mix well; stir into saucepan. Cook and stir over medium heat until very thick, about 10 minutes. Add vanilla and nuts. Cool. Spread between cake layers. Dust with confectioners' sugar. Chill. Store in the refrigerator. **Yield:** 10-12 servings.

Orange Chiffon Cake

When I was a girl, I daydreamed about being the best wife, mother and homemaker. But it wasn't until a few years ago that I started entering our county fair. Since then, this cake has received several blue ribbons. —Marjorie Ebert, South Dayton, New York

2 cups all-purpose flour
1-1/2 cups sugar
4 teaspoons baking powder
1 teaspoon salt
6 eggs, *separated*
3/4 cup fresh orange juice
1/2 cup vegetable oil
2 tablespoons grated orange peel
1/2 teaspoon cream of tartar
ORANGE GLAZE:
1/2 cup butter
2 cups confectioners' sugar
2 to 4 tablespoons fresh orange juice
1/2 teaspoon grated orange peel

In a large mixing bowl, combine the first four ingredients. Add egg yolks, orange juice, oil and peel; beat until smooth, about 5 minutes. In another mixing bowl, beat egg whites and cream of tartar until stiff but not dry. Fold into orange mixture. Spoon into an ungreased 10-in. tube pan.

Bake at 350° for 45-50 minutes or until a toothpick inserted in cake comes out clean. Immediately invert pan to cool. When cool, remove cake from the pan.

For glaze, melt butter in a small saucepan; add remaining ingredients. Stir until smooth. Pour over top of cake, allowing it to drizzle down sides. **Yield:** 16 servings.

Recipe for: Lemon Orange Cake

I love to bake this lovely three-layer cake instead of a more traditional pie for Thanksgiving. It has that tangy Florida citrus flavor we can't resist. —Norma Poole, Auburndale, Florida

1 cup butter, softened
1/4 cup shortening
2 cups sugar
5 eggs
3 cups all-purpose flour
1 teaspoon baking powder
1/2 teaspoon baking soda
1/2 teaspoon salt
1 cup buttermilk
1 teaspoon vanilla extract
1/2 teaspoon lemon extract
FROSTING:
1/2 cup butter, softened
3 tablespoons orange juice
3 tablespoons lemon juice
1 to 2 tablespoons grated orange peel
1 to 2 tablespoons grated lemon peel
1 teaspoon lemon extract
5-1/2 to 6 cups confectioners' sugar

In a mixing bowl, cream butter, shortening and sugar until light and fluffy. Add eggs, one at a time, beating well after each addition. Combine dry ingredients; add to creamed mixture alternately with buttermilk, beginning and ending with dry ingredients. Stir in extracts.

Pour into three greased and floured 9-in. baking pans. Bake at 350° for 25-30 minutes or until a toothpick inserted in center of cake comes out clean. Cool for 10 minutes in pans before removing to wire racks to cool completely.

For frosting, beat butter in a mixing bowl until fluffy; add the next five ingredients and mix well. Gradually add confectioners' sugar; beat until frosting has desired spreading consistency. Spread between layers and over the top and sides of cake. **Yield:** 10-12 servings.

Spicy Applesauce Cake

A "picnic perfect" dessert, this moist delicious cake travels and slices very well. With chocolate chips, walnuts and raisins, it's a real crowd-pleaser.
—Marian Platt, Sequim, Washington

 2 cups all-purpose flour
1-1/2 cups sugar
 1 tablespoon baking cocoa
1-1/2 teaspoons baking soda
 1 teaspoon *each* ground cinnamon,
  nutmeg, allspice and cloves
 1 teaspoon salt
 1/2 cup shortening
 2 cups applesauce
 2 eggs, lightly beaten
 1/2 cup semisweet chocolate chips
 1/2 cup chopped walnuts
 1 cup raisins
TOPPING:
 1/2 cup semisweet chocolate chips
 1/2 cup chopped walnuts
 2 tablespoons brown sugar

In a mixing bowl, combine dry ingredients. Add shortening, applesauce and eggs; beat until well mixed. Stir in chocolate chips, walnuts and raisins.

Pour into a greased 13-in. x 9-in. x 2-in. baking pan. Combine topping ingredients and sprinkle over batter. Bake at 350° for 35-40 minutes or until a toothpick inserted in center of cake comes out clean. **Yield:** 20-24 servings.

Pumpkin Cheesecake

When I was young, we produced several ingredients for this longtime favorite right on our farm. We raised pumpkins and made butter and sour cream.
—Evonne Wurmnest, Normal, Illinois

CRUST:
 1 cup graham cracker crumbs
 1 tablespoon sugar
 4 tablespoons butter, melted
FILLING:
 2 packages (8 ounces *each*) cream cheese,
  softened
 3/4 cup sugar
 1 can (16 ounces) pumpkin
1-1/4 teaspoons ground cinnamon
 1/2 teaspoon ground ginger
 1/2 teaspoon ground nutmeg
 1/4 teaspoon salt
 2 eggs
TOPPING:
 2 cups (16 ounces) sour cream
 2 tablespoons sugar
 1 teaspoon vanilla extract
 12 to 16 pecan halves

Combine crust ingredients. Press into bottom of a 9-in. springform pan; chill. For filling, beat cream cheese and sugar in a large mixing bowl until well blended. Beat in pumpkin, spices and salt. Add eggs, one at a time, beating well after each. Pour into the crust. Bake at 350° for 50 minutes or until center is almost set.

Meanwhile, for topping, combine sour cream, sugar and vanilla. Spread over filling; return to the oven for 5 minutes. Cool on rack; chill overnight. Garnish each slice with a pecan half. **Yield:** 12-16 servings.

Pies

At left: Mom's Peach Pie (p. 178).

At right: Fluffy Cranberry Cheese Pie (p. 180).

Citrus Cranberry Pie

With a lattice top, this ruby-red pie showcases abundant fall cranberries and adds a twist of citrus. A dollop of homemade orange cream complements the slightly tart flavor.

Pastry for double-crust pie (9 inches)
3-1/2 cups fresh *or* frozen cranberries
   1 small navel orange, peeled, sectioned
     and chopped
   1 cup sugar
   2 tablespoons butter, melted
4-1/2 teaspoons all-purpose flour
   2 teaspoons grated lemon peel
   1 teaspoon grated orange peel
  1/4 teaspoon salt
   1 egg, lightly beaten
Additional sugar
ORANGE CREAM:
   1 cup heavy whipping cream
   1 tablespoon sugar
   2 teaspoons grated orange peel
   1 teaspoon orange extract

Line a 9-in. pie plate with bottom pastry; trim pastry even with edge of plate. In a bowl, combine the cranberries, orange, sugar, butter, flour, lemon and orange peel and salt. Pour into pastry shell.

Roll out remaining pastry; make a lattice crust. Trim, seal and flute edges. Brush lattice crust with egg. Sprinkle with additional sugar. Cover edges loosely with foil. Bake at 450° for 10 minutes. Reduce heat to 350° and remove foil. Bake 40-45 minutes longer or until golden brown.

Meanwhile, in a mixing bowl, beat cream until it begins to thicken. Add the sugar, orange peel and extract; beat until stiff peaks form. Cover and refrigerate. Serve with warm pie. **Yield:** 6-8 servings.

Mom's Peach Pie

(Pictured on page 176)

A delightful summertime pie, this dessert is overflowing with fresh peach flavor. Each sweet slice is packed with old-fashioned appeal. The streusel topping makes this pie a little different than the ordinary and adds homemade flair. —Sally Holbrook
Pasadena, California

   1 egg white
   1 unbaked pastry shell (9 inches)
3/4 cup all-purpose flour
1/2 cup packed brown sugar
1/3 cup sugar
1/4 cup cold butter, cut into 6 pieces
   6 cups sliced peeled fresh peaches

Beat egg white until foamy; brush over the bottom and sides of the pastry. In a small bowl, combine flour and sugars; cut in butter until mixture resembles fine crumbs.

Sprinkle two-thirds into the bottom of the pastry; top with peaches. Sprinkle with remaining crumb mixture. Bake at 375° for 40-45 minutes or until filling is bubbly and peaches are tender. **Yield:** 6-8 servings.

Recipe for: Freezer Pumpkin Pie

This wonderful do-ahead dessert puts a cool twist on a traditional favorite. Ground gingersnaps and pecans form the delicious baked crust for this pie's pumpkin and ice cream filling.

—Vera Reid
Laramie, Wyoming

    1 cup ground pecans
1/2 cup ground gingersnaps
1/4 cup sugar
1/4 cup butter, softened
FILLING:
    1 cup canned pumpkin
1/2 cup packed brown sugar
1/2 teaspoon salt
1/2 teaspoon ground cinnamon
1/2 teaspoon ground ginger
1/4 teaspoon ground nutmeg
    1 quart vanilla ice cream, softened
      slightly

In a bowl, combine the pecans, gingersnaps, sugar and butter; mix well. Press into a 9-in. pie pan; bake at 450° for 5 minutes. Cool completely.

In a mixing bowl, beat first six filling ingredients. Stir in ice cream and mix until well blended. Spoon into crust. Freeze until firm, at least 2-3 hours. Store in freezer. **Yield:** 6-8 servings.

Cookie Sheet Apple Pie

I belong to several volunteer service groups, and this dessert has been a real time-saver when there's a large crowd to be fed.

—Bertha Jeffries
Great Falls, Montana

3-3/4 cups all-purpose flour
1-1/2 teaspoons salt
  3/4 cup shortening
    3 eggs, lightly beaten
  1/3 cup milk
    8 cups sliced peeled tart apples
1-1/2 cups sugar
    1 teaspoon ground cinnamon
1/2 teaspoon ground nutmeg
    1 cup crushed cornflakes
    1 egg white, beaten

In a bowl, combine flour and salt. Cut in shortening until mixture resembles coarse crumbs. Add eggs and milk; mix to form dough. Chill for 20 minutes.

Divide dough in half; roll one half to fit the bottom and sides of a greased 15-in. x 10-in. x 1-in. baking pan. Arrange apples over crust. Combine sugar, cinnamon, nutmeg and cornflakes; sprinkle over apples. Roll remaining dough to fit top of pan and place over apples. Seal edges; cut slits in top. Brush with egg white. Bake at 400° for 15 minutes. Reduce heat to 350°; bake for 25-30 minutes or until golden. **Yield:** 16-20 servings.

Fluffy Cranberry Cheese Pie

(Pictured on page 177)

This pie has a light texture and zippy flavor that matches its vibrant color. It's festive for the holidays or anytime, and easy because you make it ahead.
—Mary Parkonen, W. Wareham, Massachusetts

CRANBERRY TOPPING:
- 1 package (3 ounces) raspberry gelatin
- 1/3 cup sugar
- 1-1/4 cups cranberry juice
- 1 can (8 ounces) jellied cranberry sauce

FILLING:
- 1 package (3 ounces) cream cheese, softened
- 1/4 cup sugar
- 1 tablespoon milk
- 1 teaspoon vanilla extract
- 1/2 cup frozen whipped topping, thawed
- 1 pastry shell (9 inches), baked

In a mixing bowl, combine gelatin and sugar; set aside. In a saucepan, bring cranberry juice to a boil. Remove from the heat and pour over gelatin mixture, stirring to dissolve. Stir in the cranberry sauce. Chill until slightly thickened.

Meanwhile, in another mixing bowl, beat cream cheese, sugar, milk and vanilla until fluffy. Fold in the whipped topping. Spread evenly into pie shell. Beat cranberry topping until frothy; pour over filling. Chill overnight. **Yield:** 6-8 servings.

Candy Apple Pie

This is the only apple pie my husband will eat, but that's all right since he makes it as often as I do. Like a combination of apple and pecan pie, it's a sweet treat that usually tops off our holiday meals from New Year's all the way through to Christmas!
—Cindy Kleweno, Burlington, Colorado

- 6 cups thinly sliced peeled tart apples
- 2 tablespoons lime juice
- 3/4 cup sugar
- 1/4 cup all-purpose flour
- 1/2 teaspoon ground cinnamon *or* nutmeg
- 1/4 teaspoon salt
- Pastry for double-crust pie (9 inches)
- 2 tablespoons butter

TOPPING:
- 1/4 cup butter
- 1/2 cup packed brown sugar
- 2 tablespoons heavy whipping cream
- 1/2 cup chopped pecans

In a large bowl, toss apples with lime juice. Combine dry ingredients; add to the apples and toss lightly. Place bottom pastry in a 9-in. pie plate; fill with apple mixture. Dot with butter. Cover with top crust. Flute edges high; cut steam vents. Bake at 400° for 40-45 minutes or until golden brown and apples are tender.

Meanwhile, for topping, melt butter in a small saucepan. Stir in brown sugar and cream; bring to a boil, stirring constantly. Remove from the heat and stir in pecans. Pour over top crust. Return to the oven for 3-4 minutes or until bubbly. Serve warm. **Yield:** 8 servings.

Peanut Butter Pie

I entered this pie in our county fair, and it was selected Grand Champion. It's hard to resist the tempting chocolate crumb crust and creamy filling with big peanut butter taste. Be prepared to take an empty pan home when you serve this pie. —Doris Doherty
Albany, Oregon

CRUST:
1-1/4 cups chocolate cookie crumbs
    (20 cookies)
1/4 cup sugar
1/4 cup butter, melted
FILLING:
1 package (8 ounces) cream cheese,
    softened
1 cup creamy peanut butter
1 cup sugar
1 tablespoon butter, softened
1 teaspoon vanilla extract
1 cup heavy whipping cream, whipped
Grated chocolate *or* chocolate cookie
  crumbs, optional

Combine crust ingredients; press into a 9-in. pie plate. Bake at 375° for 10 minutes. Cool.

In a mixing bowl, beat cream cheese, peanut butter, sugar, butter and vanilla until smooth. Fold in whipped cream. Gently spoon into crust. Garnish with chocolate or cookie crumbs if desired. Refrigerate. **Yield:** 8-10 servings.

Recipe for: Lemon Blueberry Pie

When blueberries are in season, I try to find every way possible to enjoy them. This tart delicious pie is one of my favorites.
—Patricia Kile, Greentown, Pennsylvania

6 eggs, lightly beaten
1 cup sugar
1/2 cup butter
1/3 cup fresh lemon juice
2 teaspoons grated lemon peel
1 pastry shell (9 inches), baked
3 cups fresh blueberries
1/3 cup sugar
1/4 cup orange juice
1 tablespoon cornstarch

In a saucepan, combine eggs, sugar, butter, lemon juice and peel; cook, stirring constantly, over medium-low heat until mixture thickens, about 20 minutes. Cool for 20 minutes, stirring occasionally. Pour into pie shell.

In a saucepan, toss blueberries and sugar. Mix orange juice and cornstarch; add to blueberries. Cook over medium heat until mixture comes to a boil, about 8 minutes, stirring gently. Cook 2 minutes longer. Cool for 15 minutes, stirring occasionally. Spoon over lemon layer. Chill for 4-6 hours. **Yield:** 8 servings.

Coconut-Pecan Pie

I grew up on a farm with lots of pecan trees and have always had plenty of nuts to use for recipes.
—Barbara Ann McKenzie, Keytesville, Missouri

>   3 eggs
> 1-1/2 cups sugar
>   1/2 cup butter, melted
>   2 teaspoons lemon juice
>   1 teaspoon vanilla extract
> 1-1/4 cups flaked coconut
>   1/2 cup coarsely chopped pecans
>   1 unbaked pastry shell (9 inches)

In a mixing bowl, beat eggs. Add sugar, butter, lemon juice and vanilla; mix well. Stir in coconut and pecans; pour into pie shell. Bake at 350° for 45-50 minutes or until set. Cool completely. Store in the refrigerator. **Yield:** 6-8 servings.

Recipe for: Creamy Pineapple Pie

I'm often asked for the recipe for my creamy coconut-topped pie when I bring it to work or serve it at get-togethers. I use fresh pineapple, but you can also use canned pineapple for this refreshing treat. In our family, it's a special favorite.
—Bonnie Sandlin, Lakeland, Florida

>   1/4 cup sugar
>   3 tablespoons cornstarch
> 1-1/3 cups pineapple juice
>   1 egg yolk
>   2 cups fresh pineapple chunks
>   (1/2-inch pieces)
>   1 pastry shell (9 inches), baked
>   1/4 cup flaked coconut, toasted

In a saucepan, combine sugar and cornstarch. Add pineapple juice; bring to a boil, stirring occasionally. Boil for 2 minutes.

In a small bowl, beat egg yolk; stir in 1/4 cup of the hot mixture. Return all to pan; cook and stir for 1 minute. Remove from the heat; stir in pineapple. Pour into crust. Chill for 2 hours or until firm. Store in the refrigerator. Sprinkle with coconut just before serving. **Yield:** 6-8 servings.

Editor's Note: Canned pineapple can be substituted for fresh. Use one 20-ounce can and one 8-ounce can of pineapple tidbits. Drain, reserving juice. Add additional pineapple juice if necessary to equal 1-1/3 cups. Prepare recipe as directed.

Cran-Raspberry Pie

Jewel-toned fruits team up to pack this pretty pie with festive flavor. The dessert is one our four grown children especially enjoy when they come home for family holiday meals.
—Verona Koehlmoos
Pilger, Nebraska

> 2 cups chopped fresh *or* frozen
>   cranberries
> 1 package (12 ounces) frozen
>   unsweetened raspberries
> 1-1/2 cups sugar
> 2 tablespoons quick-cooking tapioca
> 1/2 teaspoon almond extract
> 1/4 teaspoon salt
> **Pastry for double-crust pie (9 inches)**

In a bowl, gently stir cranberries, raspberries, sugar, tapioca, extract and salt. Line pie plate with bottom pastry; add filling. Top with a lattice crust. Bake at 375° for 15 minutes. Reduce heat to 350° and bake 35-40 minutes more or until bubbly. **Yield:** 6-8 servings.

Sky-High Strawberry Pie

This pie is my specialty. It's fairly simple to make but so dramatic to serve. The ultimate taste of spring, this luscious pie has a big, fresh berry taste. I've had many requests to bring it to gatherings.
—Janet Mooberry, Peoria, Illinois

> 3 quarts fresh strawberries, *divided*
> 1-1/2 cups sugar
> 6 tablespoons cornstarch
> 2/3 cup water
> **Red food coloring, optional**
> 1 deep-dish pastry shell (10 inches),
>   baked
> 1 cup heavy whipping cream
> 1-1/2 tablespoons instant vanilla pudding
>   mix

In a large bowl, mash enough berries to equal 3 cups. In a saucepan, combine the sugar and cornstarch. Stir in the mashed berries and water; mix well. Bring to a boil over medium heat, stirring constantly. Cook and stir for 2 minutes.

Remove from the heat; add food coloring if desired. Pour into a large bowl. Chill for 20 minutes, stirring occasionally, until mixture is just slightly warm. Fold in the remaining berries. Pile into pie shell. Chill for 2-3 hours.

In a small mixing bowl, whip cream until soft peaks form. Sprinkle pudding mix over cream and whip until stiff. Pipe around edge of pie or dollop on individual slices. **Yield:** 8-10 servings.

Pecan Fudge Pie

This fudgy pie is the perfect showcase for crunchy pecans. It's a special chocolaty twist on traditional pecan pie, and one slice goes a long way. Top each piece with a dollop of whipped cream, and you won't wait long for compliments!
—Jacquelyn Smith, Soperton, Georgia

1-1/4 cups light corn syrup
1/2 cup sugar
1/3 cup baking cocoa
1/3 cup all-purpose flour
1/4 teaspoon salt
   3 eggs
   3 tablespoons butter, softened
1-1/2 teaspoons vanilla extract
   1 cup chopped pecans
   1 unbaked pastry shell (9 inches)
Whipped cream, optional

In a large mixing bowl, beat the first eight ingredients until smooth. Stir in nuts; pour into pie shell. Bake at 350° for 55-60 minutes or until set. Cool completely. Garnish with whipped cream if desired. **Yield:** 6-8 servings.

Old-Fashioned Raisin Pie

My family came to Texas from Virginia after the Civil War. Two brothers helped drive a herd of cattle up the Chisholm Trail to Kansas, and they decided to stay in Kansas and open a meat market. One brother sent for his girlfriend back in Texas to come and marry him. She did, and she brought this recipe. The family has been making this pie ever since.
—Debra Ayers, Cheyenne, Wyoming

   2 eggs
   1 cup (8 ounces) sour cream
   2 cups raisins
   1 cup packed brown sugar
   1 teaspoon ground cinnamon
1/2 teaspoon ground nutmeg
1/4 teaspoon salt
Pastry for double-crust pie (9 inches)
Additional nutmeg, optional

In a bowl, beat eggs. Add sour cream. Stir in raisins, brown sugar, cinnamon, nutmeg and salt. Place bottom pastry in a pie plate; pour in filling. Top with a lattice crust.

Bake at 450° for 10 minutes. Reduce the heat to 350°; bake for about 25 minutes more or until filling is set. If desired, sprinkle with nutmeg. **Yield:** 8 servings.

Sour Cream Apple Pie

A cool, creamy version of the original, this delicious dessert is the perfect finish to a summer meal. Its crumbly topping and smooth apple filling are real crowd-pleasers. Be prepared to serve seconds!
—Sharon Bickett, Chester, South Carolina

        2 eggs
        1 cup (8 ounces) sour cream
        1 cup sugar
        6 tablespoons all-purpose flour, ***divided***
        1 teaspoon vanilla extract
    1/4 teaspoon salt
        3 cups chopped peeled tart apples
        1 unbaked pie shell (9 inches)
    1/4 cup packed brown sugar
        3 tablespoons cold butter

In a large bowl, beat eggs. Add sour cream. Stir in sugar, 2 tablespoons flour, vanilla and salt; mix well. Stir in apples. Pour into pie shell. Bake at 375° for 15 minutes.

Meanwhile, combine brown sugar and remaining flour; cut in butter until mixture is crumbly. Sprinkle over top of pie. Return to oven for 20-25 minutes or until filling is set. Cool completely on a wire rack. Serve or cover and refrigerate. **Yield:** 8 servings.

Recipe for: Four-Fruit Pie

My husband likes this fruity combination almost as much as traditional apple pie—and that's saying something! I keep rhubarb, blueberries and raspberries in the freezer and always have apples on hand for this colorful dessert.
—Joan Rose, Langley, British Columbia

        1 cup sliced rhubarb (1-inch pieces)
        1 cup chopped peeled apple
        1 cup blueberries
        1 cup raspberries
        1 teaspoon lemon juice
    3/4 cup sugar
    1/4 cup all-purpose flour
    Pastry for double-crust pie (9 inches)
        2 tablespoons butter
    Additional sugar, optional

In a large bowl, gently toss rhubarb, apple, berries and lemon juice. Combine sugar and flour; stir into the fruit and let stand for 30 minutes. Line a pie plate with bottom crust. Add filling; dot with butter. Roll out remaining pastry to fit top of pie; cut slits in top. Place over filling. Seal and flute edges.

Bake at 400° for 50-60 minutes or until crust is golden brown and filling is bubbly. Sprinkle with sugar if desired. **Yield:** 6-8 servings.

Raspberry Ribbon Pie

While he was growing up, this was my husband's favorite Christmas dessert. When we married, his mother passed it on to me. I take it to family gatherings during the holidays and have yet to bring any home! It's a cool recipe for summer as well.
—Victoria Newman, Antelope, California

2 packages (3 ounces *each*) cream cheese, softened
1/2 cup confectioners' sugar
Dash salt
1 cup heavy whipping cream, whipped
1 pastry shell with high fluted edge (9 inches), baked
1 package (3 ounces) raspberry gelatin
1-1/4 cups boiling water
1 tablespoon lemon juice
1 package (10 ounces) frozen raspberries in syrup, thawed

In a mixing bowl, beat the cream cheese, sugar and salt until light and fluffy. Fold in cream. Spread half into pie shell. Chill 30 minutes.

Meanwhile, dissolve gelatin in water; add lemon juice and raspberries. Carefully spoon half over the cream cheese layer. Chill until set, about 30 minutes.

Set aside the remaining gelatin mixture at room temperature. Carefully spread remaining cream cheese mixture over top of pie. Chill 30 minutes. Top with remaining gelatin. Chill until firm. **Yield:** 6-8 servings.

Granny would roll out her pie crusts into thin layers, and she'd always poke a hole in the middle of one of the smaller crusts. Then she'd bake them until they were light brown and crisp. When they cooled, she'd spread jelly on the crust with the hole. I stood in her kitchen with my chin on the counter and my mouth watering—I could hardly wait for that special treat she made just for me! —Sherrie Callison, Cabot, Arkansas

---

Fall Pear Pie

A wide slice of this festive fruity pie is a great end to a delicious meal. The mellow flavor of pears is a refreshing alternative to the more common pies for the holidays. It's nice to serve a dessert that's a little unexpected. —Ken Churches, San Andreas, California

8 cups thinly sliced peeled pears
3/4 cup sugar
1/4 cup quick-cooking tapioca
1/4 teaspoon ground nutmeg
Pastry for double-crust pie (9 inches)

1 egg, lightly beaten
1/4 cup heavy whipping cream, optional

In a large bowl, combine pears, sugar, tapioca and nutmeg. Line a pie plate with bottom crust; add pear mixture. Roll out remaining pastry to fit top of pie; cut large slits in top. Place over filling; seal and flute edges. Brush with egg.

Bake at 375° for 55-60 minutes or until the pears are tender. Remove to a wire rack. Pour cream through slits if desired. **Yield:** 8 servings.

Grandma's Favorites

Recipe for: *Peach Cream Pie*

This yummy pie is especially good when fresh peaches are in season. The sour cream filling and cinnamon crumb topping complement the fruit flavor.
—Denise Goedeken, Platte Center, Nebraska

1-1/2 cups all-purpose flour
1/2 teaspoon salt
1/2 cup butter
FILLING:
    4 cups fresh *or* frozen unsweetened
      sliced peaches
    1 cup sugar, *divided*
    2 tablespoons all-purpose flour
    1 egg
1/2 teaspoon vanilla extract
1/4 teaspoon salt
    1 cup (8 ounces) sour cream
TOPPING:
1/3 cup sugar
1/3 cup all-purpose flour
    1 teaspoon ground cinnamon
1/4 cup butter

Combine flour and salt; cut in butter until crumbly. Press into a 9-in. pie plate. Place peaches in a bowl; sprinkle with 1/4 cup sugar. Combine flour, egg, vanilla, salt and remaining sugar; fold in sour cream. Stir into peaches; pour into the crust. Bake at 400° for 15 minutes. Reduce heat to 350°; bake for 20 minutes.

For topping, combine sugar, flour and cinnamon in a small bowl; cut in butter until crumbly. Sprinkle over the pie. Return oven temperature to 400°; bake 15 minutes longer. Cool. **Yield:** 6-8 servings.

Strawberry-Pecan Pie

I stock up on locally grown berries for treats like this pie, which pairs them with pecans. I received a ribbon from the Strawberry Festival food show at near-by Poteet. —Becky Duncan, Leming, Texas

1-1/2 cups sugar
  1/4 cup all-purpose flour
    1 teaspoon ground nutmeg
    1 teaspoon ground cinnamon
    2 cups chopped fresh strawberries
    1 cup chopped pecans
Pastry for double-crust pie (9 inches)
    1 to 2 tablespoons butter

In a bowl, combine sugar, flour, nutmeg and cinnamon. Add strawberries and pecans; toss gently. Line pie plate with bottom crust. Add filling; dot with butter. Top with a lattice crust. Bake at 375° for 50 minutes or until crust is golden brown and filling is bubbly. **Yield:** 6-8 servings.

Golden Apricot Pie

This wonderful pie is full of apricot flavor and so pretty. The fruit's golden-orange color shows through the lattice top. —Jo Marin, Patterson, California

> 2 packages (6 ounces *each*) dried apricots
> 2-3/4 cups water
> Pastry for double-crust pie (9 inches)
> 1 cup sugar
> 3 tablespoons cornstarch
> 1/8 teaspoon nutmeg
> 1 tablespoon butter

In a saucepan, combine apricots and water; bring to a boil. Reduce heat and simmer for 20-22 minutes. Remove from the heat; cool. Place bottom pastry in a 9-in. pie plate. Drain apricots, reserving 3/4 cup liquid. Arrange apricots in the pie shell.

Combine sugar, cornstarch, nutmeg and reserved apricot liquid; mix well. Pour over apricots; dot with butter. Top with a lattice crust. Bake at 400° for 50-55 minutes or until crust is golden brown and filling is bubbly. **Yield:** 8 servings.

Creamy Banana Pie

Everyone who tastes this delectable pie enjoys its delicious old-fashioned flavor and creamy filling. It's a yummy ending to just about any meal. —Rita Pribyl Indianapolis, Indiana

> 1 envelope unflavored gelatin
> 1/4 cup cold water
> 3/4 cup sugar
> 1/4 cup cornstarch
> 1/2 teaspoon salt

> 2-3/4 cups milk
> 4 egg yolks, beaten
> 2 tablespoons butter
> 1 tablespoon vanilla extract
> 4 medium firm bananas
> 1 cup heavy cream, whipped
> 1 pastry shell (10 inches), baked
> Juice and grated peel of 1 lemon
> 1/2 cup apple jelly

Soften gelatin in cold water; set aside. In a saucepan, combine sugar, cornstarch and salt. Blend in the milk and egg yolks; cook over low heat, stirring constantly, until thickened and bubbly, about 20-25 minutes.

Remove from the heat; stir in softened gelatin until dissolved. Stir in butter and vanilla. Cover the surface of custard with plastic wrap and chill until no longer warm. Slice 3 bananas; fold into custard with whipped cream. Spoon into pie shell. Chill until set, about 4-5 hours.

Shortly before serving, place lemon juice in a small bowl and slice the remaining banana into it. Melt jelly in a saucepan over low heat. Drain banana; pat dry and arrange on top of pie. Brush banana with the jelly. Sprinkle with grated lemon peel. Serve immediately. **Yield:** 8 servings.

Editor's Note: The filling is very light in color. It is not topped with additional whipped cream.

Cherry Pie

A slice of this pretty cherry pie is a delicious traditional treat. —Frances Poste, Wall, South Dakota

PASTRY:
1-1/2 cups all-purpose flour
  1/2 teaspoon salt
  1/2 cup shortening
  1/4 cup ice water
FILLING:
    2 cans (16 ounces *each*) tart cherries
    1 cup sugar
    3 tablespoons quick-cooking tapioca
    1/4 teaspoon almond extract
    1/4 teaspoon salt
Red food coloring, optional
    1 tablespoon butter

In a bowl, combine flour and salt; cut in shortening until crumbly. Gradually add water, tossing with a fork until dough forms a ball. Divide dough in half. Roll out one half to fit a 9-in. pie plate for bottom crust. Drain cherries, reserving 1/4 cup juice. Mix cherries, juice, sugar, tapioca, extract, salt and food coloring if desired; pour into the crust. Dot with butter. Top with a lattice crust. Bake at 375° for 55-60 minutes. **Yield:** 6-8 servings.

Recipe for: Praline Pumpkin Pie

For me, baking is a relaxation rather than a chore. This is one of my favorites, a dessert I adapted from a neighbor's recipe for praline chocolate pie. —Sandra Haase, Baltimore, Maryland

    1/3 cup finely chopped pecans
    1/3 cup packed brown sugar
     3 tablespoons butter, softened
     1 unbaked pastry shell (10 inches)
FILLING:
     3 eggs, lightly beaten
    1/2 cup packed brown sugar
    1/2 cup sugar
     2 tablespoons all-purpose flour
    3/4 teaspoon ground cinnamon
    1/2 teaspoon salt
    1/2 teaspoon ground ginger
    1/4 teaspoon ground cloves
     1 can (16 ounces) pumpkin
1-1/2 cups half-and-half cream
Additional chopped pecans, optional

Combine the pecans, sugar and butter; press into the bottom of pie shell. Prick sides of pastry with a fork. Bake at 450° for 10 minutes; cool for 5 minutes.

Combine first eight filling ingredients; stir in pumpkin. Gradually add cream. Pour into pie shell. If desired, sprinkle chopped pecans on top. Bake at 350° for 45-50 minutes or until a knife inserted near the center comes out clean. Cool completely. Store in the refrigerator. **Yield:** 8-10 servings.

Cookies & Bars

At left: Chocolaty Double Crunchers (p. 194).

At right: Deluxe Chocolate Marshmallow
Bars (p. 192).

Chocolate Malted Cookies

These cookies are the next best thing to a good old-fashioned malted milk. With malted milk powder, chocolate syrup plus chocolate chips and chunks, these are the best cookies I've ever tasted...and with six kids, I've made a lot of cookies over the years.
—Teri Rasey-Bolf, Cadillac, Michigan

> 1 cup butter-flavored shortening
> 1-1/4 cups packed brown sugar
> 1/2 cup malted milk powder
> 2 tablespoons chocolate syrup
> 1 tablespoon vanilla extract
> 1 egg
> 2 cups all-purpose flour
> 1 teaspoon baking soda
> 1/2 teaspoon salt
> 1-1/2 cups semisweet chocolate chunks
> 1 cup (6 ounces) milk chocolate chips

In a mixing bowl, combine the first five ingredients; beat for 2 minutes. Add egg. Combine the flour, baking soda and salt; gradually add to creamed mixture, mixing well after each addition. Stir in chocolate chunks and chips.

Shape into 2-in. balls; place 3 in. apart on ungreased baking sheets. Bake at 375° for 12-14 minutes or until golden brown. Cool for 2 minutes before removing to a wire rack. **Yield:** about 1-1/2 dozen.

Deluxe Chocolate Marshmallow Bars

(Pictured on page 191)

I'd have to say that I've been asked to share this chocolaty layered bar recipe more than any other recipe in my collection. It's a tried-and-true favorite.
—Esther Shank, Harrisonburg, Virginia

> 3/4 cup butter, softened
> 1-1/2 cups sugar
> 3 eggs
> 1 teaspoon vanilla extract
> 1-1/3 cups all-purpose flour
> 1/2 teaspoon baking powder
> 1/2 teaspoon salt
> 3 tablespoons baking cocoa
> 1/2 cup chopped nuts, optional
> 4 cups miniature marshmallows
> TOPPING:
> 1-1/3 cups (8 ounces) chocolate chips
> 3 tablespoons butter
> 1 cup peanut butter
> 2 cups crisp rice cereal

In a mixing bowl, cream butter and sugar. Add eggs and vanilla; beat until fluffy. Combine flour, baking powder, salt and cocoa; add to creamed mixture. Stir in nuts if desired. Spread in a greased 15-in. x 10-in. x 1-in. pan.

Bake at 350° for 15-18 minutes. Sprinkle marshmallows evenly over cake; bake 2-3 minutes longer. Using a knife dipped in water, spread melted marshmallows evenly over cake. Cool.

For the topping, combine the chocolate chips, butter and peanut butter in a small saucepan. Cook over low heat, stirring constantly, until melted and well blended. Remove from heat; stir in rice cereal. Spread topping immediately over bars. Chill. **Yield:** about 3 dozen.

Recipe for: *Turtle Bars*

This recipe of my mother's is a "must make" for the holidays. I always have good intentions of taking some to Christmas parties, but my family finishes them too soon! —Faye Hintz, Springfield, Missouri

2 cups all-purpose flour
1 cup packed brown sugar
1/2 cup butter, softened
1 cup pecan halves
TOPPING:
2/3 cup butter
1/2 cup packed brown sugar
1 cup (6 ounces) semisweet chocolate chips

In a mixing bowl, beat flour, sugar and butter on medium speed for 2-3 minutes. Press firmly into an ungreased 13-in. x 9-in. x 2-in. baking pan. Arrange pecans over crust.

Combine butter and brown sugar in a heavy saucepan. Bring to a boil; boil for 1 minute, stirring constantly. Pour over pecans.

Bake at 350° for 18-22 minutes or until bubbly. Sprinkle chocolate chips on top; let stand for 3 minutes. Spread chocolate but allow some chips to remain whole. Cool completely; cut into small squares. **Yield:** about 8 dozen.

Hazelnut Shortbread

We have several acres of hazelnut trees here in the Willamette Valley, where the climate is perfect for this crop. Harvesttime is a big family event with everyone pitching in to help. I try to incorporate this wonderful flavorful nut into our recipes, and this cookie is always a hit. —Karen Morrell
Canby, Oregon

1 cup butter, softened
1/2 cup sugar
2 tablespoons maple syrup *or* honey
2 teaspoons vanilla extract
2 cups all-purpose flour
1-1/4 cups finely chopped hazelnuts *or* filberts
1/2 cup semisweet chocolate chips

In a mixing bowl, cream butter and sugar. Add syrup and vanilla. Add flour and mix just until combined; fold in the nuts. Shape into two 1-1/2-in. rolls; wrap tightly in waxed paper. Chill for 2 hours or until firm. Cut into 1/4-in. slices and place 2 in. apart on ungreased baking sheets.

Bake at 325° for 14-16 minutes or until edges begin to brown. Remove to wire racks to cool. Melt chocolate chips; drizzle over cookies. Allow chocolate to harden. **Yield:** about 6 dozen.

Cookies & Bars

Chocolaty Double Crunchers

(Pictured on page 190)

I first tried these fun crispy cookies at a family picnic when I was a child. Packed with oats, cornflakes and coconut, they quickly became a regular at our house. Years later, I still make them for my own family.
—Cheryl Johnson, Upper Marlboro, Maryland

1/2 cup butter, softened
1/2 cup sugar
1/2 cup packed brown sugar
 1 egg
1/2 teaspoon vanilla extract
 1 cup all-purpose flour
1/2 teaspoon baking soda
1/4 teaspoon salt
 1 cup quick-cooking oats
 1 cup crushed cornflakes
1/2 cup flaked coconut

FILLING:
 2 packages (3 ounces *each*) cream
  cheese, softened
1-1/2 cups confectioners' sugar
 2 cups (12 ounces) semisweet chocolate
  chips, melted

In a mixing bowl, cream butter and sugars. Add egg and vanilla; mix well. Combine flour, baking soda and salt; add to creamed mixture and mix well. Add oats, cornflakes and coconut.

Shape into 1-in. balls and place 2 in. apart on greased baking sheets. Flatten with a glass dipped lightly in flour. Bake at 350° for 8-10 minutes or until lightly browned. Remove to wire racks to cool.

For filling, beat cream cheese and sugar until smooth. Add the chocolate; mix well. Spread about 1 tablespoon on half of the cookies and top each with another cookie. Store in the refrigerator. **Yield:** about 2 dozen.

Cookie Jar Gingersnaps

My grandma kept two cookie jars in her pantry. One of the jars, which I now have, always had these crisp and chewy gingersnaps in it. They're still my favorite. My

daughter, Becky, prepared this recipe for a 4-H fair and was awarded a blue ribbon.
—Deb Handy
Pomona, Kansas

3/4 cup shortening
 1 cup sugar
 1 egg
1/4 cup molasses
 2 cups all-purpose flour
 2 teaspoons baking soda
1-1/2 teaspoons ground ginger
 1 teaspoon ground cinnamon
1/2 teaspoon salt
Additional sugar

In a large mixing bowl, cream the shortening and sugar. Beat in the egg and molasses. Combine flour, baking soda, ginger, cinnamon and salt; gradually add to creamed mixture.

Roll teaspoonfuls of dough into balls. Dip one side of each ball into sugar; place with sugar side up on a greased baking sheet. Bake at 350° for 12-15 minutes or until lightly browned and the surface cracks. **Yield:** 3-4 dozen.

Peanut Butter Cookies

This treasured recipe is the only one my grandmother ever wrote down! When my mother was married in 1942, she insisted that her mother write down one recipe for her. That was a real effort, because Grandma was a traditional pioneer-type cook who used a little of this or that until it felt right. —Janet Hall
Clinton, Wisconsin

    1 cup shortening
    1 cup peanut butter
    1 cup sugar
    1 cup packed brown sugar
    3 eggs
    3 cups all-purpose flour
    2 teaspoons baking soda
1/4 teaspoon salt

In a mixing bowl, cream shortening, peanut butter and sugars. Add eggs, one at a time, beating well after each addition. Sift together flour, baking soda and salt; add to creamed mixture. Roll into 1-1/2-in. balls and place 3 in. apart on ungreased baking sheets. Flatten with a fork if desired. Bake at 375° for 10-15 minutes. **Yield:** 3-4 dozen.

Recipe for: # Apricot Bars

My family likes snacking on these rich-tasting bars. This recipe's one I've used and shared for over 30 years, and we never get tired of it. —Helen Cluts, Sioux Falls, South Dakota

    1 cup all-purpose flour
    1 teaspoon baking powder
1/2 cup butter
    1 egg
    1 tablespoon milk
    1 cup apricot preserves
TOPPING:
    1 egg, lightly beaten
2/3 cup sugar
1/4 cup butter, melted
    1 teaspoon vanilla extract
    2 cups flaked coconut

In a bowl, combine flour and baking powder. Cut in butter until the mixture resembles coarse crumbs. Beat the egg and milk; stir into flour mixture. Spread in a greased 9-in. square baking pan. Spread apricot preserves over crust.

Combine topping ingredients; carefully drop by tablespoonfuls over apricot layer. Bake at 350° for 25-30 minutes or until golden brown. Cool; cut into small bars. **Yield:** 2 to 2-1/2 dozen.

Pecan Squares

These bars are good for snacking when you're on the road or for taking to gatherings. They're different from ordinary dessert bars...if you love pecan pie, you'll likely find them irresistible! —Sylvia Ford
Kennett, Missouri

CRUST:
- 3 cups all-purpose flour
- 1/2 cup sugar
- 1 cup butter, softened
- 1/2 teaspoon salt

FILLING:
- 4 eggs
- 1-1/2 cups light *or* dark corn syrup
- 1-1/2 cups sugar
- 3 tablespoons butter, melted
- 1-1/2 teaspoons vanilla extract
- 2-1/2 cups chopped pecans

In a large mixing bowl, blend together flour, sugar, butter and salt until mixture resembles coarse crumbs. Press firmly and evenly into a greased 15-in. x 10-in. x 1-in. baking pan. Bake at 350° for 20 minutes.

Meanwhile, in another bowl, combine first five filling ingredients. Stir in pecans. Spread evenly over hot crust. Bake at 350° for 25-30 minutes or until set. Cool on a wire rack. Cut into squares. **Yield:** 4 dozen.

Recipe for: Chewy Brownie Cookies

These look like cookies, but biting into them reveals they're like chewy brownies inside. This recipe is like getting two chocolaty treats in one! —Jonie Adams, Albion, Michigan

- 2/3 cup shortening
- 1-1/2 cups packed brown sugar
- 1 tablespoon water
- 1 teaspoon vanilla extract
- 2 eggs
- 1-1/2 cups all-purpose flour
- 1/3 cup baking cocoa
- 1/2 teaspoon salt
- 1/4 teaspoon baking soda
- 2 cups (12 ounces) semisweet chocolate chips
- 1/2 cup chopped walnuts *or* pecans, optional

In a large mixing bowl, cream shortening, sugar, water and vanilla. Beat in the eggs. Combine flour, cocoa, salt and baking soda; gradually add to creamed mixture and beat just until blended. Stir in chocolate chips and nuts if desired.

Drop by rounded teaspoonfuls 2 in. apart on ungreased baking sheets. Bake at 375° for 7-9 minutes; do not overbake. Cool 2 minutes before removing to wire racks. **Yield:** 3 dozen.

Pumpkin Chocolate Chip Cookies

I'm one of the cooking project leaders for my daughter's 4-H club, where these soft delicious cookies were a great hit with the kids. —Marietta Slater
Augusta, Kansas

1 cup butter, softened
3/4 cup packed brown sugar
3/4 cup sugar
1 egg
1 teaspoon vanilla extract
2 cups all-purpose flour
1 cup quick-cooking oats
1 teaspoon baking soda
1 teaspoon ground cinnamon
1 cup canned pumpkin
1-1/2 cups semisweet chocolate chips

In a mixing bowl, cream butter and sugars. Beat in egg and vanilla. Combine flour, oats, baking soda and cinnamon; stir into creamed mixture alternately with pumpkin. Fold in chocolate chips. Drop by tablespoonfuls onto greased baking sheets. Bake at 350° for 12-13 minutes or until lightly browned. **Yield:** 4 dozen.

Coffee breaks at Grandma's were a local ritual at 10 and 3 o'clock. With a fresh pot of coffee, homemade cookies, open-faced sandwiches or fresh bread with preserves, it was an event. Husbands and wives, children, field workers, neighbors, the postman, the parson...everyone gathered for food and fellowship.
—Susan Huppert, Palmetto, Florida

Icebox Cookies

This cookie recipe from my grandmother was my grandfather's favorite. I keep the dough in the freezer and make a fresh batch when folks drop in.
—Chris Paulsen, Glendale, Arizona

1/2 cup butter, softened
1 cup packed brown sugar
1 egg, beaten
1/2 teaspoon vanilla extract
2 cups all-purpose flour
1/2 teaspoon baking soda
1/2 teaspoon cream of tartar
1/2 teaspoon salt
1 cup chopped walnuts, optional

In a mixing bowl, cream the butter and brown sugar. Add egg and vanilla; beat well. Combine dry ingredients; add to creamed mixture. Stir in nuts if desired. On a lightly floured surface, shape the dough into three 10-in. x 1-in. rolls. Tightly wrap each roll in waxed paper. Freeze for at least 12 hours. Cut into 3/8-in. slices and place on greased baking sheets. Bake at 350° for 6-8 minutes. Remove to a wire rack to cool. **Yield:** about 7 dozen.

Chocolate Date Squares

My mother-in-law used to send these moist bars to my husband when he was in the Army.
—Pat Walter, Pine Island, Minnesota

  2 cups chopped dates
  1 cup hot water
  1 cup sugar
  2/3 cup shortening
  2 eggs
1-1/2 cups all-purpose flour
  1 teaspoon baking soda
1/2 teaspoon salt
TOPPING:
  1 cup (6 ounces) semisweet chocolate
    chips

1/2 cup packed brown sugar
1/2 cup chopped nuts

In a bowl, combine dates and water; set aside to cool (do not drain). In a mixing bowl, cream sugar and shortening. Add eggs, flour, baking soda and salt; mix well. Add dates.

Pour into a greased and floured 13-in. x 9-in. x 2-in. baking pan. Combine the topping ingredients; sprinkle over batter. Bake at 350° for 40 minutes or until a toothpick inserted in the center comes out clean. **Yield:** 24 servings.

Mom's Soft Raisin Cookies

With four sons in the service during World War II, my mother sent these favorite cookies as a taste from home to "her boys" in different parts of the world. These days, my grandchildren are enjoying them as we did, along with my stories of long ago.
—Pearl Cochenour, Williamsport, Ohio

  2 cups raisins
  1 cup water
  1 cup shortening
1-3/4 cups sugar
  2 eggs, lightly beaten
  1 teaspoon vanilla extract
3-1/2 cups all-purpose flour
  1 teaspoon baking powder
  1 teaspoon baking soda
  1 teaspoon salt
1/2 teaspoon ground cinnamon
1/2 teaspoon ground nutmeg
1/2 cup chopped walnuts

In a small saucepan, combine raisins and water; bring to a boil. Cook for 3 minutes; remove from the heat and let cool (do not drain). In a mixing bowl, cream shortening; gradually add sugar. Add eggs and vanilla.

Combine dry ingredients; gradually add to creamed mixture and blend thoroughly. Stir in nuts and raisins. Drop by teaspoonfuls 2 in. apart on greased baking sheets. Bake at 350° for 12-14 minutes. **Yield:** about 6 dozen.

Scotch Shortbread

This simple three-ingredient recipe makes wonderfully rich, tender cookies. Serve them with fresh berries of the season for a nice, light dessert. You'll get miles of smiles when you provide these for afternoon tea or a bridal shower.
—Marlene Hellickson
Big Bear City, California

4 cups all-purpose flour
1 cup sugar
1 pound cold butter

In a large mixing bowl, combine flour and sugar. Cut in butter until mixture resembles fine crumbs. Knead dough until smooth, about 6-10 minutes. Pat dough into an ungreased 15-in. x 10-in. x 1-in. baking pan. Pierce with a fork. Bake at 325° for 25-30 minutes or until lightly browned. While warm, cut into squares. Cool. **Yield:** 4 dozen.

Editor's Note: This recipe makes a dense, crisp cookie, so it does not call for baking powder or soda.

Recipe for: Coconut Washboards

My husband and I were married in 1944, and I've been making him these favorite cookies for many years. Our great-grandchildren like to come over to munch on these chewy treats, too. The recipe makes a lot, so there's plenty for everyone.
—Tommie Sue Shaw, McAlester, Oklahoma

1/2 cup butter, softened
1/2 cup shortening
2 cups packed brown sugar
2 eggs
1/4 cup water
1 teaspoon vanilla extract
4 cups all-purpose flour
1-1/2 teaspoons baking powder
1/2 teaspoon baking soda
1/4 teaspoon salt
1 cup flaked coconut

In a mixing bowl, cream butter, shortening and sugar for 2 minutes or until fluffy. Add eggs; mix well. Gradually add water and vanilla; mix well. Combine flour, baking powder, baking soda and salt; add to the creamed mixture. Fold in coconut. Cover and refrigerate for 2-4 hours.

Shape into 1-in. balls. Place 2 in. apart on greased baking sheets; flatten with fingers into 2-1/2-in. x 1-in. oblong shapes. Press lengthwise with a floured fork. Bake at 400° for 8-10 minutes or until lightly browned. Cool 2 minutes before removing to a wire rack. **Yield:** about 9 dozen.

Gingerbread Cutouts

Baking is the tastiest part of my hobby of collecting gingerbread boys. I decorate gingerbread cookies to use for gifts and always serve them during the holidays. —LaJunta Malone, Camden, Alabama

1 cup butter, softened
1 cup sugar
1/2 cup dark corn syrup
1 teaspoon *each* ground cinnamon, nutmeg, cloves and ginger
2 eggs, beaten
1 teaspoon vinegar
5 cups all-purpose flour
1 teaspoon baking soda
Red-hot candies

In a large saucepan, combine the butter, sugar, corn syrup and spices; bring to a boil, stirring constantly. Remove from the heat and cool to lukewarm. Stir in eggs and vinegar. Combine the flour and baking soda; stir into sugar mixture to form a soft dough. Chill for several hours.

On a lightly floured surface, roll dough to 1/4-in. thickness. Cut with a floured 2-1/2-in. gingerbread man cookie cutter and place on greased baking sheets. Use red-hot candies for eyes and buttons. Bake at 350° for 8-10 minutes. Remove to wire racks to cool. **Yield:** about 6 dozen.

No trip to Grandma's would be complete without enjoying a batch of her snickerdoodle cookies. How we loved the spicy scent of cinnamon and the sweet taste of those sugar-coated treats! —Jada O'Toole Wappingers Falls, New York

Pecan Sandies

Whenever Mother made these cookies, there never seemed to be enough! Even now when I make them, they disappear quickly. These melt-in-your-mouth treats are great with a cold glass of milk or a steaming mug of hot chocolate. —Debbie Carlson San Diego, California

2 cups butter, softened
1 cup confectioners' sugar
2 tablespoons water
4 teaspoons vanilla extract
4 cups all-purpose flour
2 cups chopped pecans
Additional confectioners' sugar

In a mixing bowl, cream butter and sugar. Add water and vanilla; mix well. Gradually add flour; fold in pecans. Roll dough into 1-in. balls. Place on ungreased baking sheets and flatten with fingers. Bake at 300° for 20-25 minutes. Cool on a wire rack. When cool, dust with confectioners' sugar. **Yield:** about 5 dozen.

Recipe for: *Lemon Butter Cookies*

These tender cutout cookies have a slight lemon flavor that makes them stand out from the rest. They're very easy to roll out compared to other sugar cookies I've worked with. I know you'll enjoy them as much as we do.
—Judy McCreight, Springfield, Illinois

1 cup butter, softened
2 cups sugar
2 eggs, beaten
1/4 cup milk
2 teaspoons lemon extract
1/2 teaspoon salt
4-1/2 cups all-purpose flour
2 teaspoons baking powder
1/4 teaspoon baking soda
Colored sugar, optional

In a mixing bowl, cream butter and sugar. Add eggs, milk and extract. Combine dry ingredients; gradually add to creamed mixture. Cover and chill for 2 hours.

Roll out on a lightly floured surface to 1/8-in. thickness. Cut with a 2-in. cookie cutter dipped in flour. Place 2 in. apart on ungreased baking sheets. Sprinkle with colored sugar if desired. Bake at 350° for 8-9 minutes or until the edges just begin to brown. Remove to wire racks to cool. **Yield:** about 13 dozen.

Chocolate Chip Brownies

People love these very rich brownies so much that I never take them anywhere without bringing along several copies of the recipe to hand out. These treats are wonderful to take on a picnic because you don't have to worry about frosting melting.
—Brenda Kelly, Ashburn, Virginia

1 cup butter, softened
3 cups sugar
6 eggs
1 tablespoon vanilla extract
2-1/4 cups all-purpose flour
1/2 cup baking cocoa
1 teaspoon baking powder
1/2 teaspoon salt
1 cup (6 ounces) semisweet chocolate chips
1 cup (6 ounces) vanilla *or* white chips
1 cup chopped walnuts

In a mixing bowl, cream butter and sugar. Add eggs and vanilla; mix well. Combine flour, cocoa, baking powder and salt; stir into creamed mixture just until blended (do not overmix).

Pour into two greased 9-in. square baking pans. Sprinkle with chocolate and vanilla chips and nuts. Bake at 350° for 35-40 minutes or until a toothpick inserted near the center comes out clean. Cool. **Yield:** 3-4 dozen.

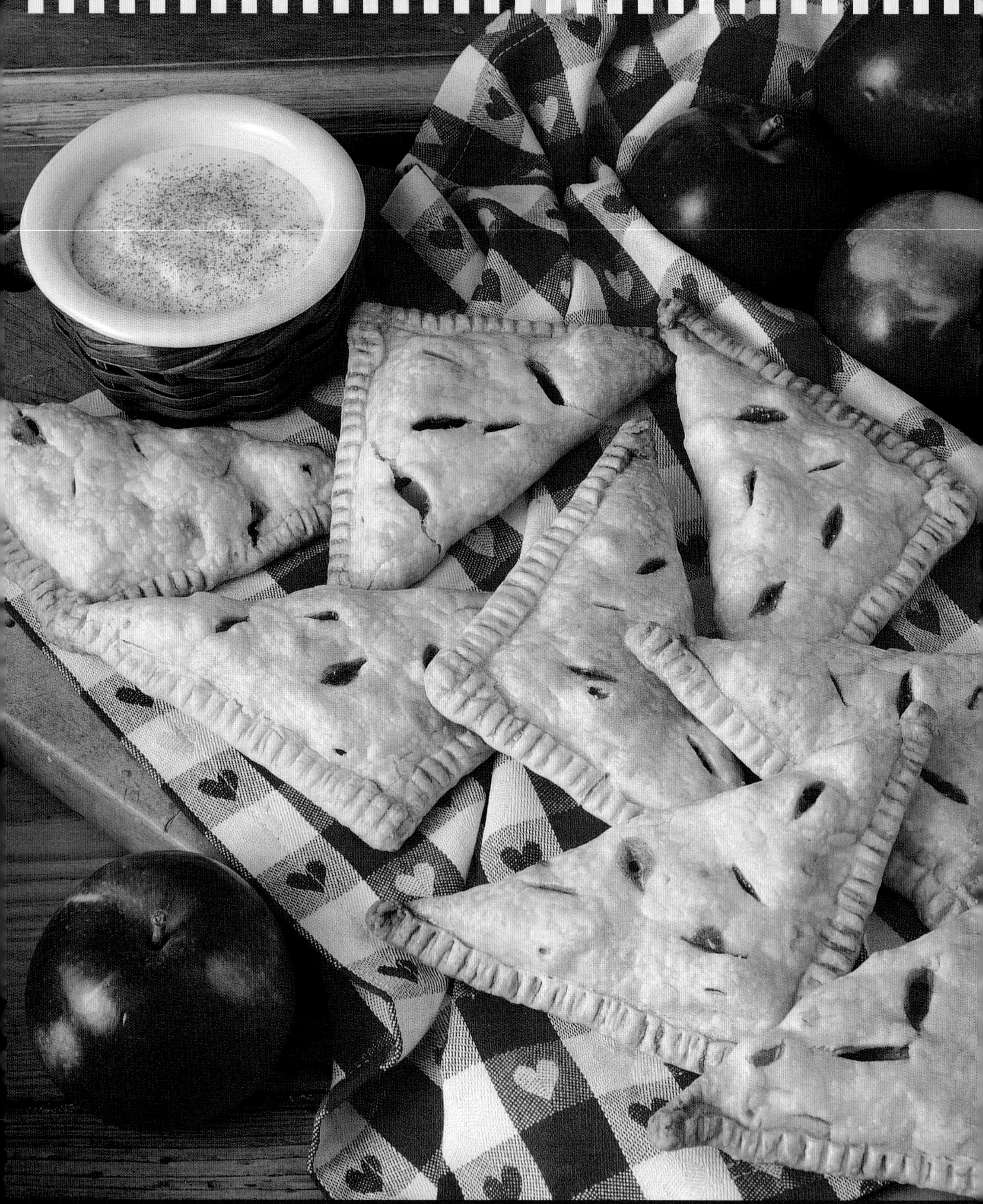

Desserts

At left: Apple Turnovers with Custard (p. 205).

At right: Pineapple Cheese Torte (p. 206).

Seven-Minute Pudding

This rich, smooth pudding couldn't be quicker to make, and it has such nice homemade flavor. You'll surely enjoy it as an evening snack or anytime!
—Renee Schwebach, Dumont, Minnesota

  1/3 cup sugar
    2 tablespoons cornstarch
    2 cups milk
    2 egg yolks
    2 tablespoons butter
    1 teaspoon vanilla extract

In a microwave-safe mixing bowl, combine sugar and cornstarch. With a hand mixer, beat in milk and egg yolks until smooth. Microwave on medium for 5 minutes. Beat well with mixer. Microwave on high for 2 minutes; stir. Blend in butter and vanilla. Pour into serving dishes; cool. **Yield:** 3-4 servings.

Making ice cream was the highlight of summer picnics at my great-grandparents' farm. The excitement rose when the cranking became labored, because that meant the "dasher" would soon be lifted out. For me, no ice cream has ever tasted as good as that sweet treat clinging to the cold metal!
—Bette Hillegass
Black Mountain, North Carolina

Frozen Chocolate Torte

In summer, this cool make-ahead dessert is one of my favorites. —Tammy Neubauer, Ida Grove, Iowa

    1 package (10-1/2 ounces) miniature marshmallows
    1 cup (6 ounces) semisweet chocolate chips
    1 can (12 ounces) evaporated milk
    1 cup flaked coconut
  1/2 cup butter
    2 cups graham cracker crumbs
  1/2 gallon vanilla ice cream, softened

In a saucepan over low heat, melt marshmallows and chocolate chips with milk. Remove from heat; cool. In a skillet, stir coconut in butter until browned. Remove from the heat; stir in crumbs. Pat three-fourths into a 13-in. x 9-in. x 2-in. baking pan; cool.

Spoon half of the ice cream onto crust. Top with half of the chocolate mixture. Layer with remaining ice cream and chocolate. Sprinkle with remaining crumbs. Cover and freeze for at least 2 hours. **Yield:** 12 servings.

Recipe for: *Apple Turnovers with Custard*

(Pictured on page 202)

With the flaky turnovers and rich sauce, this recipe outshines every other apple recipe I make. It's a comforting treat everyone loves. —Leora Muellerleile, Turtle Lake, Wisconsin

CUSTARD:
  1/3 cup sugar
  2 tablespoons cornstarch
  2 cups milk *or* half-and-half cream
  3 egg yolks, lightly beaten
  1 tablespoon vanilla extract
TURNOVERS:
  4 medium tart apples, peeled and cut
    into 1/4-inch slices
  1 tablespoon lemon juice
  2 tablespoons butter, diced
  1/3 cup sugar
  3/4 teaspoon ground cinnamon
  1 tablespoon cornstarch
Pastry for double-crust pie
Milk

In a saucepan, combine sugar and cornstarch. Stir in milk until smooth. Cook and stir over medium-high heat until thickened and bubbly. Reduce heat; cook and stir for 2 minutes. Remove from heat; stir 1 cup into yolks. Return all to pan. Bring to a gentle boil; cook and stir for 2 minutes. Remove from heat; stir in vanilla. Cool slightly. Cover surface of custard with waxed paper; chill.

Place apples in a bowl; sprinkle with lemon juice. Add butter. Combine sugar, cinnamon and cornstarch; mix with apples and set aside.

Divide pastry into eight portions; roll each into a 5-in. square. Spoon filling off-center on each. Brush edges with milk. Fold over to form a triangle; seal. Crimp with tines of fork. Make steam vents in top. Place on greased baking sheets. Chill 15 minutes. Brush with milk. Bake at 400° for 35 minutes. Serve warm with custard. **Yield:** 8 servings.

Chocolate Sauce

I make different toppings so we can enjoy our favorite snack—ice cream sundaes. This smooth chocolate sauce is always a big hit. —Nancy McDonald Burns, Wyoming

  1/2 cup butter
  2 squares (1 ounce *each*) unsweetened
    chocolate
  2 cups sugar
  1 cup half-and-half cream *or*
    evaporated milk
  1/2 cup light corn syrup
  1 teaspoon vanilla extract

In a saucepan, melt butter and chocolate. Add sugar, cream, corn syrup and vanilla. Bring to a boil, stirring constantly. Boil for 1-1/2 minutes. Remove from the heat. Serve warm or cold over ice cream or pound cake. Refrigerate leftovers. **Yield:** about 3-1/3 cups.

Pineapple Cheese Torte

(Pictured on page 203)

This light and yummy pineapple dessert looks prettiest when it's garnished with fresh strawberries. I serve this cool dessert at summer picnics or family get-togethers. It's always popular! —Diane Bradley
Sparta, Michigan

CRUST:
- 1 cup all-purpose flour
- 1/4 cup confectioners' sugar
- 1/4 cup finely chopped almonds
- 1/3 cup butter, softened

FILLING:
- 2 packages (8 ounces *each*) cream cheese, softened
- 1/2 cup sugar
- 2 eggs
- 2/3 cup unsweetened pineapple juice

PINEAPPLE TOPPING:
- 1/4 cup all-purpose flour
- 1/4 cup sugar
- 1 can (20 ounces) crushed pineapple
- 1/2 cup heavy whipping cream

Fresh strawberries, optional

Combine crust ingredients; pat into the bottom of an 11-in. x 7-in. x 2-in. baking dish. Bake at 350° for 20 minutes. In a mixing bowl, beat cream cheese until fluffy; beat in sugar and eggs. Stir in juice. Pour filling over hot crust. Bake at 350° for 25 minutes or until center is set. Cool.

For topping, in a saucepan, combine flour and sugar. Drain pineapple, reserving juice. Stir in 1 cup of reserved pineapple juice. Bring to a boil, stirring constantly. Boil and stir 1 minute. Remove from heat; fold in pineapple. Cool.

Whip cream until stiff peaks form; fold into topping. Spread carefully over dessert. Refrigerate 6 hours or overnight. Garnish with strawberries if desired. **Yield:** 12-16 servings.

Cherry Cobbler

I've made this recipe for years, adapting it to suit our taste. It's a delicious way to use lots of tart cherries.
—Peggy Burdick, Burlington, Michigan

- 5 cups pitted canned *or* frozen tart red cherries
- 2-1/2 tablespoons lemon juice
- 1/3 cup sugar
- 1/3 cup packed brown sugar
- 2-1/2 tablespoons cornstarch
- 1 teaspoon ground cinnamon
- 1/4 teaspoon ground nutmeg

TOPPING:
- 1 cup all-purpose flour
- 1 tablespoon sugar
- 1 teaspoon baking powder
- 1/4 teaspoon salt
- 2 tablespoons butter
- 1/3 to 1/2 cup milk

Drain cherries, reserving 1/4 cup juice; discard remaining juice. Combine cherries and lemon juice; set aside. In a saucepan, combine sugars, cornstarch, cinnamon and nutmeg; stir in cherry juice. Bring to a boil, stirring occasionally; boil 2 minutes. Add cherries; pour into an ungreased 8-in. square baking pan.

For topping, combine flour, sugar, baking powder and salt; cut in butter until crumbly. Stir in enough milk to moisten. Drop by tablespoonfuls over cherries. Bake at 450° for 10-13 minutes or until golden brown. **Yield:** 6-8 servings.

Layered Banana Pudding

My mother gave me this recipe, which an old friend had shared with her. When my children were still at home, we enjoyed this satisfying pudding often, and now I make it for company. There's no comparison between this recipe and the instant pudding mixes from the grocery store! —Esther Matteson, Bremen, Indiana

1/3 cup all-purpose flour
2/3 cup packed brown sugar
2 cups milk
2 egg yolks, beaten
2 tablespoons butter
1 teaspoon vanilla extract
1 cup heavy whipping cream, whipped
4 to 6 firm bananas, sliced
Chopped walnuts, optional

In a medium saucepan, combine the flour and brown sugar; stir in milk. Cook and stir over medium heat until thickened and bubbly; cook and stir 1 minute more. Remove from the heat.

Gradually stir about 1 cup hot mixture into egg yolks. Return all to the saucepan. Bring to a gentle boil; cook and stir for 2 minutes. Remove from the heat; stir in butter and vanilla. Cool to room temperature, stirring occasionally. Fold in the whipped cream.

In a 2-qt. glass bowl, layer a third of the pudding; top with half of the bananas. Repeat layers. Top with remaining pudding. Sprinkle with nuts if desired. Cover and chill at least 1 hour before serving. **Yield:** 8 servings.

Recipe for: **Blueberry Grunt**

A tightly covered skillet will "grunt" while this traditional dessert cooks. It's said early settlers served this to the captain of the "Yankee Clipper." —Iola Egle, McCook, Nebraska

4 cups fresh blueberries
1 cup sugar
1 cup water
1-1/2 cups all-purpose flour
2 teaspoons baking powder
2 tablespoons grated orange peel
1/2 teaspoon ground cinnamon
1/4 teaspoon ground nutmeg
1/4 teaspoon salt
3/4 cup milk
Heavy whipping cream, optional

In a skillet, combine blueberries, sugar and water; bring to a boil. Simmer, uncovered, for 20 minutes. In a bowl, combine the next six ingredients; stir in milk just until moistened (dough will be stiff). Drop by tablespoonfuls over blueberries. Cover and cook for 10-15 minutes or until dumplings are puffed and a toothpick comes out clean. Serve warm with cream if desired. **Yield:** 6-8 servings.

Coconut Cream Pudding

A golden baked meringue makes the crowning touch to this mouth-watering dessert.—Verona Koehlmoos
Pilger, Nebraska

1-1/4 cups sugar, *divided*
1/4 cup cornstarch
3 cups milk
4 eggs, *separated*
1 cup flaked coconut
1 teaspoon vanilla extract

In a heavy saucepan, combine 3/4 cup sugar and cornstarch; stir in milk. Cook and stir over medium heat until thick and bubbly; cook and stir 2 minutes more. Remove from heat.

Beat egg yolks. Stir 1 cup hot milk mixture into yolks; return to pan. Cook and stir over medium heat until gently boiling; cook and stir 2 minutes more. Remove from the heat; cool to lukewarm. Stir in coconut and vanilla. Pour into an ungreased 8-in. square baking dish.

In a mixing bowl, beat egg whites until soft peaks form. Gradually add remaining sugar, beating until stiff peaks form. Spread over pudding, sealing edges. Bake at 350° for 10-15 minutes. Serve warm. **Yield:** 9 servings.

Recipe for: Apple Cobbler

A treasured family recipe, this cobbler is a delicious old-fashioned dessert. It travels well and slices nicely, so it's perfect for picnics or tailgate parties. We like apples, but you can use your favorite fruit.
—Rita Reifenstein, Evans City, Pennsylvania

3 cups all-purpose flour
1 cup sugar, *divided*
1-1/2 teaspoons baking powder
1/2 teaspoon salt
1/2 cup butter
2 eggs
1 tablespoon vanilla extract
3 to 4 tablespoons milk
8 cups thinly sliced peeled tart apples
2 tablespoons quick-cooking tapioca
1/2 teaspoon ground cinnamon
TOPPING:
1 tablespoon milk
3/4 teaspoon sugar
1/4 teaspoon ground cinnamon

In a bowl, combine flour, 1/4 cup sugar, baking powder and salt. Cut in butter until crumbly. In another bowl, lightly beat eggs and vanilla; add to crumb mixture. With a fork, gently mix in milk to moisten. Stir until dough forms a ball.

Press half of the dough into the bottom of a greased 13-in. x 9-in. x 2-in. baking pan. Chill the remaining dough. Toss apples with tapioca, cinnamon and remaining sugar; place over dough in pan.

On a lightly floured surface, roll chilled dough to fit top of pan. Place over apples. Brush with milk. Combine sugar and cinnamon; sprinkle on top. Bake at 350° for 45-50 minutes or until apples are tender and crust is golden. **Yield:** 12-16 servings.

Blueberry Custard Parfait

I'm a retired nurse, and cooking is my hobby. I love to share homemade treats like this fresh-tasting parfait with family and friends. —*Mildred Stubbs*
Hamlet, North Carolina

2 eggs, lightly beaten
1-1/2 cups milk
1/4 cup sugar
1/4 teaspoon salt
1 teaspoon vanilla extract
1 teaspoon grated lemon peel
1 teaspoon grated orange peel
1/4 teaspoon ground nutmeg
1/2 cup heavy whipping cream
2 teaspoons confectioners' sugar
2 cups fresh blueberries

In a saucepan, combine eggs, milk, sugar and salt. Cook over medium-low heat, stirring constantly, until custard is slightly thickened and coats the back of a spoon, about 18 minutes. Remove from the heat. Add vanilla, peels and nutmeg; mix well. Cool for 30 minutes, stirring occasionally.

In a small mixing bowl, whip the cream and confectioners' sugar until stiff. Fold two-thirds into the custard. Layer custard and blueberries in 4 parfait glasses. Garnish with remaining cream. Chill for 1 hour. **Yield:** 4 servings.

Banana Split Cream Puffs

These fruity cream puff "sandwiches" are a treat that our family has always found scrumptious. For a nice variation, use whipped cream instead of the ice cream. —*Sandra McKenzie, Braham, Minnesota*

1 cup water
1/2 cup butter
1 cup all-purpose flour
1/4 teaspoon salt
4 eggs
12 scoops vanilla ice cream
1 cup sliced fresh strawberries
1 large *or* 2 medium bananas, thinly sliced
1 can (8 ounces) pineapple tidbits, drained
1/2 cup hot fudge sauce

In a saucepan over medium heat, bring water and butter to a boil. Add flour and salt all at once; stir until a smooth ball forms. Remove from the heat; let stand 5 minutes. Add eggs, one at a time, beating well after each addition. Beat until mixture is smooth and shiny, about 3 minutes.

Drop by rounded tablespoonfuls onto a greased baking sheet. Bake at 400° for 30-35 minutes or until golden brown. Transfer to a wire rack. Immediately split puffs open; remove tops and set aside. Discard soft dough from inside. Cool puffs.

Fill each with a scoop of ice cream and top with fruit. Drizzle with hot fudge sauce. Replace tops and serve immediately. **Yield:** 12 servings.

Grandma's Chocolate Pudding

My grandmother always made this creamy, very chocolaty pudding when we visited. —Donna Hughes
Rochester, New Hampshire

1 cup sugar
1/2 cup baking cocoa
1/4 cup all-purpose flour
2 cups water
3/4 cup evaporated milk
1 tablespoon vanilla extract
Pinch salt

In a saucepan, combine sugar, cocoa and flour. Add water and milk; stir until smooth. Cook over medium heat, stirring constantly, until mixture comes to a boil. Cook until thick, about 1 minute.

Remove from heat; stir in vanilla and salt. Cool to room temperature, stirring several times. Pour into a serving bowl or individual dishes. Serve warm or chill. **Yield:** 4-6 servings.

Lemony Apple Dumplings

The first time I made this recipe, I was serving guests who had two little daughters. The girls weren't sure about eating a dessert that looked so different. But after just one bite, they proclaimed the treat "yummy" and cleaned their plates. —Kristy Deloach
Baker, Louisiana

1-1/2 cups all-purpose flour
1-1/4 teaspoons salt, *divided*
1/3 cup shortening
4 to 5 tablespoons cold milk
1/2 cup packed brown sugar

3 tablespoons butter, softened
1/2 teaspoon ground cinnamon
4 medium tart apples, peeled and cored
1 egg white, beaten
LEMON SAUCE:
1/2 cup sugar
4 teaspoons cornstarch
1 cup water
3 tablespoons butter
4 teaspoons lemon juice
2 teaspoons grated lemon peel
1/8 teaspoon salt

Combine flour and 1 teaspoon salt. Cut in shortening until crumbly. Stir in milk until pastry forms a ball; set aside. Stir brown sugar, butter, cinnamon and remaining salt to form a paste. Divide and press into center of each apple; pat any extra filling on outside of apples.

On a floured surface, roll pastry into a 14-in. square. Cut into four 7-in. squares. Place one apple in center of each square. Brush edges of pastry with egg white. Fold up corners to center; pinch to seal. Place in a greased 9-in. square baking dish. Bake at 375° for 35-40 minutes or until golden brown.

Meanwhile, combine sugar and cornstarch in a saucepan. Stir in water. Bring to a boil; boil 2 minutes. Remove from heat; stir in remaining ingredients until smooth. Serve warm over warm dumplings. **Yield:** 4 servings.

Berries in Custard Sauce

This sweet sauce makes the perfect topping for a medley of fresh-picked berries. —Leona Luecking
West Burlington, Iowa

1 cup milk
1 egg, lightly beaten
2 tablespoons sugar
Pinch salt
1/2 teaspoon vanilla extract
3 cups fresh blueberries, raspberries and strawberries

In saucepan, scald milk. Combine egg and sugar in a bowl; stir in small amount of hot milk. Return all to saucepan. Cook over low heat, stirring constantly, until mixture reaches at least 160° and coats the back of a metal spoon, about 15 minutes. Remove from heat; stir in salt and vanilla. Chill at least 1 hour. Serve over berries. **Yield:** 6 servings.

Recipe for: Pumpkin Bread Pudding

Old-fashioned but never out of style, this comforting dessert is especially good with whipped cream. I got this favorite pumpkin recipe from an elderly aunt. —Lois Fetting, Nelson, Wisconsin

4 cups cubed day-old whole wheat bread
1/2 cup chopped dates *or* raisins
1/2 cup chopped pecans, *divided*
2 cups milk
1 cup canned pumpkin
2 eggs, *separated*
2/3 cup packed brown sugar
1-1/2 teaspoons ground cinnamon
3/4 teaspoon ground nutmeg
1/4 teaspoon salt
1/8 teaspoon ground cloves
Half-and-half cream *or* whipped cream, optional

Combine bread cubes, dates and 1/3 cup pecans; place in a greased 2-qt. shallow baking dish. In a mixing bowl, combine the milk, pumpkin, egg yolks, brown sugar, cinnamon, nutmeg, salt and cloves; beat well.

In a small mixing bowl, beat egg whites until stiff; fold into pumpkin mixture. Pour over bread cubes and toss gently. Sprinkle with remaining nuts.

Bake, uncovered, at 350° for 1 hour or until a knife inserted near the center comes out clean. Serve warm or chilled with cream if desired. **Yield:** 6-8 servings.

General Recipe Index

This handy index lists every recipe by food category, major ingredient and/or cooking method, so you can easily locate recipes to suit your needs.

Grandma's Favorites

Alphabetical Index

*This handy index lists every recipe in alphabetical order
so you can easily find your favorite dish.*

Lemony Apple Dumplings, 210
Lime Broiled Catfish, 149
Lime Gelatin Salad, 51
Luscious Almond
    Cheesecake, 165

M

Maple Country Ribs, 138
Marinated Turkey, 124
Mashed Potatoes with
    Horseradish, 66
Meatless Spaghetti Sauce, 155
Mexican Corn Bread, 84
Mini Apple Pizzas, 12
Mini Hamburgers, 9
Mocha Cupcakes, 172
Mock Lobster, 154
Molded Peach Gelatin, 53
Mom's Chicken 'n' Buttermilk
    Dumplings, 120
Mom's Peach Pie, 178
Mom's Soft Raisin Cookies, 198
Mozzarella Meat Loaf, 102
Muenster Bread, 86
Mushroom and Potato
    Chowder, 37

N

North Carolina Shrimp
    Saute, 152
Norwegian Parsley Potatoes, 65
Nutty Apple Muffins, 83
Nutty Oven-Fried Chicken, 114
Nutty Sweet Potato Biscuits, 86

O

Oatmeal Waffles, 25
Old-Fashioned Cabbage
    Rolls, 104
Old-Fashioned Raisin Pie, 184
Old-World Tomato Soup, 38
One-Dish Pork Chop Dinner,
    145
Onion Potato Pancakes, 60
Orange Chiffon Cake, 174
Orange Date Bread, 85

Oven Barbecued Chicken, 123
Overnight Apple French
    Toast, 20
Overnight Blueberry French
    Toast, 22
Overnight Coleslaw, 50

P

Pan-Fried Trout, 158
Paprika Potatoes, 62
Parmesan Chicken, 126
Party Potatoes, 69
Pat's Potato Salad, 55
Peach Cream Pie, 187
Peanut Butter Cookies, 195
Peanut Butter Pie, 181
Peas with Mushrooms, 72
Pecan Fudge Pie, 184
Pecan Sandies, 200
Pecan Squares, 196
Peppered Rib Eye Steaks, 98
Perfect Pot Roast, 108
Pineapple Bundt Cake, 164
Pineapple Cheese Torte, 206
Pineapple Gelatin Salad, 49
Poppy Seed Bread, 79
Pop-Up Rolls, 76
Pork and Spinach Salad, 141
Pork Chops with Caraway
    Cabbage, 140
Pork Chow Mein, 142
Pork Patties, 26
Potato Cheese Soup, 38
Potato Pork Pie, 139
Poteca Nut Roll, 82
Praline Pumpkin Pie, 189
Puffed Wheat Balls, 15
Pumpkin Bread, 80
Pumpkin Bread Pudding, 211
Pumpkin Cheesecake, 175
Pumpkin Chocolate Chip
    Cookies, 197
Pumpkin Raisin Cake, 163
Pumpkin Sheet Cake, 166

Q

Quiche Lorraine, 30
Quick Mushroom Stew, 101

R

Raspberry Lemon Muffins, 80
Raspberry Ribbon Pie, 186
Red Beans and Rice, 148
Rhubarb Upside-Down
    Cake, 171
Roasted Chicken with
    Rosemary, 123
Roasted Duck with
    Apple-Raisin Dressing, 119
Ruby Red Raspberry Salad, 57

S

Sage Dressing for Chicken, 60
Salisbury Steak Deluxe, 102
Sandy's Chocolate Cake, 162
Saucy Apple Cake, 166
Saucy Chicken and
    Asparagus, 124
Sauerkraut 'n' Sausage, 134
Sausage and Mushroom
    Stew, 144
Sausage Gravy, 23
Sausage Lentil Soup, 39
Savory Cheese Soup, 41
Savory Pot Roast, 103
Savory Spaghetti Sauce, 111
Scalloped Pineapple
    Casserole, 70
Scalloped Potatoes and Pork
    Chops, 137
Scotch Broth, 42
Scotch Shortbread, 199
Scrambled Egg Casserole, 28
Seven-Minute Pudding, 204
Sheepherder's Breakfast, 21
Skillet Pork Chops with
    Zucchini, 138
Sky-High Strawberry Pie, 183
Smoked Turkey and Apple
    Salad, 125
Snowflake Cake, 170
Sole in Herbed Butter, 156
Sour Cream Apple Chicken, 122
Sour Cream Apple Pie, 185
Spaghetti 'n' Meatballs, 98
Special Potato Salad, 52
Spiced Pecans, 9

Metric Equivalents

VOLUME

IMPERIAL	METRIC
⅛ teaspoon	0.5 milliliter
¼ teaspoon	1 milliliter
½ teaspoon	2 milliliters
1 teaspoon	5 milliliters
1 tablespoon (½ fluid ounce)	1 tablespoon (15 milliliters)*
¼ cup (2 fluid ounces)	2 tablespoons (50 milliliters)
⅓ cup (3 fluid ounces)	¼ cup (75 milliliters)
½ cup (4 fluid ounces)	⅓ cup (125 milliliters)
¾ cup (6 fluid ounces)	¾ cup (200 milliliters)
1 cup (8 fluid ounces)	1 cup (250 milliliters)
1 pint (16 fluid ounces)	500 milliliters
1 quart (32 fluid ounces)	1 liter minus 3 tablespoons

*The Australian tablespoon is 20 milliliters,
but the difference is negligible in most recipes.*

WEIGHT

IMPERIAL	METRIC
¼ ounce	7 grams
½ ounce	15 grams
¾ ounce	20 grams
1 ounce	30 grams
6 ounces	170 grams
8 ounces (½ pound)	225 grams
12 ounces (¾ pound)	340 grams
16 ounces (1 pound)	450 grams
35 ounces (2 ¼ pounds)	1 kilogram

LENGTH

IMPERIAL	METRIC
½ inch	12 millimeters
1 inch	2.5 centimeters
6 inches	15 centimeters
12 inches (1 foot)	30 centimeters

TEMPERATURE

IMPERIAL	METRIC
0°F (freezer temperature)	minus 18°C
32°F (temperature water freezes)	0°C
180°F (temperature water simmers)*	82°C
212°F (temperature water boils)*	100°C
250°F (low oven temperature)	120°C
350°F (moderate oven temperature)	180°C
425°F (hot oven temperature)	220°C
500°F (very hot oven temperature)	260°C

At sea level

BAKING PAN SIZES

IMPERIAL	METRIC
8 x 1½-inch round cake pan	20 x 5-centimeter cake tin
9 x 1½-inch round cake pan	23 x 5-centimeter cake tin
11 x 7 x 1½-inch baking pan	28 x 18 x 4-centimeter baking tin
13 x 9 x 2-inch baking pan	30 x 20 x 3-centimeter baking tin
15 x 10 x 1-inch baking pan (jelly-roll pan)	38 x 25 x 2.5-centimeter baking tin (Swiss-roll tin)
9 x 5 x 3-inch loaf pan	25 x 7.5-centimeter loaf tin in Canada
	19 x 12 x 9-centimeter loaf tin in Australia
9-inch pie plate	23 x 3-centimeter pie plate
7- or 8-inch springform pan or loose-bottom tin	20-centimeter springform tin
10-inch tube or Bundt pan	26-centimeter (15-cup capacity) ring tin

NOTE: *Pan sizes vary between manufacturers, so use this list as an approximate guide only. Always use the nearest equivalent available.*